MAKING IT
IN THE MUSIC
BUSINESS

A Business and Legal Guide for
Songwriters and Performers

LEE WILSON

A PLUME BOOK

PLUME
Published by the Penguin Group
Penguin Books USA Inc., 375 Hudson Street, New York, New York 10014, U.S.A.
Penguin Books Ltd, 27 Wrights Lane, London W8 5TZ, England
Penguin Books Australia Ltd, Ringwood, Victoria, Australia
Penguin Books Canada Ltd, 10 Alcorn Avenue, Toronto, Ontario, Canada M4V 3B2
Penguin Books (N.Z.) Ltd, 182–190 Wairau Road, Auckland 10, New Zealand

Penguin Books Ltd, Registered Offices:
Harmondsworth, Middlesex, England

First published by Plume, an imprint of Dutton Signet,
a division of Penguin Books USA Inc.

First Printing, March, 1995
10 9 8 7 6 5 4 3 2 1

 REGISTERED TRADEMARK—MARCA REGISTRADA

LIBRARY OF CONGRESS CATALOGING-IN-PUBLICATION DATA:
Wilson, Lee
    Making it in the music business : a business and legal guide for songwriters and performers /
Lee Wilson.
        p.   cm.
    Includes index.
    ISBN 0-452-26848-6
    1. Music trade—United States.   2. Copyright—Music—United States.
3. Musicians—Legal status, laws, etc.—United States.   I. Title.
ML3790.W57   1995
780'.68—dc20   94-30368
                                                                    CIP
                                                                    MN

Printed in the United States of America
Set in Goudy
Designed by Leonard Telesca

AUTHOR'S NOTE
Anecdotes illustrating various points of law appear throughout this book. Although they recount
realistic situations and occasionally use the names of actual copyright or trademark owners, celebri-
ties, companies, and organizations, they are wholly fictitious and do not refer to any actual events.
No parallels should be drawn from these anecdotes to any actual persons, companies, or organizations or to any clients or acquaintances of the author.

The information contained in this book is intended only to educate readers generally in selected
areas of the law related to the music industry and is not meant to substitute for legal advice applicable to specific situations, for which it may be inadequate. Further, because laws and business practices change, the information given in this book may become outdated. The author and publisher
therefore disclaim any responsibility for any consequence of the use by anyone of the information
contained in this book and, with regard to any particular legal concern or problem, urge the reader
to seek legal advice from an attorney competent in the pertinent area of the law.

BOOKS ARE AVAILABLE AT QUANTITY DISCOUNTS WHEN USED TO PROMOTE PRODUCTS OR SERVICES.
FOR INFORMATION PLEASE WRITE TO PREMIUM MARKETING DIVISION, PENGUIN BOOKS USA INC.,
375 HUDSON STREET, NEW YORK, NEW YORK 10014.

This book is dedicated to my very good friend Dane Bryant, who has himself been around the block a couple of times in the music business. I could not have written *Making It in the Music Business* without his love and support. Anyone who undertakes to write a book should first secure a cheerful Italian paramour who knows just when dinner and a movie are in order.

Contents

Acknowledgments

I'd like to thank my agent, Richard Curtis, for his encouragement and patience during the writing of this book; I have benefited from his knowledge and judgment and value his friendship. I'd also like to thank my faithful First Reader, Eric Stein, whose friendship and estimable abilities I have enjoyed for many years, and my old friend Bill King, who spent a lot of his valuable time helping me turn my manuscript into a better one. I am grateful to Bertis Downs, general counsel for R.E.M., for sharing his valuable insights with me, and to Henry Root, who practices music law in Los Angeles, for giving me the West Coast perspective. I appreciate the assistance I received from Steven Gladstone, Nashville music lawyer; from Fred Koller, Nashville writer, songwriter, and performer *extraordinaire*; from Ellen Caldwell, of the Recording Industry Association of America; from Pat Huber Rogers, of the Nashville Songwriters Association International; from Kathy Hyland, of the Songwriters Guild of America; and from Dennis Wile, whose photographic portraits make all his subjects look more interesting. I am also grateful to my sister Sonia St. Charles, who took over the management of many time-consuming areas of housekeeping in the country at a critical point during the construction of this book, and to my little nephew Will, who, at three, could already read the Do Not Disturb sign on the door of my study.

Preface

This book was written for a band that doesn't exist anymore. The Boyz, as I'll call them, were a talented band of four guys. Three of them had college degrees and all had several years' experience making a living from their music. But their career crashed and burned just as they were attracting the attention of people who could have helped get it off the ground.

The Boyz were a successful cover band who signed a booking agreement that was like an indentured servitude agreement. Two years into playing small clubs and fraternity parties every fall and winter and debutante parties every spring, they wearied of hauling themselves around the country in a crowded van and decided to begin to play original material exclusively. Their booking agent didn't like their decision, primarily because he was making good commissions off their cover-band dates. When they tried to leave him and began to book themselves into some of the clubs where they had become well known, they found that there was a paragraph in their booking agreement that allowed their booker to claim a commission on every date they played in any club into which he had ever booked them for a very long time to come. He also claimed that they owed him money under a management agreement that he had induced two of The Boyz to sign, and that he was entitled to their publishing, too, under the terms of a vague "deal memo" that they had all signed, thinking it wasn't binding. He held on to money that was due them, refused to talk to their new manager, and threatened to sue.

The band and I tried for months to reach a settlement with their booker. Their new manager left them. A record company lost interest in them when it discovered that the status of their publishing was in doubt. They began to squabble among themselves. After a few months of this, the band split up. One band member joined another band; one went back to his teaching job; one returned to school for a degree in art history; one resumed his career as a waiter. All their hopes had drowned in a puddle of problems.

How did four smart guys get into such a fix? By having too little information at a very important stage in their careers—the stage that precedes serious money and a real future in music. I call this stage the Abyss of Ignorance because it traps so many people. Had The Boyz known as much about the business side of their careers as they knew about their music, their time on-stage would not have been so short. As it was, they were eliminated from competition in the first round. I tried hard to help them because I liked them and thought they had a future as a band, and my advice to them was the best I could muster, but it had one flaw—it was *too late*. Nothing I could tell them could undo what they had already done.

This book won't help The Boyz. They already learned the lessons it can teach the hard way. But it can help you. Getting the information you need when you need it is as important to a career in music as knowing how to sing and play. This book is intended to furnish you with that information—to tell you what you need to know before you can afford to hire a lawyer. It is not intended to *substitute* for a lawyer but is meant to educate you enough so that you can avoid some of the traps songwriters and musicians fall into and to alert you to the events that are clear signals that you need a lawyer's advice and guidance *now*.

Think of this book as a map for the first few years of your career in music, with the pitfalls and predators you're likely to encounter clearly marked and a few pointers in the right direction at important crossroads. It won't tell you everything you need to know to make it in the music business, but it will help you avoid some dead ends and will speed you down the avenues that are open to you because of your talent and persistence.

Lee Wilson
Nashville, Tennessee
January 1995

I

INTRODUCTION

One reason people are so intrigued by the idea of making money making music is that the music business is like the lottery. One lucky break can turn a bunch of struggling musicians who haven't had the nerve to give up their day jobs into a band with a record deal and a sudden need for an accountant and a lawyer. It doesn't happen to every hopeful who rides into L.A. or New York or Nashville on a Greyhound bus, but it does happen, and it is the stories of those hometown boys and girls who conquer Hollywood or the Apple or Music City that feed the dreams of all the high school kids who play air guitar in front of MTV and plan their own eventual escapes into stardom. Few rock star wannabes ever consider the possibility that they will never make it past the waiting-tables stage of a career in music; the dream is too strong to admit any thought of failure. And most singers and songwriters, even those who have worked at their craft for several years, don't pay enough attention to the business side of their music until their dream springs a leak because they have neglected some important part of it.

That's too bad. People who will work for six months to perfect a song lyric or guitar technique should be more concerned about protecting the result of their work, because that result, the song or the performance, can be very valuable. Writing a hit song is like creating an annuity for yourself out of thin air. And no one knows what makes a star, but when you've got whatever it is, people will notice you and pay you for it.

Unfortunately, creative people are often frustrated by the paperwork necessary to document their business arrangements. They believe contracts are simply unnecessary aggravations inflicted on them by lawyers and the other people in suits who stand between them and their paychecks. Consequently, they don't know as much as they should about what those contracts say and they aren't as careful as they should be in signing them. This is a naive attitude, and a dangerous one. Talent is elusive in any industry, but in the music industry the products of talent—songs and stage presence and name recognition—are *invisible*. That means the only business life those fruits of talents have are on paper, in contracts.

Thanks largely to that workhorse the First Amendment, the music industry in the United States is comparatively unregulated. However, that doesn't mean the music industry is untouched by legal concerns. In fact, a good argument can be made that the industry wouldn't exist at all without copyright law. Of course, contract law is important in the business of music, too, as are trademark law, partnership law, and several other kinds of business law. You don't need a law degree, yet, to become a hit songwriter or a rock troubadour or a country music heartthrob, but you do need to know enough law to protect yourself in the early days of your career, when your star is just beginning to shine.

After you become successful, expensive lawyers will compete to buy you lunch and listen to your problems (for a fee). However, before you can pay for it by the hour, reliable information about music industry law and business practices is hard to come by. That's what this book is about—giving you the information you need when it will do you the most good, which, believe it or not, was *yesterday*.

Skeptical? Dear reader, there are sharks in the waters of the American music industry. They eat greenhorns like you for breakfast. You can lose your songs, your spotlight, and your shirt if you don't know how to avoid them.

And you have to watch out for more than sharks. One of the biggest hazards that endanger music industry novices is their own vast ignorance. At least half the big mistakes you can make in trying to create and manage a music career are your own bad decisions. To make the right decisions, you need the right information at the right time. In the music business, as in any other business, what you don't know *will* hurt you.

• To prosper as a songwriter, you need to know more about copyright law than most lawyers, because copyrights are a songwriter's stock-in-trade. You must understand how copyrights are created, what rights copyright gives you, what copyright protects, how long the protection lasts, and how to secure the best protection copyright law allows. You must know how to stay out of copyright infringement lawsuits, how to tell whether someone has infringed your copyright, and what to do if someone has. You must understand music publishing agreements and the sources of income earned by your songs. And you need to know how copyright ownership is transferred and how songwriters or their heirs can terminate copyright transfers.

• • If you're a performer, you need to understand that the other members of your band may be your partners even if you never sign a partnership agreement, and you need to know what rights and liabilities a partnership entails. When you choose a name for your band, you need to know that using the wrong name can puncture your career as surely as bad guitar playing, and you need to know how you can avoid becoming involved in a trademark infringement lawsuit just when you start earning money from your music. And you need to know how to protect the most valuable asset any band owns outside its talent—its name—from interlopers and imitators who want a free ride on your hard-won reputation.

You must understand the first important relationships you must develop to succeed as a performer, those with your booking agent and your manager. You need to know how to find and choose one of each, what bookers and managers do, how booking and management agreements work, and what to do when the honeymoon is over.

And you need to know more about lawyers than you probably want to: the role of the music lawyer, how to find and hire a good one, how to pay your lawyer, and how to get the best from him or her.

It's easier than you think to learn what you need to know. Anyone who is smart enough to write a good song or play lead guitar has more than enough intelligence to figure out how to escape the sharks and avoid the abyss. Every beginning songwriter and unknown singer wants to become rich making music and retire to a ranch on Maui. You can begin your journey by having the gumption to get on a Greyhound and leave home, but you need equal parts of talent, drive, and good advice to make it to Maui. This book contains the advice you need until you can hire your own advisors. It is no *substitute* for those advisors, but if you absorb the information it contains and follow the advice it gives, you'll be in good shape to fly when your career starts to take off. However, you'll have to furnish the talent and drive and the Greyhound ticket. It's going to be an interesting ride!

COPYRIGHT FOR
SONGWRITERS

Copyright Basics

Many songwriters believe that copyright law is simply tedious stuff that nobody except lawyers and maybe music publishers needs to know anything about. In fact, copyright so permeates the music business that a working knowledge of copyright law is essential for anyone who hopes for any sort of music career. Since copyrights are their stock-in-trade, songwriters especially need to know plenty about copyright law, both to protect their own rights and to avoid violating the rights of others. That's why the first four chapters of this book explain copyright law and the business practices that surround the exploitation of music copyrights. Don't think that four chapters on copyright is overkill. In fact, unless you read and understand these chapters on copyright, you can skip the others, since without a working knowledge of copyright law you'll be too uninformed to create a career in music anyway.

The rights of all U.S. copyright owners are created by the U.S. copyright statute (a statute is a written law), which is the latest in a long series of copyright statutes passed by Congress. (There is no such thing as a state copyright statute; there is only one copyright statute in the United States and that statute is a federal statute.)

Our copyright statute exists because of a provision inserted into the U.S. Constitution by the men who wrote it. Article I, Section 8, Clause 8 of the Constitution gives Congress the power to make a law that "promote[s] the Progress of Science and useful Arts, by securing, for limited Times to Authors and Inventors, the exclusive Right to their respective Writings and Discoveries." This section of the Constitution is the origin of both the U.S. patent and copyright statutes. The idea behind this provision was to encourage American citizens to create books and inventions by giving them property rights in their creations.

Congress passed the first American copyright statute in 1790; it protected only books, charts, and maps. Musical compositions were granted copyright protection in 1831, photographs in 1865, paintings, drawings, and statuary in 1870, movies in 1912, but sound recordings were not granted protection until 1971. The newest U.S. copyright statute became effective January 1, 1978. It aims to encompass both existing and emerging technologies for creative expression by stating simply that copyright protects "original works of authorship fixed in any tangible medium of expression, now known or later developed, from which they can be perceived, reproduced, or otherwise communicated, either directly or with the aid of a machine or device." (The new copyright statute refers generally to all copyrightable products of the imagination as "works" and to the creators of these "works" as "authors," even when the "work" created by the "author" is something besides a book. We will occasionally adopt the terminology of the copyright statute in our discussion of copyright, and that discussion will focus on musical compositions, since those are the sorts of "works" that primarily concern songwriters.)

The implications of the phrase "fixed in any tangible medium of expression" affect every songwriter. Since the new copyright statute became effective, copyright protection for any song you write begins the moment your song is recorded on tape or written on paper, but not *before*, even if you've carried your tune around in your head and sung it in the shower for months.

Since the "fixation" of your song is the trigger for copyright protection, you should record your song on tape or reduce it to a lead sheet *before* performing it live in a club. You don't have to rent a studio and hire musicians to produce a 16-track tape of your song or hire an arranger to reduce it to a completely notated score to trigger copyright protection. <u>All that is necessary</u> is that your music and lyrics be recorded in sufficient detail that your song is accurately represented. A guitar-vocal cassette recorded on a boom box or a simple lead sheet with the lyrics and melody of your song will do it. Copyright begins once your song is "fixed." Unless you write a song as a "work-for-hire," *because* you wrote it, you own the copyright in it until you transfer ownership of the copyright to a music publisher under a song publishing agreement. (We'll talk more about work-for-hire and transfers of copyright in Chapter Four.)

But what, exactly, *is* a copyright? A copyright is a set of what are called "exclusive" rights. Exclusive rights may be exercised only, or *exclusively*, by the owner of those rights. Although copyright protection does not begin until a work is "fixed in [a] tangible medium of expression," copyright itself is *in*tangible; that is, you can't see a copyright or hold it in your hands or put it in your pocket. It is invisible, but valuable. In essence, a copyright is your admission ticket to participate in a complicated system based in federal law that exists to ensure that you as a songwriter get paid for any use of your songs. Even the lowliest unpublished, unrecorded songwriter can count on the full majesty and power of the U.S. government to help perfect and protect his or her song copyright, even if it is a *bad* song, because the copyright statute is a *federal* law, administered by a *federal* agency, the Copyright Office, and the courts that hear copyright suits are *federal* courts.

(Consequently, however, all this law ends at the border, because U.S. laws have no jurisdiction outside the United States or its territories other than the more or less reciprocal recognition other countries grant U.S. copyrights under the various copyright treaties to which the U.S. is a party. Under certain conditions that are too complicated to explain here, the copyright statute also limits the right of some foreign nationals to enjoy the protection of U.S. copyright law even if they create otherwise copyrightable works within the United States. If you're not a U.S. citizen, you may want to ask a copyright lawyer to help you determine under what conditions your songs are protected by U.S. law.)

Under the present copyright statute, copyright protection automatically begins when you first fix a song in tangible form. No formalities are necessary to acquire the protection of copyright law; you don't need anyone's permission to protect your new song with copyright and you don't have to file anything with any government agency. Copyright protection follows automatically, by action of federal law, from the act of creating a copyrightable work.

Many songwriters assume that their songs are unprotected by copyright until they send off application forms and fees to the Copyright Office to register them. This is not the case. Neither is it necessary to use copyright notice to secure the protection of copyright. The existence of the song as written in lead sheet form or recorded on a cassette is sufficient to trigger copyright protection. However, although copyright protection actually begins the moment a song is first fixed in any tangible form, the full range of benefits of copyright are not secured until the song is registered and unless proper copyright notice is used, as we will discuss at greater length in Chapter Two.

In short, the vast federal copyright machinery is like a bulldozer standing guard over the rights given you by the copyright statute, ready to help you squash anyone who would disregard them—but *you* have to set it going. Your key to federal copyright protection is the set of exclusive rights the government grants you, as a new copyright owner, whenever you write a song.

The exclusive rights of copyright applicable to musical compositions are:

- The right to reproduce the copyrighted song in "phonorecords" (a term that includes vinyl records, cassette tapes, CDs, and all other "material objects," *except* audiovisual recordings, that embody recordings of copyrighted works) or otherwise make copies of it
- The right to distribute copies or phonorecords of the copyrighted song to the public
- The right to create "derivative works" (alternate versions) of the copyrighted song
- The right to perform the song publicly

With certain narrow exceptions, no one but the owner of a song copyright may exercise any of these rights. Any unauthorized exercise of any of these rights by anyone but the copyright owner is called copyright infringement, because any poacher on the copyright owner's territory is said to "infringe" upon the owner's rights, or violate them.

It's easier to understand these four exclusive rights of copyright if you consider them in terms of the ways songs are used.

Because the copyright statute gives you the exclusive right to reproduce your song in "phonorecords" and the exclusive right to distribute any such phonorecords to the public, only you may record it and sell copies of the recording in the form of vinyl records, tapes, CDs, and other phonorecords. This is true *unless* your song has been recorded previously with your permission and the recording was distributed in the form of phonorecords to the public within the United States. In that situation anyone can issue another recording of the song, subject only to the obligations imposed by law to notify you in advance of releasing the new phonorecord, to pay you royalties at a prescribed rate, and to furnish you with monthly royalty statements. This provision of the copyright statute is referred to as the "compulsory (mechanical) license" provision. Although you, as the owner of the song copyright, are the one who (theoretically) grants permission, also known as a "license," to record your song, the law makes the granting of such permission compulsory. That is, the law decrees that you must issue such a license. (There are three other, less important, uses specified in the copyright statute for which compulsory licensing is prescribed. Compulsory licenses also apply to uses of songs by PBS television broadcasters and in jukeboxes, and to some cable television uses.)

As a practical matter, however, because the copyright statute sets out strict and specific accounting regulations by which record companies must abide when they record songs under the compulsory mechanical license provision of the statute, record companies prefer to obtain permission to record songs by "direct license" rather than exercising their right to record the songs under a compulsory license. A direct license is a permission to record a song obtained directly from the owner of the song copyright. Record companies like direct licenses because they usually can persuade copyright owners to agree to more lenient accounting obligations and lower royalties than the copyright statute imposes for compulsory licenses.

The right to reproduce a song in the form of records, tapes, CDs, and other phonorecords is referred to as the "mechanical rights" to the song. The royalties paid by record companies for the use of songs as phonorecords are referred to as "mechanical royalties" or "mechanicals." (Most reproductions of songs have been electronic rather than mechanical for many years now, but when phonographs were invented they *were* mechanical, so we're stuck with the term "mechanicals.") Mechanical royalties are currently fixed by the Library of Congress at 6.6¢ per song for songs of five minutes or less or 1.25¢ per minute of playing time for songs longer than five minutes, per phonorecord sold. These rates are periodically adjusted for inflation; the statutory rate will increase again on January 1, 1996. (It is very common for record companies to pay even less than this small royalty for songs written or owned by the artists who record them, through the "controlled composition" clauses found in most contracts between recording artists and record companies.)

Because the copyright statute gives you the exclusive right to make and distribute other sorts of copies of your song, only you may synchronize the song with visual images, as for a movie, television program, commercial, or other audiovisual project, and only you may print and sell sheet music or make and distribute other visual copies of it. The right to use a song for a television or movie soundtrack is called the "synch (or synchronization) rights" to the song; the right to print sheet music is referred to as the "print rights." (But remember not to call the right to use your song as the "soundtrack" for a radio ad a "synch license," because there are no visuals in radio with which to synchronize your song. A radio commercial license is called a "transcription license," for some reason that nobody remembers anymore.)

Because the copyright statute gives you the exclusive right to create "derivative works" from your song, only you may change its words or music or create other versions of it or *derive* other works from it, such as a television script based on the characters and story of the song. Another common sort of derivative work that often produces bags of money for songwriters who agree to allow such uses of their songs is the reworking of a song into an advertising jingle by means of new or altered lyrics and/or a revised or shortened melody. (For instance, Mega Airlines could rewrite the lyrics of "The Wind Beneath My Wings" to refer to the joys of flying with Mega Airlines.) The right to prepare alternate versions of a song or create a derivative work from it is referred to as the "derivative rights" to the song.

The copyright statute also gives you the exclusive right to perform your song publicly. The "performance rights" to a song are divided into "small performing rights" and "grand performing rights."

The small performing rights are primarily the right to perform a song on radio and television, in clubs, concert halls, and parks, and in restaurants and other businesses on public address systems. The "performing rights organizations" (BMI, ASCAP, and SESAC) exist to collect the royalties created by these sorts of public performances of songs because it would be next to impossible for individual copyright owners themselves to collect the royalties due them from the many end users of their songs. These "public-performance royalties" typically represent one of the largest sources of income for songwriters.

The grand performing rights to a song are primarily the right to perform it in a musical play or as part of a television show or movie in a way that advances the plot. (In practice, however, the performance of a song in a television show, for instance, will create royalties for the small performing rights, and the grand performing rights will be included in the synchronization license issued by the copyright owner.)

Of course, the exclusive rights of copyright are exercised every day, legally, by people who didn't write the songs they use. How? These users obtain permission from the owners of the song copyrights, who are usually very happy to allow their songs to be used in return for appropriate payment. In other words, it's not trespassing if you have permission.

The exclusive rights of copyright apply only to what is actually protected by copyright. It may surprise you to learn that certain elements of your songs are *not* protected by copyright, no matter how hard you worked to come up with them. In fact, to understand what copyright protects, you need to know first what it does *not* protect.

The most basic premise of copyright law is that copyright protects only particular *expressions* of ideas, *not* the ideas themselves. This is a hard concept to grasp; it confuses even lawyers and judges. Nevertheless, it *is* logical, if you think about it. Our Constitution empowered Congress to pass a copyright law "to promote the Progress of Science and useful Arts." In other words, the goal of our copyright statute is to encourage free expression and creation so that all of society may benefit from the insights of the creators among us. If our copyright law allowed people to monopolize ideas, which are the building blocks of all literature, art, and music, free expression would be stifled.

Instead, copyright law gives you exclusive rights only in your own particular, original expression of any idea. Therefore, anyone else's expression of the same idea is equally protectable by copyright, even if that person's expression duplicates yours. In fact, if two people independently come up with identical expressions of the same idea, both own valid copyrights in their expressions of it. The key to understanding this concept of copyright law is the word "independently." No one can *copy* your expression of an idea without risking a lawsuit for copyright infringement, but if another songwriter *coincidentally* duplicates the melody of your song, the law says he or she owns the copyright in that duplicate melody just as you own the copyright in yours.

There are other elements of songs besides the ideas they express that are not protected by copyright. All of these unprotectable elements are like ideas in that they are "building blocks" for songs that should be free for anyone to use.

Themes of songs are not protected by copyright. To understand this, think about love songs. Most popular songs in our culture are love songs, but there are only so many love song themes. Since the advent of radio, songwriters have filled the airwaves with variations on only a few: I'm-in-love-and-life-is-new, I-love-you-please-love-me-too, she-broke-my-heart-and-now-I'm-blue, he-left-me-what-can-I-do, you-lied-to-me-I'm-leaving-you. If copyright law granted a monopoly on the use of these themes to the first songwriters who created songs around them, the building blocks available to other songwriters would be so severely limited that no one after about 1952 could have written a love song without infringing the rights of someone who used the theme first. However, because there is no copyright in themes and since each theme can be expressed in an infinite number of ways, the world has not lacked for love songs, in the form of thousands of copyrightable *expressions* of each possible theme.

A word of caution, however. Although using the same theme for your song that another songwriter used first is never copyright infringement, taking any more from another song than the bare bones of the theme *can* amount to infringement.

The moment you begin lifting from someone else's song any part of that songwriter's *expression* of a universal theme, you risk copyright infringement. Conversely, the more a song is a creative expression of a theme rather than just a bare, unadorned presentation of the theme itself, the more protection it is given.

Almost every songwriter has heard that there is no copyright protection for song titles. This is true. Copyright law specifically withholds protection from short phrases such as titles and slogans. The reasoning behind this rule is that titles and slogans are too close to mere unembellished ideas to be granted copyright protection.

This means that if you find you've chosen for your song the same title as that used for an existing song, you don't have to worry about having infringed the other songwriter's copyright. However, if you intentionally or accidentally use the title of a famous song by another songwriter as the name of your song, you could run afoul of another kind of law, the law of unfair competition. It works like this: If you use the title of a well-known song as the name of your new one, consumers could buy the album that includes a cut of your song in the mistaken belief that it includes a cut of the famous song. Unfair competition law seeks to prevent this sort of consumer confusion by prohibiting your selling your product by taking a free ride on your competitors' coattails. Smart songwriters avoid very famous song titles in naming their own compositions because choosing an already-famous name for the title of a new song can result in a lawsuit for unfair competition, which can be as expensive and troublesome as a copyright infringement suit. And since most music publishers will shy away from song titles that are already famous, you'll probably have to re-name your song before it is cut, anyway.

If copyright law does not protect titles, neither does it protect any other sort of short slogan or lyrical phrase. This means that short catchphrases or slogans used in songs are not protected by copyright. Short phrases of any sort are considered to embody too little creative expression to be entitled to copyright protection; that is, they are deemed by the law to be simply another variety of building block. As a general rule, the shorter the phrase, the less protection it is granted, since the shorter the phrase, the less protectable "expression" it embodies. Further, even if the phrase is a relatively long one, if it's merely a popular slogan that you have incorporated into your song as a lyric, any other songwriter can also use the slogan without infringing your rights, because you are not deemed to *have* any exclusive rights in it. If you use a popular slogan as the "hook" of your song, no one can legally copy your melody or the original parts of your song's lyrics, but they can use your hook in another song with impunity.

The denial of copyright protection to short phrases means that there is no more protection for short *musical* phrases than for short verbal phrases. Copyright does not protect short riffs, chord progressions, or other brief musical phrases.

Because copyright law does not protect methods or systems, the structure of your song is not copyrightable. Whether the structure of a musical composition is a method or a system or something in between is hard to say, but whatever it is, it's not sheltered under the copyright umbrella. In other words, copyright does not protect the way a song is constructed, only the particular musical and lyrical expression that is hung on the basic unprotectable framework of the song.

A related principle is that copyright does not protect your arrangements of other people's songs or, at least, arrangements that you can create without running the risk of infringing someone's copyright. It works like this: An arrangement of a song that is different enough from the underlying musical composition to evidence real originality would be protectable by copyright as a derivative work of the composition. No derivative work of a copyrighted composition can be created without the permission of the owner of the copyright, so no such extensive arrangement of anyone else's song is possible without copyright infringement. An arrangement that is *not* an extensive reworking of the underlying composition probably amounts only to a new method of performing the composition and therefore does not embody a new expression sufficient to earn copyright protection.

The exception to this rule is arrangements of public domain songs. These are old songs for which copyright protection has expired. Since anyone can exercise any of the rights in a public domain composition that were formerly reserved to the owner of the copyright in that composition, you can create any new version of the song you want, arranging its music or changing its lyrics at will, and earn at the same time copyright protection for your new version of the old song. You will not, by tinkering with an old standard, somehow retrieve from the public domain the basic underlying song; that's impossible under the law. However, you can keep others from using your *version* of the song without your permission.

Surprisingly, this is *not* a useless piece of information. More than one big pop hit has actually consisted of new lyrics for a new arrangement of an old favorite. For example, the Elvis Presley hit "Love Me Tender" is nothing more than a reworking of a popular Civil War–era ballad called "Aura Lee." And more than one songwriter has used the melody from a piece of classical music as the basis of a new song. (Don't rush off to write hit versions of old pop tunes or classical melodies until you read Chapter Two, in which we will discuss how you can determine whether a song is indeed in the public domain and available for reworking without pesky copyright infringement problems.)

Under ordinary circumstances, the owner of a song copyright is the person who wrote the song. Although ownership of the copyright begins the moment the song is fixed in a tangible form, ownership of the physical object in which the song is embodied does *not* convey any ownership in the copyright to the song. If two or more people collaborate to write a song, they each own equal shares of the song copyright unless they agree when the song is written that one of them owns a larger or smaller share because of his or her larger or smaller contribution. It is a quirk of copyright law that if a lyricist writes all the lyrics to a song and a composer writes the entire melody, each owns half of the *entire song,* rather than the lyricist owning only the lyrics and the composer owning only the music. This means that if you've written a song with another writer you can't simply take the melody you wrote and get your buddy Leon to write new lyrics; in fact, if you did, the first lyricist would own an interest in the new version of the song because he would own half the music you used for the new version. But this is not so if you compose a piece of music that you do not *intend* to merge with lyrics later, or if you write a poem with no idea that it may be set to music to become the lyrics to a song. In these instances, the composer would own 100 percent of his music and the poet would own 100 percent of her poem, even if either should later be turned into part of a song. The intent of the composer and lyricist *at the time of writing the music or lyrics* is the determining factor.

If you do collaborate with another songwriter to write a song, you may make any non-exclusive use you wish of the *entire* song, without the other songwriter's consent and even if the other writer hates the idea, subject only to the obligation to share the proceeds from any such exploitation of the song with the other writer according to his or her percentage ownership of it. This means, for example, that you can offer your song to your girlfriend for her new album without asking your co-writer for permission. What you can't do is withhold income the song produces from your co-writer, since each of you owns half the song and is, therefore, entitled to half the money it earns. And neither of you, without permission from the other, can grant anybody the *exclusive* right to use the song for any purpose, since that would tie up the song and limit the income it could earn.

Once your song is written, your copyright in it will endure until your children are grandparents, and during all those years no one can legally record your song without paying you, or change your music or lyrics, or base a movie or stage play on it without permission from you or your heirs. (In Chapter Two you'll find out exactly how long copyright protection lasts under various circumstances, and what you must do to protect your copyrights.)

The exception to the rule that the person who creates a work owns the copyright in it is a doctrine of copyright law known as "work-for-hire." This doctrine has little to do with ordinary songwriting, except in some cases that we will discuss in Chapter Three involving music publishers who try to take advantage of the unsuspecting songwriter by inserting work-for-hire provisions in song publishing agreements. However, songwriters who write advertising jingles or scores for slide shows and films often do encounter work-for-hire provisions that are legitimately a part of agreements to write such music.

When a piece of music or a jingle (words and music for use in an ad) is prepared as a work-for-hire, the client who commissions the music or jingle owns the copyright in it from the moment of its creation and is considered its author for copyright purposes. This exception to the "if you write it, you own it" rule recognizes the reality that exists in such situations, i.e., that the client specifies the sort of musical composition required for the purposes of the client and the composer or jingle writer prepares the composition according to those specifications, more or less under the supervision of the client.

The law requires that this departure from the usual rule be well documented to avoid situations in which a client simply assumes that he or she owns the copyright in a composition and the composer or jingle writer disagrees. Consequently, no piece of music or jingle can be a work-for-hire unless there is a written agreement, signed by *both* the composer or jingle writer and the commissioning client, documenting the fact that the composition was prepared as a work-for-hire. The copyright statute is explicit on this point, and the moral of this little tale about works-for-hire is "know what you are signing *before* you pull out your Bic."

Confusingly enough, there is an important exception to the requirement that work-for-hire arrangements be documented in written agreements. If you compose a piece of music or write a song as a part of the ordinary duties of your job, your employer owns the copyright in the music or the song, which is considered a work-for-hire. As a practical matter, there are very few jobs that involve any sort of songwriting as a regular duty of employment, but they do exist. A staff writer for a jingle company writes jingles as works-for-hire. The same is true for a staff composer who creates soundtracks for a film production company. The people who create musical compositions every day at the office already know who they are and that their employers automatically own the copyrights in their compositions. The important thing for *you* to remember is that, in ordinary circumstances, songwriters are not actual employees of music publishers and do not write the songs they create as works-for-hire for their publishers, even if they sign exclusive songwriting contracts.

Pop Quiz

The following quiz is designed to find out whether you've been paying attention. In this book, we operate on the honor system. If you get only one answer right, go back and read this chapter again. If you answer two questions correctly, pat yourself on the back. If you get all three questions right, you're beginning to think like a lawyer; lie down in a darkened room until you feel better.

Q. Jack's girlfriend Amy dumps him for a guy who wears a gold pinky ring and drives a Jaguar. Jack is miserable without her and convinced that romance only leads to heartbreak. He writes a song to express his misery and disillusionment. He calls it "No More Amour." The chorus is four lines of death-less poetry that come to him one night as he is crying in his beer:

> "Love is like a little bug,
> With arms just like a lizard.
> It twines itself around your heart,
> And nibbles at your gizzard."

Jack records a demo of "No More Amour" in his buddy's basement 16-track studio and takes copies around to some music publishers. He also gives a demo tape to his cousin Sol, who works with the brother of the drummer for Rock City, a local metal band just signed by a little record company distributed by a big one. Jack forgets about becoming rich off record royalties when, after several months, it appears that nobody wants to publish his song, much less record it, and he meets another woman *not* named Amy who makes romance look interesting again. Until, that is, he hears the title cut from Rock City's first album, a song called "No More Love."

Jack can't believe the similarities between Rock City's song and his. Like Jack's song, "No More Love" is the lament of a man whose heart has been broken by a woman who left him for someone else. And the chorus!

> "Love is a worm
> That eats at my heart,
> And entangles my soul
> In its tentacles."

Jack isn't sure whether worms have tentacles, but he is sure his rights have been violated. He makes an appointment with the only lawyer he knows who knows anything about copyright law to ask whether she'll handle the copyright infringement suit he intends to file against Rock City and starts wondering how he'll spend the money the judge will award him. Does Jack have a case?

A. Jack's lawyer may break his heart again when she tells him he doesn't have a case and she won't help him bring an infringement suit. Whether Rock City wrote "No More Love" after hearing "No More Amour" is immaterial; even if they did copy Jack's song, the only elements of it they stole are unprotectable by copyright law. Copyright does not give Jack exclusive rights in the theme of his song: the pain of losing a lover. Lots of songs written before Jack was even born employed exactly this theme; think of "I'll Never Smile Again" (recorded by The Ink Spots), "Heartbreak Hotel" (Elvis Presley), "Bye, Bye, Love" (The Everly Brothers), "It's My Party (And I'll Cry If I Want To)" (Lesley Gore), and "Yesterday" (The Beatles).

The similar chorus of Rock City's song won't make a case for copyright infringement, either. Jack's chorus and Rock City's chorus express the same idea, that of love as a parasite that gnaws at your innards. As we have seen, ideas are not protected by copyright. Copyright infringement does result when one person copies another's *expression* of an idea and the second expression is "substantially similar" to the first, but Rock City's song *as a whole* would have to be much more like Jack's to infringe Jack's song—the similarity between the choruses of the songs is not sufficient to constitute infringement of "No More Amour" by "No More Love." (More about copyright infringement in Chapter Three.)

Even though Rock City's song title is nearly the same as Jack's, because copyright does not include titles in its scope of protection, this similarity is likewise immaterial.

Jack's lawyer tells him that although it does seem likely that Rock City copied his song, they have copied only parts of it that are not protected by copyright. She says that because the verses of the two songs are very different and the only similarities are between the unprotectable themes, the unprotectable titles, and the similar (unprotectable) ideas expressed in the choruses, he has no copyright infringement claim against the band. Jack is bowed but unbeaten. In honor of his new girlfriend, he rewrites "No More Amour" as a love song called "More Amour," which is signed by a publisher and recorded by a bigger act than Rock City, who disappear without a trace after their first album flops, for which Jack is not even a little bit sorry.

Q. One afternoon at the restaurant where they're working as waiters until the world discovers they're really hit songwriters, Rob and Mike write a beautiful love ballad they call "Come to Me, Ramona." Rob picks out the melody on the piano in the bar before happy hour and Mike jots the lyrics on the back of a menu. After they polish the song a little, they decide they've written a hit.

Rob prevails on a friend who owns a studio to let them demo their song late at night when no one wants to book studio time. Then Rob starts to shop the tape. He plays the song for his mom; she says she thinks he shows definite promise and that "Come to Me, Ramona" is perfect for Julio Iglesias. Rob doesn't know much about Julio Iglesias except that his records sell, but that's enough to make Rob like him. Rob starts trying to get publishers interested in "Come to Me, Ramona" and recalls that his old college roommate once said he knew Julio Iglesias's valet.

Nothing happens for a month or two, but then one day a publisher calls to say he's interested in signing Rob and Mike's song. Rob can't wait to tell Mike.

As Rob is driving to work the next day, he hears an ad for a local carwash on the radio. The jingle sounds a lot like "Come to Me, Ramona"! The words are different (there's no mention of "Tony's All-Cloth Carwash" in the lyrics Rob wrote), but the jingle tune is *identical* to the melody of the song that was going to make Rob and Mike enough money to let them leave their jobs as waiters. Rob is steamed. He thinks some unscrupulous ad agency got hold of a copy of the demo tape and stole the song's melody. He can't wait to tell Mike.

When he sees Mike, however, Mike says nonchalantly that he already knows about the carwash jingle because he gave a copy of the demo to his brother-in-law Tony and told him he could use the melody for his jingle. Mike is surprised that Rob is angry. He sees nothing wrong with what he did because, he says, *he* was the one who wrote the melody.

Rob can't believe what he's hearing. "Come to Me, Ramona" has been turned into a carwash jingle and Mike did it and he doesn't even care! He remembers from his college music law class that turning a song into a jingle is creating a "derivative work" from it and that this is a right the law reserves to the owner of the copyright in the song. He figures that since he is one of the owners of the copyright in "Come to Me, Ramona," he should have some control over how the song is used.

But what really makes Rob see red is that Mike tells him he intends to keep the whole $500 Tony paid him for his melody, because nobody used Rob's lyrics for anything. Rob decides to consult a lawyer.

Does Rob have any reason to be angry?

A. Maybe Rob has reason to be angry because his ballad has been used to advertise a carwash, but not because Mike has violated his rights as joint owner of the copyright in it. The lawyer Rob consults is his Uncle Harry, who practices real estate law but knows something about copyright law because he once had a band. The first thing Uncle Harry tells Rob is to stop saying that he is going to "rearrange" Mike's face, because assault is illegal and what Mike did is not. Rob stops pounding on Uncle Harry's desk and begins to listen to what he has to say.

Uncle Harry tells Rob that he and Mike are joint owners of the copyright in "Come to Me, Ramona" because they both wrote the song and intended that their individual contributions, Rob's lyrics and Mike's melody, be merged into one song. This means that Mike, as one of the owners of the song copyright, can make whatever use he wants of the song, including allowing his brother-in-law to use the melody for an advertising jingle without consulting Rob. The only thing Mike cannot do without Rob's consent is to give someone the exclusive right to use the song, that is, tie the song up so that no other use can be made of it by granting someone an exclusive license to use it.

Rob is glad to hear, however, that Mike owes him $250. Even though Rob wrote the lyrics to "Come to Me, Ramona" and Mike wrote the music, each writer owns half the entire song, since they created their individual contributions with the intention that their melody and lyrics would be merged into one song. This joint ownership of all parts of the song means that any income produced by any use of the song by either of the joint owners must be split between them.

Mike pays Rob the $250, which Rob uses to get his guitar out of hock. "Come to Me, Ramona" is recorded by Garth Brooks, who sells a lot of records himself, and Mike and Rob are signed to an exclusive songwriting agreement by Uncle Harry, who decides to give up practicing law and return to his first love, music.

Q. Natalie comes across some great old acetate LPs in her parents' attic. They are her father's college record collection, and he gives them to Natalie along with an old phonograph that will play the 78s. The B side of one of them is a 1934 recording of a young Alberta Hunter singing "Two Cigarettes in the Dark."

Because she fancies that her voice is like Alberta Hunter's (circa 1934), Natalie wants to include "Two Cigarettes in the Dark" in her club act. Because she vehemently opposes smoking, Natalie wants to change the lyrics from the story of a woman who discovers that her lover is involved with another woman to the tale of a woman who rejects a man when she discovers he's a smoker; she intends to call her new version of the song "No Cigarettes or I'll Leave."

Natalie is not worried that she may be violating anybody's rights by changing the lyrics to "Two Cigarettes in the Dark." She remembers hearing that there was no copyright protection for sound recordings before 1972, and, since old acetate LPs are so fragile, she's sure she must own the only copy of the Alberta Hunter record in existence. Besides, she thinks anyone old enough to have written a song recorded in 1934 must have died before she was born, and anyway, she doesn't plan to touch the music of the song because she likes it just as it was written.

Is Natalie right about anything besides the evils of smoking?

A. Natalie may be a good singer, but she's a bad copyright lawyer. What Natalie proposes to do to the song on the old Alberta Hunter album is to create an alternate version of it, i.e., a "derivative work." Preparing a derivative work from a song that is protected by copyright is, as you will recall, one of the exclusive rights reserved to copyright owners. It makes no difference that Natalie does not plan to change the song melody; *any* significant change will be infringement if the song is still protected by copyright. This means Natalie should determine whether she will be violating anyone's copyright rights before she writes new lyrics for "Two Cigarettes in the Dark."

Natalie is correct that sound recordings were not eligible for copyright protection before 1972. There were some state laws prohibiting unauthorized duplication of sound recordings before 1972, but they weren't very effective in stopping record pirates from ripping off hit records. Congress finally figured out in 1971 that it needed to pass a nationwide law to stop record pirates; it did, and protection began in February 1972. But whether one could once have duplicated a sound recording without breaking the law has nothing at all to do with whether Natalie can change the lyrics to the song. Whether or whenever copyright began protecting the Alberta Hunter recording, the sound recording copyright is a copyright only in the *recording* of the song, *not* in the song itself.

Even if Natalie does own the only existing LP of the Alberta Hunter recording of the song, that has absolutely nothing to do with anybody's copyright rights in either the sound recording or the song. Ownership of a physical object that embodies a copyrighted work does not carry with it any ownership or other rights in the copyright itself. Even if *all* the recordings of "Two Cigarettes in the Dark" ever made had somehow disappeared, the owner of the copyright in that song, its publisher, would still have all the rights accorded every other copyright owner.

Although Natalie believes "Two Cigarettes in the Dark" is practically prehistoric, it was probably created when songs were protected for a period of seventy-five years, and unless it was written before 1918 it may *still* be protected by copyright. If so, any unauthorized exercise by Natalie of any of the exclusive rights of copyright will infringe the song. Whether the writers of the song have yet become stars in heaven is immaterial, since the duration of copyright in a song created before 1978 has nothing to do with when its authors died. What Natalie needs to find out is when "Two Cigarettes in the Dark" was first published and whether it is still protected by copyright. If the copyright in the song has expired, anyone, including Natalie, can create an alternate version without its publisher's permission because the song will have become a public domain song, available for use by anybody in any way. If the copyright has not expired, Natalie will be infringing it.

If you're as confused as Natalie is about all this, don't feel bad. Neither you nor Natalie has read the next chapter, in which we discuss the complicated topic "How long will my copyrights live after I myself am no longer 'fixed in a tangible form'?"

2

Copyright Protection

The bad news is that although this chapter is filled with lots of information you need to prosper as a songwriter, it's also one of the more boring chapters in this book. The good news is that it won't take any longer to read this chapter than to eat a ham sandwich, so raid your fridge and read on.

As you've seen, you can bring yourself under the gigantic wing of the U.S. government by the mere act of writing a song, because our copyright law is a federal law and copyright protection for your song magically begins the moment it is "fixed in any tangible medium of expression." You don't have to notify any government office that Title 17 of the United States Code, Section 101, *et seq.*, the Copyright Law of the United States of America, has to be stretched a little to accommodate your new work. Nor do you have to use copyright notice on copies of it; in fact, you don't even have to register your copyright to gain copyright protection. Protection is yours simply because you wrote the song.

"Copyright protection" means the protection the law gives copyright owners from unauthorized use of their works. The period during which the law protects a particular work is called the "term of copyright." The term of copyright for any song written after January 1, 1978, begins the moment the song is "fixed" in a tangible form; when this protection ends depends to a large extent on who wrote it and under what circumstances.

There are two basic sorts of terms of copyright, one that probably applies to the songs you write and another that applies only in certain circumstances.

Under ordinary circumstances, if you write a song, copyright in that song will endure until fifty years after your death. If you write your song with one or more co-writers, copyright protection will endure until fifty years after the last of you dies.

If, however, a musical composition is written as a work-for-hire, anonymously, or under a fictitious name, the term of copyright for the song will be either one hundred years from the date the song was created or seventy-five years from the date it is "published," whichever period expires first.

Because publication can determine the expiration of the term of copyright for a song, it can be very important to determine whether and when a song has been published within the meaning of the copyright statute. "Published," in this context, has a specialized meaning; acceptance of a song by a music publisher is not synonymous with "publication" of the song for copyright purposes. Generally, the copyright statute says that selling or otherwise distributing copies of a song to the public in the form of sheet music or phonorecords is "publication," but that a public performance of a song onstage or on the radio does not *of itself* constitute publication.

Since so many songwriters adopt stage names (which the Copyright Office calls, of course, "pseudonyms"), you should remember that you can probably lengthen the term of copyright for any song you write by simply using your real, legal name instead of your stage name in the "author" space on the PA form (more about this below) when you register your copyright in the song. This is because using your real name for copyright purposes gives you the basic life-plus-fifty years term of copyright rather than the seventy-five-or-one-hundred-years-whichever-expires-first period of protection granted to pseudonymous works.

Of course, you'll have to avoid killing yourself off early with drugs or alcohol or unsafe sex in order for this strategy to work, because fifty years plus the twenty-five you lived before you died of controlled-substance abuse is no increase. However, if you live to sixty-five before you die of heart disease (like any self-respecting American carnivore), you will have beaten the system, because the total term of copyright for your song will be 115 years (65 plus 50). If you really want to play the copyright statute for all it's worth, clean up your act now and live to be seventy-five or eighty; you'll enjoy the royalties from your songs until you die, and then your children can use them to pay for college for your grandchildren.

If you do write and register a song anonymously or using a pseudonym, you can easily convert the term of copyright granted to pseudonymous or anonymous works to the longer life-plus-fifty-years by disclosing to the Copyright Office your real name at any time before the copyright expires. The same goes for a song you write with someone else; if either of you discloses your real name to the Copyright Office, the term of copyright for the song will endure for fifty years after the last of you dies.

No such fiddling is possible with the term of copyright for works-for-hire. If you create a song or a piece of music as a part of your regular full-time job, your employer is the copyright owner from the inception of the work and is considered the author of it for copyright purposes; the copyright statute protects it for one hundred years from the date of its creation or seventy-five years from the date it is published, whichever period is shorter, with no second-guessing possible. The same is true for songs you are commissioned to create as an independent contractor; once you sign a document agreeing that your song is to be considered a work-for-hire, that song gets the same seventy-five-or-one-hundred-years-whichever-expires-first period of protection and you have no further control over any aspect of the song or its use.

But you don't really have to remember anything in the preceding paragraph, because if you're lucky enough to get someone to pay you a salary to write music full-time, you won't mind that your employer owns everything you write (or if you do object, you'll quit your job) and the term of copyright for what you write won't concern you. And if somebody who *won't* give you a job asks you to sign a work-for-hire agreement, you won't sign it until you've read Chapter Four carefully and have figured out whether it is a fair agreement under the circumstances or is overreaching. If it's fair, you'll sign and forget you ever wrote the song, because you and it will have permanently parted company; if it's not fair, you'll astonish the person who asked you to sign the agreement with your grasp of copyright law when you refuse to sign it, and you won't need to remember anything about the term of copyright for works-for-hire because your song won't become one.

Before the current copyright statute became effective, figuring out how long songs were protected by copyright was a lot more difficult. Songs were granted an initial twenty-eight-year term of copyright and a second twenty-eight-year renewal term, for a total of fifty-six years of protection. To secure the second twenty-eight years of protection, copyright owners had to renew their registrations with the Copyright Office. Failure to renew a copyright registration resulted in loss of copyright protection for the song.

The old system was cumbersome and often led to unfortunate circumstances for copyright owners. As a result, when the current copyright statute was being drafted, two important changes were written into the new law. The basic period of copyright protection was lengthened to life-plus-fifty-years to ensure that songwriters (and other authors) didn't outlive their copyrights. Further, the requirement that writers file for a renewal of copyright to secure the full available term of copyright protection was eliminated to ensure that songs would not accidentally fall into the public domain, thereby eliminating the payment of royalties. To even things up for those who owned still valid copyrights in works created before January 1, 1978, existing terms of copyright were extended to allow seventy-five years of protection rather than the fifty-six years (two twenty-eight-year terms) previously available.

You may think none of this stuff about the old copyright statute has anything to do with you, but you're wrong. It's important to understand the periods of copyright protection available to songs created before 1978 in order to know whether those older songs have ceased to be protected by copyright, because the date copyright protection stops delineates the boundary between copyright infringement and lawful use of a song written by someone else.

Songs for which copyright protection has expired are said to have fallen into the "public domain." The U.S. copyright statute is based on the assumption that creative people will be encouraged to create if they are given exclusive control for a period over the use of their works. After that control ends, the public will benefit from the right to make unlimited use of the previously protected creations. When a song falls into the public domain, this is what has happened; that is, the songwriter's right to control the use of the song has expired and the song has become available for use in any way by any member of the public, including you.

This means that with a public domain song you can legally lift the lyrics or use the melody, create a parody, change the lyrics, change the melody—in short, do without breaking the law all those things that would constitute copyright infringement if the song were still protected by copyright. The only thing you can't do with a public domain song is rescue it from the public domain; whatever you take from a public domain song for use in your own composition is *still* in the public domain, and you're entitled to copyright protection only for the part of your composition you created.

Determining the copyright status of a song can be tricky. It's never safe to assume that a song is in the public domain just because it seems ancient. Generally, you should never assume that copyright protection has expired for any song published less than seventy-five years ago; even though the owners of copyright in the song *may* have failed to renew their copyright registration after the first twenty-eight-year term of copyright, you won't *know* that unless you check with the Copyright Office. For example, copyright protection for a song written in 1924 may not expire until 1999. The best way to get a really accurate answer about the copyright status of a song is to read and follow the advice in the free Copyright Office publication called "How to Investigate the Copyright Status of a Work." Information on obtaining this handy little pamphlet is given in the Resources section of this book.

Most songwriters are confused about the effects of copyright registration. Despite the fact that the "new" copyright statute has been in effect for almost twenty years, they still believe that registration creates copyright rights. As you've seen, this is not so; your copyright rights are created automatically by the act of writing a song. Copyright registration does, however, *enhance* those rights.

In the United States, all copyrights are registered in the Copyright Office in Washington, D.C. The Copyright Office is the federal agency responsible for maintaining all records of U.S. copyright registrations and creating and disseminating regulations interpreting the copyright statute. This means that anything registered for copyright in the United States, from the latest textbook by your college physics professor to the newest album from Ozzie Osbourne, is registered in the Copyright Office. Strangely enough, both the physics textbook and the Ozzie Osbourne album may end up in the Library of Congress. The Copyright Office is a division of the Library of Congress, and copies of works being registered for copyright may be selected for the collections of the Library, depending on the work and the needs and acquisitions policies of the Library.

The Copyright Office prescribes the types of application forms to be used to apply for registration of copyright in various sorts of works. The only two of these forms that really concern you are the PA form, for registrations of songs, which are considered by the Copyright Office to be works of the Performing Arts, and the SR form, for registrations of Sound Recordings of all types except those embodied in audiovisual works. (You can order these free forms, and other Copyright Office publications, by calling the Copyright Office forms hotline at 202/707-9100 and leaving your name and address and information on the forms you want with the robot that answers this number twenty-four hours a day.)

Copyright registration forms are relatively simple, and you probably won't need a lawyer to help you fill one out. However, because a copyright registration certificate is an official document that evidences certain important legal rights and because your registration certificate will be reproduced directly from the application form you complete and send to the Copyright Office, you should take care that the information you furnish is accurate and that your application form is legible. Form PA is reproduced in the Appendixes of this book.

Songwriters may never need Form SR, since it's primarily used for registering the copyright in sound recordings, as opposed to the musical compositions underlying the sound recordings. Form PA is always used to register the copyrights in songs, that is, the music and lyrics of songs, even if the only embodiment of those songs is a sound recording, such as a cassette. You can register *both* your song *and* your recorded performance of it by filing an appropriately completed Form SR and sending the Copyright Office a recorded version of your song, but most songwriters do not want to register their demo recordings and most performers have no need to register the copyrights in their commercially released recordings, which ordinarily belong to their record companies under their recording agreements. The best way to figure out which form you need and how to fill it out correctly is to order the Copyright Office flyer "Copyright Registration of Musical Compositions and Sound Recordings." You can also consult the free Copyright Office publications "Copyright Registration for Musical Compositions" and "Copyright Registration for Sound Recordings." Information on obtaining these useful pamphlets is given in the Resources section of this book.

The copyright registration fee is presently $20 per registration; it will increase in January 1996. If you are a prolific writer, you may have trouble paying $20 every time you want to register the copyright in one of your songs. One good solution to this fiscal problem is to register a group of songs together for one $20 fee. A group of songs may be registered together *if* they were written by the same person (or if one person was a co-writer of every song in the group) *and* the owner(s) of copyright in each is or are the same *and* the songs are assembled in an orderly form (usually one cassette tape that includes all the songs being registered) under one title. For example, you can call your first 1995 collection of songs "Collected Songs of Megan Bowers, 1995, Volume I"; if you register more songs in 1995, you can call the second collection "Collected Songs of Megan Bowers, 1995, Volume II." The individual titles of your songs will not appear on the copyright registration certificate, but the compositions themselves will be registered. You can later file another PA Form or a CA Form (for Correction and Amplification) for any one of the compositions included in the original registration for your song collection; either form will get the title of your song on the Copyright Office's index of titles, where it can be located by anyone researching the copyright status of your song. (Another method for getting the individual titles of your songs on the Copyright Office's index when you file a group registration is to enter the title of the collection on the copyright registration form as "Collected Songs of Megan Bowers, 1995, Volume II, comprising 'My Cat Fido'; 'Love Me, Love My Cat'; and 'All Cats are Grey in the Dark'.")

Besides your completed registration form and the registration fee, you must send the Copyright Office one copy of an unpublished song or two copies of the "best edition" of a published song. This is called the "deposit requirement"; furnishing copies of the work you're registering allows the Copyright Office to record precisely the content of your song.

Besides the requirement that copyright registration applications be accompanied by "deposit copies" of the works being registered, the copyright statute also requires that all published works be deposited with the Copyright Office within three months after publication. This "mandatory deposit requirement" is separate from the requirement that a copyright registration application be accompanied by deposit copies of the work registered, although it's *fulfilled* by the deposit of copies made with a registration application. That is, if for some reason you publish your song but do *not* register the copyright in it, you're still required by law to send to the Copyright Office for the collections of the Library of Congress a certain number of copies of the best edition of the song. As a practical matter, however, this requirement can be ignored by songwriters and performers. Music publishers will register the copyrights in the compositions that are assigned to them by songwriters and commercially recorded and released or otherwise published. Record companies will register the copyrights in the master recordings performers record under their recording agreements. This eliminates any need for songwriters or performers to make separate deposits of copies of the published materials.

The best way to make sense of the copyright statute's deposit requirements is to order the short, free Copyright Office publication titled "Mandatory Deposit of Copies or Phonorecords for the Library of Congress." If you read this pamphlet, you'll know more than most lawyers do about this aspect of the copyright statute. The best way to figure out whether you're sending the copies you should when you register the copyright in a song is to carefully read the instructions that come with the Form PA or, if you still have questions, to call 202/707-3000 between 8:30 and 5:00 Eastern Standard Time for free advice from a Copyright Information Specialist about filling out and filing your registration form.

Now that you've learned how to register your song copyright, maybe you'd like to know just what copyright registration does for you. Copyright registration *enhances* the rights you gain by the act of creating a copyrightable song. Aside from the fact that copyright registration is a prerequisite for filing a copyright infringement suit, there are four significant advantages of registration:

1. Registration establishes *prima facie* evidence in court of the validity of the copyright and of the statements made in your copyright registration certificate, such as the identity of the owner of the copyright and the date of creation of the song, *if* you register your song before it is published or within five years after its publication. This assumption of the truth of the statements made in the copyright registration certificate means that registration has an important effect on what's known as the "burden of proof." Anyone who contests the validity of your registration, such as an accused infringer making a defense in a copyright infringement lawsuit, bears the initial burden of introducing evidence sufficient to prove that your registration is invalid. Until such evidence is produced, the court will assume that your registration *is* valid, and you have no obligation to prove the truth of any of the statements you made in your application.

2. If registration is made within three months of publication of your song or before any infringement of it and if you later sue for copyright infringement and win your suit, the court may require the infringer to pay you the amount you spent for attorneys' fees and you may be awarded "statutory damages." These constitute a range of money damages the copyright statute allows the court to award to you, at its discretion, instead of the actual monetary damages you have sustained plus the actual amount by which the infringer profited from the use of your song. Since actual damages and an infringer's profits can be very difficult, time-consuming, and expensive to prove during a lawsuit, and because an infringer will often not have profited from infringing your song, this can be an important advantage.

3. Registration protects you against false accusations of copyright infringement. Registration of your copyright establishes a public record that your copyrighted song existed in a certain form at least as early as the date of registration. If the song you're accused of infringing was created later than your song, this is all the proof necessary to convince a court (or, even before an accusation ripens into a lawsuit, the lawyers of the person who accuses you of infringing his or her song) that you're not guilty of infringement. Mailing your song to yourself and preserving the unopened envelope to prove that the song inside it existed on the date of the postmark, a homemade remedy for proving authorship popularly known as "poor man's copyright," is virtually worthless as evidence in a lawsuit and is *not* a substitute for copyright registration.

4. Registration gives "constructive notice" to the world that you claim authorship and ownership of your song. Constructive notice means that because your registration is reflected in the records of the Copyright Office, which are public, everyone is presumed to have knowledge of your copyright claims, whether he or she has ever actually examined the Copyright Office records that document your registration. This can be advantageous if, for example, an unscrupulous co-writer tries to assign 100 percent of a song you co-wrote to a music publisher without your participation in the deal. The publisher is presumed to have constructive notice of your claim to half ownership of the song copyright, and you can have any agreements or filings documenting any such bogus transfer declared invalid. Like the other three advantages of registration, this one may seem impossibly technical and its usefulness somewhat remote. If the song in question is an "undiscovered" hit that is, so far, worth zilch, half of nothing wouldn't be worth fighting over. But you'd think differently if someone were trying to cheat you out of half of a *hit* song. Then you'd be very glad to have registered the copyright in it and equally gratified to have the fraudulent transfer of copyright nullified.

That's the thing about a lot of the tiresome provisions of the law we will discuss in this book. If you don't need to know them, they are tiresome; if you do need them, you *want* to know them. If you've at least heard—or read—of these tedious but valuable points of law, you may remember enough about them to look them up when you need some ammunition. Bear that in mind as you read, so as to receive this information with the proper attitude. Musicians have historically considered themselves outsiders. That may be true and it may be that any artist's work depends to some extent on his or her "outsideness." But don't make the mistake of assuming that just because you don't want to *be* a lawyer, you'll never need one or need to know any of the things lawyers know. The law applies to everybody, and you can't make money making your music if you keep bumping up against the problems that can be caused by complete blissed-out ignorance of the law.

End of lecture. Now about copyright notice. Copyright notice is so interesting that we have saved it for the last part of this chapter. It's one of the parts of copyright law that people never really understand. By the same process that gives rise to folklore, they know it's there and they know they're supposed to do something about it, but they never know exactly what. Or how. In fact, it's one of the simpler mysteries of the universe. Like Gaul, copyright notice is divided into three parts:

1. **The word "copyright"** (this is c-o-p-y-r-i-g-h-t, not "copywrite," and while we're at it, it's "copyrighted," and not "copywritten," a nonexistent term that has been known to issue even from the mouths of lawyers) or **the © symbol or the ℗ symbol** (for sound recordings only)

2. **The year of first publication of the work**, which may *not* be the year it was created or the year it was registered

3. **The name of the copyright owner** (it's best to use your legal name in a copyright notice, since it's harder to figure out who "Babe" Bowers is than to find Megan Clark Bowers in the Copyright Office index of registrants)

Proper copyright notice, then, looks like this: Copyright 1995 Megan Clark Bowers *or* © 1995 Megan Clark Bowers.

There is no substitute for these three elements of copyright notice. You can't make up your own version of copyright notice and depend on it to have the same legal effect as the notice specified in the copyright statute. You don't have to have anyone's permission to use copyright notice, and you don't have to have registered your copyright beforehand. All you have to do is write or type your notice legibly on your lead sheet or on the label of a cassette or tape in a place where it's easy to see.

Remember that the ℗ symbol rather than the © symbol is used in copyright notice for sound recordings. However, don't get confused and use the ℗ symbol in copyright notice for a demo recording, when what you're really claiming is copyright *in the song itself*, rather than the recorded version of the song. As a matter of fact, most songwriters and musicians will never really need to use the ℗ symbol in copyright notice, because they will be concerned only with protecting the copyrights in their songs. This means they will use the © symbol on their demo tapes to claim copyright in their songs rather than in their demo recordings of those songs.

This may not be true for performers, who may properly use the ℗ symbol to protect their recordings of their performances. If the performers also own the copyrights in the songs they perform on tape, they may use an additional, separate notice that includes the © symbol to denote that they are *also* the owners of the songs performed in the recording.

No copyright notice is required for unpublished works. However, it's common practice to use copyright notice on unpublished works. The best approach for unpublished songs may be to use "Unpublished Work © 1995 Megan C. Bowers," to eliminate any confusion as to whether your song has been published. You can update the year in the copyright notice for an unpublished song as often as necessary, since if the song has not yet been published, there is no "date of publication."

As important as copyright notice is in warning off would-be infringers and honest blunderers who would otherwise assume that your song is in the public domain, it must be said that copyright notice is no longer required on works first published after March 1, 1989, the date the United States signed the Berne Convention. The Berne Convention is an old and widespread copyright treaty, or agreement between certain nations that each will honor the copyrights of the others' citizens. For complicated reasons having to do with the requirements imposed on treaty signatory nations, the United States has relaxed or abolished some of the formalities it previously required for copyright protection. Copyright notice is one of those formalities.

However, even though U.S. law no longer requires the use of copyright notice on publicly distributed copies of copyrighted works to avoid losing copyright protection, copyright notice is still very important. To encourage the use of copyright notice, the copyright statute now provides a valuable procedural advantage (in infringement lawsuits) to copyright owners who do use it. Specifically, an infringer cannot successfully claim that he or she did not know that his or her acts constituted copyright infringement if the copyright owner has used proper copyright notice. In other words, if you use copyright notice as a No Trespassing sign, no one who trespasses on your rights as a copyright owner can say he or she strayed into infringement by accident in the innocent belief that your song was not protected by copyright.

The final word on copyright notice is the free Copyright Office pamphlet titled "Copyright Notice." It's not very long, but it will tell you everything you'll ever need to know about No Trespassing signs and where to put them. You already know where to find out how to get a copy.

What to do about trespassers, and how to avoid becoming one, is another matter. The Copyright Office doesn't publish any free pamphlet about copyright infringement, and the copyright statute itself says merely that "anyone who violates any of the exclusive rights of the copyright owner . . . is an infringer of the copyright." The law doesn't define exactly what acts constitute such a violation. Fortunately, the next chapter does.

3

Copyright Infringement

In the world of music, copyright infringement looms like an ogre on the horizon. Songwriters often mistakenly report sightings of the beast while failing to notice that they're sheltering it in their own backyards. Since the only thing worse than having to sue someone for copyright infringement is being sued yourself, if you're a songwriter you must know not only how to protect your own rights but also how to avoid trampling those of others. To determine whether your rights have been infringed or your song infringes someone else's song, you must first have a good understanding of what rights copyright gives to copyright owners.

As you've seen, copyright owners have certain "exclusive rights of copyright"; that is, there are certain rights relating to the copyrighted work that only the owner of the copyright may legally exercise. These are the right to perform or display the work publicly (however, the copyright statute does not grant the owners of sound recording copyrights the right to control performances of those recordings), the right to make copies of the work, the right to prepare alternate or "derivative" versions of the work, and the right to distribute and sell copies of the work. Because the copyright statute does not define copyright infringement except to say that infringement is the exercise of any exclusive right of copyright without permission of the copyright owner, courts have had to do so. The body of law made up of court decisions in copyright infringement cases is called copyright "case law." Copyright case law is the source for the test for copyright infringement and the standard for applying the test to the facts in particular copyright infringement cases.

Almost all song copyright infringement lawsuits involve accusations of unauthorized copying; that is, a songwriter is accused of having written a song by "lifting" all or part of the melody or lyrics, or both, of another, copyrighted, song. Understanding copyright infringement means understanding the standard courts use in evaluating whether accusations of copyright infringement are true. Assuming that the copyright in the song that is said to have been infringed is valid and that that song was created *before* the song accused of infringing it, and in the absence of any admission by the defendant songwriter that he or she *did* copy the plaintiff's song, courts ordinarily judge copyright infringement by a circumstantial evidence test.

The circumstantial evidence test for copyright infringement has three parts: (1) Did the accused infringer have *access* to the song that is said to have been infringed, so that copying was possible? (2) Is the defendant actually guilty of *copying* part of the plaintiff's protectable expression from the plaintiff's song? and (3) Is the accused song *substantially similar* to the song the plaintiff says was copied? If you can remember these three parts of the test for copyright infringement, "access," "copying," and "substantial similarity," you should always be able to decide correctly for yourself whether a song of yours infringes someone else's song or whether someone else has infringed your copyright.

"Access" simply means what it says. Did an accused infringer have access to and hear the "infringed" song before creating the "infringing" song? It's very important to remember that the action for which the copyright statute prescribes penalties is *copying*, not the mere *coincidental* creation of a work that is similar or even nearly identical to a preexisting work. In most cases, access is not presumed but must be proved before the questions of copying and substantial similarity even enter the equation.

This means that if you write a song called "Nearly Gone Ozone" to protest our vanishing ozone layer and some songwriter on the other side of the continent *independently* writes a song called "The Ballad of the Ozone Layer" with the *same* lyrics and the *same* melody, *each* of you owns a valid copyright in your song, despite the fact that the two songs are identical twins. This is easier to understand if you remember that our copyright statute rewards the act of creation. You own the copyright in a product of your own imagination so long as your imagination—and not that of another songwriter—really is the source of your song. This is true regardless of what anybody else in the world comes up with before, at the same time as, or after you write your song.

If you're a songwriter, the obvious implication of the access requirement in proving copyright infringement is that good documentation of your pitches to artists and producers can be critically important in the event someone decides your song is good enough to steal. If you know where your demo tape has been, you may be able to prove that an infringer had "reasonable opportunity" (which is usually sufficient proof of access) to hear and copy your song.

The circumstantial evidence test for copyright infringement is like a three-legged stool. All three legs of the test are necessary to support a claim of copyright infringement, and the absence of proof of one of the three parts of the test means an infringement suit will fail. Proving the second element of copyright infringement, copying of protected subject matter, is just as important as proving access and substantial similarity, but would-be plaintiffs often gloss over this requirement in the mistaken assumption that *any* copying is sufficient to support an infringement suit.

To understand what constitutes copying of protected expression, you must understand what elements of your songs are not protected. As was discussed in Chapter One, there are several categories of elements of songs, some of them important to the overall quality of any composition, that are not protected by copyright:

- Ideas (although particular expressions of ideas are protected)
- Song themes (which are a variety of idea)
- Song titles and short slogans or lyrical phrases
- Short musical phrases

There are, after all, only twelve musical notes. Because some possible combinations of notes are unsuited to popular music, it's inevitable that certain combinations of notes will recur in musical compositions. Such coincidental repeated occurrences of short musical phrases do not amount to infringement. However, although copyright does not protect short riffs, chord progressions, or other brief musical phrases, you can't assume that lifting fewer than the legendary six bars from someone else's song is always safe. The courts have never bound themselves to any strictly quantitative rule in judging copyright infringement, and, depending on the importance of the stolen segment of melody, stealing even fewer than six bars could well be judged copyright infringement. The old "six-bar rule" (usually passed on in songwriter folklore as "They can't get you for copyright infringement if you don't steal more than six bars") apparently has its origins in a 1923 copyright decision in which the court held that six bars copied from the plaintiff's song, when used in the defendant's new composition of 450 bars, did not constitute infringement. The six-bar rule isn't really a rule at all, and using it to gauge possible copyright infringement is dangerous. Except for remembering to ignore it, forget you ever heard of this "rule" and never consciously lift *any* number of bars from anyone else's song.

- The way a song is constructed
- Your arrangement of someone else's song

Unless your arrangement of a song actually amounts to an alternate version of it, your arrangement is not protectable by copyright. If your arrangement does constitute an alternate version of the song, you're guilty of copyright infringement for creating it because you must have permission from the owner of the song copyright to create an alternate version of it. The exception to this is an arrangement of a public domain song. Since you can use a public domain song any way you want, it's legal to make a detailed arrangement of such a song, and the resulting arrangement is protectable.

Now that you know the *exceptions* to the general rule that copyright protects what you create, you can tell that there aren't many categories of elements of songs that *are* protected by copyright. In fact, copyright protects the melodies of your songs, the lyrics (especially the "hooks"), and not much else. Once you understand this, it's easy to apply the second part of the test for copyright infringement, because the question becomes a simple one: *Did the accused infringer steal from the melody, or from the lyrics, or from both?* If your answer is yes to any part of this question and it can be proved that the accused infringer had access to the song that is said to have been infringed, you must then evaluate whether the theft was substantial.

The third part of the test for copyright infringement is determining whether the "infringing" song is "substantially similar" to the "infringed" song. Substantial similarity is hard to define. Even the courts have never been able to come up with a hard-and-fast test for determining substantial similarity. This may be because no such test is possible—each copyright infringement case must be decided entirely on the facts of *that* case, and what happened in a similar suit has no real bearing on the question whether *this* defendant did, indeed, write a song that is substantially similar to that of *this* plaintiff.

Although it's not possible to pinpoint the border between infringing and noninfringing similarity, a map of the danger zone between the two exists in the form of copyright case law.

Courts do not require plaintiffs to demonstrate that their defendants' songs are nearly identical to their own songs to prove substantial similarity. However, courts will not interpret even several small, unimportant similarities between the songs in question as substantial similarity. In short, "substantial similarity" is just that: substantial. The *sort* of similarity between two songs is just as important as the *degree* of similarity—the judgment of substantial similarity is both *qualitative* and *quantitative*.

Further, although plaintiffs in copyright infringement suits routinely hire expert witnesses—usually people who have Ph.D.'s in musicology—to testify as to what similarities exist between the songs at issue, courts judge whether those similarities are substantial by the "ordinary observer" test, which is a sort of "man on the street" view of the effect of those similarities. Courts try to decide whether an ordinary observer, hearing two similar songs for the first time, would believe that the "infringing" and "infringed" song are the same. If so, substantial similarity exists. This means you probably have the information you need and the "ears" to decide for yourself whether someone's song infringes yours.

Some examples will help you grasp the difficult concept of substantial similarity.

If you decide to create a parody version of a hit song by writing what you think are hilarious lyrics to the hit song's melody, you may find your record pulled from distribution and off the air, if your song ever makes it to vinyl (and tape), because you will have infringed the hit song by using its melody. Most of the parody songs of this sort that have entertained you in recent years were created by writers clever enough to get permission from the owners of the copyrights in the parodied songs before releasing their parody versions (a good example of this is Weird Al Yankovic's "Eat It" parody of Michael Jackson's "Beat It"). Most of the writers who create parodies of famous songs without getting permission to use the famous songs' melodies in their parodies end up in federal court, defending a copyright infringement case. The only safe way to create a parody of a song without permission from the owner of the song copyright is to satirize the song by means of your *own* lyrics and your *own* melody, using only enough of the original song to recall it and make it obvious that it's the subject of the satire.

If another songwriter takes the melody of your ballad and speeds it up for the bluegrass song he writes, he may think that by altering the tempo of your melody and combining it with his own lyrics he has found a clever way to use someone else's composition without having to worry about copyright infringement. If he does, he's wrong. There is a principle of copyright law called "fair use" that allows the very limited use of the copyrighted work of another, but this is not fair use. It's fair to quote a paragraph of a novel in a book review or to make one or two photocopies of a piece of sheet music for use by a high school choir or enough photocopies of a textbook illustration of a painting to hand out to a college art history class, but it's not fair to use someone else's copyrighted melody without permission. That's infringement. Period. In fact, because songs are so short, there are very few "fair" uses of the protected elements of songs.

If you write an hourlong original piece of Christmas music and incorporate into your composition the melodies of several popular Christmas tunes, your composition is an infringement of any of those tunes that are not in the public domain. It makes no difference that the melodies you appropriate without permission are very short in comparison to your masterwork, because you have stolen the most important parts of those songs. In other words, you can't turn a theft into something else by hiding what you stole among elements that you do own. Your bright idea could get you into trouble with Santa Claus, who takes a dim view of copyright infringers.

There is one situation in which one part of the three-part test for copyright infringement need not be proved. That is the situation in which there is "striking similarity" between the two songs. Essentially, this is just a specialized application of the three-part infringement test. In cases where the similarity between the two songs is so striking that there's no explanation for such overwhelming similarity other than that one song was copied from the other, courts say that access may be assumed and the circumstances that made the infringement possible need not be reconstructed by the plaintiff. The "striking similarity" approach to proving infringement is rarely allowed by courts, which prefer to see plaintiffs prove every element of their cases.

A corollary to any discussion of musical copyright infringement is what is *not* infringement. One provision of the copyright statute that sometimes surprises songwriters who are also performers is that the statute specifically states that the imitation of sound recordings is permissible. The law does include sound recordings within the scope of copyright protection, although this was once not the case. This means that you can't buy the newest Annie Lennox album and manufacture copies in your basement to sell from a roadside stand; if you do a federal judge may decide you're guilty of *criminal* copyright infringement, which entails more serious penalties than "ordinary" copyright infringement.

What you *can* do, with impunity, is create "soundalike" recordings, no matter how similar they are to the originals. If your band decides to put together an album of retro hits you can imitate the original *recordings* of "Louie, Louie," "Satisfaction," and "I Heard It Through the Grapevine" without a qualm. You will be copying the performances of The Kingsmen, The Rolling Stones, and Marvin Gaye, but this copying does not constitute copyright infringement of the original hit recordings of those performers because the copyright statute does not protect *performances* of songs. Neither will you be infringing the underlying songs because the copyright statute provides that anyone can record any song that has already been recorded and commercially released with the permission of the copyright owner, subject only to the obligation to pay mechanical royalties. You cannot, however, lift substantial portions of the melodies or lyrics from any of those *songs* without risking a lawsuit. This is because while the copyright statute does not protect performances, it does protect original expressions of ideas, such as the melodies and lyrics of songs. Maybe you can earn more in one evening by screaming songs into a microphone and jumping around onstage like James Brown than your cousin Harold will *ever* earn from the bad country songs he writes, but the law protects the songs Harold writes in his cluttered little room and does *not* extend the same protection to your onstage activities. A *recording* of your performance is protected by copyright, but not the performance itself; that is, anyone can imitate your performance without violating your rights under copyright law.

However, it must be said that there are two legal doctrines that prevent, for example, your representing (or implying by deceptive packaging) that your recording of "Rainy Night in Georgia" is the original recording by Brook Benton. The first is the "right of publicity," which is the right a celebrity has to prevent others from trading on his or her fame. The second is a section of the federal trademark statute that prohibits unfair competition achieved by false indication of the origin of a product. You can record a song and you can make it sound as much like the original, famous recording of the song as you're able, but you cannot market records by leading consumers to believe they are buying a performance by someone else.

Copyright infringement is an area of real danger for the songwriter. Consequently, anyone who aspires to earn his or her living as a professional songwriter needs to know enough about copyright infringement to stay out of danger. People only *think* that writing songs is a nice, safe job that can't get anyone in trouble. In reality, what you do with your guitar while you sit on your front porch or your living room sofa can land you in federal court, where you will be asked to explain just *what* you did and *why* and *when* you did it.

If you think someone has infringed your copyright, see a lawyer who's well versed in copyright law. Most lawyers will not charge you for an initial consultation about a possible copyright infringement case. You'll need the objective evaluation a lawyer can give you, since songwriters are notoriously poor judges of whether their songs have actually been infringed. Your lawyer should be willing to tell you whether there has been an infringement and, if so, whether you're likely to prevail in court. If you don't like what the first lawyer you consult says, make an appointment with another for a second evaluation. But don't wait too long before you take your suspicions of infringement to a lawyer, because the "statute of limitations" (the period within which you must file suit) for copyright infringement is only three years from the date you discover that the infringement has taken place. After three years your infringement suit may be barred. That is, the court will throw it out because you did not file it within the prescribed three-year period. You snooze, you lose.

If you win your copyright infringement suit, the court may issue a permanent injunction that prohibits any further use of the song that violates your copyright. It may order the seizure and destruction of any copies of the infringing song. It may award you "actual damages" (the profits the infringer made from the infringing song and the money you lost because of the infringement) or, alternately, "statutory damages" (a range of money damages the court is allowed to award you in lieu of actual damages), the expenses of the suit that you've had to pay, and attorneys' fees. However, if you're the defendant in an infringement suit, you'll be on the receiving end of these remedies for infringement and will have cause to regret that you were ever so foolish as to trifle with the copyright of the plaintiff.

Is It Infringement?

The following questions should help you understand copyright infringement a little better. Give yourself an "A" for four or five correct answers and a "B" for three; if you answer no more than two questions correctly, consider your guitar a loaded weapon and use extreme caution when composing your next song.

Q. You wake up one morning with a melody running through your head and decide while eating your oatmeal that it's a hit song. You write the melody on a paper napkin and compose lyrics to match the melody during the day as you work. You take the resulting song, "Cold, Cruel Heart," to a friend of yours who works as an intern for a big music publisher. He shows it to his boss, who loves it, signs you and your song, and shows it within days to the producer for The Gonzos, who are in the studio and need one more side to finish their new album.

The Gonzos cut your song and release it as the first single off the album, you quit your job to write songs full-time, and begin to look around for a new, big, flashy car. Then you get a call from your buddy the intern, who whispers that he thinks you're in trouble, because right after his boss got a phone call from the company's New York office he asked the intern to locate the demo tape of your song, *pronto*, and sent him out to buy a copy of an old Kansas album. The next call you get is from your buddy's boss, who asks you to meet with him in his office *immediately*.

It seems that the publishers of the Kansas standard "Dust in the Wind" have sued your publisher, and you, for copyright infringement. They have claimed, in a federal lawsuit, that "Cold, Cruel Heart" infringes "Dust in the Wind." They allege that you stole the melody from their song. As you sit in your publisher's office listening to tapes of the two songs, you realize that the melody for "Cold, Cruel Heart" *is* identical to the "Dust in the Wind" melody. You're embarrassed, but you assure your publisher that you had no intention of copying the Kansas song when you wrote yours and that you know for a fact that there is no infringement when one songwriter independently creates the same song as another.

Is it infringement?

A. Unfortunately, it is. You may not have *intended* to lift the melody from "Dust in the Wind," but it appears you did so unconsciously. Even if you've never owned a Kansas album, unless you can prove that you spent the last twenty years in a monastery in Tibet, the highly skilled lawyers who represent the publishers of "Dust in the Wind" are going to argue, successfully, that you had access to the Kansas song just by being alive in America during the period when it issued from every radio in the country and that you copied it unconsciously. You're right that your independent creation of an identical melody would not be copyright infringement, but where access is proved, a court may find that there has been *unconscious* copying, which *is* infringement.

The court will rule against you and you will never see a nickel of your royalties from the Gonzos cut, because you, poor sap, will foot the bill for the settlement your publisher will have to pay to the publisher of "Dust in the Wind," as well as for the lawyers your publisher had to hire to represent it, since your publishing agreement for "Cold, Cruel Heart" includes an indemnity provision that says you will. (More about these provisions in the next chapter.)

Don't feel too bad, though—you're in good company. Some years ago George Harrison learned the same lesson when a court found that he had unconsciously copied the melody from the old Chiffons song "He's So Fine" when he wrote "My Sweet Lord." Because he wrote his own lyrics, George got to keep the copyright in them and your publisher will get to keep the copyright in yours. But the owner of the copyright in "Dust in the Wind" will own the melody half of the "Cold, Cruel Heart" copyright and will get half of the publisher's share of royalties from any cuts of the song. If anybody ever cuts "Cold, Cruel Heart" again, the "Dust in the Wind" songwriters will share the writers' credits with you.

Q. Your friend Sally the English major discovers a poem by Ben Jonson called "Though I Am Young and Cannot Tell" in her literature textbook. She decides she wants to set the poem to music and sing it as a mournful ballad in the talent portion of her college's annual "Ice Maiden" beauty pageant. She especially likes the first four lines of the poem:

> Though I am young and cannot tell
> Either what Death or Love is well,
> Yet I have heard they both bear darts,
> And both do aim at human hearts.

Sally plans to wear a black dress and carry a single candle when she sings; the only thing she needs is the music for the song. She knows you're a songwriter and asks you very charmingly to help her. You agree because you don't want to have to watch her twirl flaming batons again this year. Then you wonder whether you and Sally can get in trouble for using someone else's poem for the lyrics of your song. Is it infringement?

A. No—at least not in this case. Although you have *access* to the poem and plan to *copy* it and the resulting song will be *substantially similar* to the original poem, there is no infringement since the poem you will copy is not "protectable expression"—or, rather, is no longer protected. As Sally could tell you, the great Ben Jonson has been dead since 1637. That means anything he wrote is in the public domain and is legally available for anyone to use in any way. The trick, however, is to make sure that copyright protection for a poem you want to use has expired rather than just determining that the author of the poem is dead; many copyrights outlast their authors. The question is not how long the author has been dead, but whether the author's work is still protected by copyright. (Refer to Chapter Two for a refresher course in the duration of copyright and what "public domain" means if you have trouble understanding why you and Sally can use Ben's poem.)

Q. You write a song called "Uptown Rumble" for your band. You play the song at a local club. In the audience you notice the lead guitar player and the lead singer of a rival band named

The Bad Boys, but you don't think much about it. A few months later, though, you hear The Bad Boys play a song called "Street Fight" during their performance at another club. You're incensed, because "Street Fight" is very much like "Uptown Rumble." You buy a Bad Boys tape after the performance and rush home to compare the "Street Fight" cut to your demo for "Uptown Rumble."

You sit up half the night making a list of the similarities between the two songs. Both songs are about gang violence, and the lyrics of each present the viewpoint of a reluctant gang member. Most of the lyrics for "Uptown Rumble" are very different from your lyrics, but the first line of the chorus for each song is "I don't want to fight." And even though the melodies of the two songs are not really similar, there is a five-note sequence in the verse of your song that also occurs in the chorus of the Bad Boys' song.

In the morning you knock on the door of the lawyer who has an office over the music store where you work. This lawyer doesn't look much like a lawyer—he's a young Rastafarian named Aashid who wears dreadlocks and owns only one suit—but you think he knows his stuff and he plays in a reggae band sometimes and, anyway, he'll talk to you for free. What you're anxious to ask him is: *Is it infringement?*

A. No, mon. As Aashid will tell you after he listens to your tapes of the two songs, the similarities between your song and the Bad Boys' are not the sort that add up to copyright infringement. Yes, each song has gang violence as its theme, but themes are ideas, and ideas are not protected by copyright law. Neither are "stock devices," that is, common dramatic or literary conventions, such as star-crossed lovers, or the pauper who is actually the lost heir to a fortune, or the long-suffering mother or, as here, the sensitive youth who is reluctant to fight but does so because of the circumstances in which he finds himself. And the lyric line common to the chorus of both songs? Well, it is a cliché expression, that is, one of only a few possible ways to say briefly what it says. It is, therefore, not protected by copyright. Forget basing your copyright infringement lawsuit on the fact that the same five-note sequence is found in both songs. There are, after all, only twelve musical notes. That means that one sequence of the same five notes found in both songs may be merely coincidental; in any event, five notes do not constitute "substantial similarity," especially when taken from an unknown, unrecorded song.

So. Even though two of The Bad Boys heard your songs and even if they did rip off your idea when they wrote their own song and even if some of the elements of the two songs are similar, there has been no infringement. Remember, the test is access *plus* copying of protected expression *plus* substantial similarity. The only one of these three parts of the infringement test you could prove against The Bad Boys is that they had the access necessary to allow copying. If that were enough by itself to prove infringement, you'd have to sue everyone who ever heard you perform.

Forget about suing for copyright infringement. Console yourself with the fact that The Bad Boys are a bunch of homely dudes who can't play very well and are probably doomed to keep their jobs as busboys and bartenders forever while you and your band amass a large and loyal following of attractive young women, a stack of good reviews in the local music press, and one phone message waiting downstairs at the music store that says that a major-label A&R guy who saw your last show wants to meet with you and the band. Take *that*, Bad Boys. And take Aashid to that meeting.

Q. Because you're an excellent mandolin player and because you have to feed two cats and a dog, not to mention yourself, you work as a session musician. One day you're working a demo session at a dingy little studio where they cook the coffee all day but there is always beer in the public-domain fridge, when you realize that the "new" song you're recording, a ditty called "Six-Pack Sally," is one you've heard before. In fact, you think you *wrote* the melody, which seems to you to be identical to the melody for your song "My Sweet Susie." You ask Sally, the songwriter whose session it is, where her melody came from. She tells you she wrote the lyrics (from experience, by the look of her eyeballs), but that the music was written by a guy named Reggie. You take down Reggie's phone number and pack up your mandolin to leave, since you have an aversion to participating in the infringement of your own compositions.

You leave four messages on Reggie's machine, but he doesn't call back. Then you look up his address in the phone book and discover that he lives in *your* apartment building and that his bedroom and your living room would be the same room except for the fact that a thin wall separates them.

You don't find Reggie at home, but your lawyer's secretary says he can see you the same afternoon you call. You want to ask both your lawyer and Reggie some questions because, of course, you want to know: *Is it infringement?*

A. Yes. Your lawyer will tell you that because the melody for "Six-Pack Sally" is, nearly note for note, identical to your melody, substantial similarity definitely exists between the two songs. If you can prove you wrote your song before Reggie wrote his melody and that he had access to your song to make copying possible, you can probably win an infringement suit. Since you had the foresight to register the copyright in your song soon after you wrote it six months ago and Sally says Reggie "wrote" the "Six-Pack Sally" melody only last week, you *can* prove that you wrote your song before Reggie and Sally wrote theirs.

Your lawyer will also want to know, however, what proof you can offer to demonstrate that Reggie had access to your song. You can tell your lawyer that all your neighbors will testify to the fact that tapes played on the stereo system in your living room can be heard through the walls. They can vouch for the fact that they all had the "opportunity" to hear "My Sweet Susie"—in fact, they could form a chorus and sing every verse in court if they had to, because you played your demo tape over and over again for your buddies and the occasional producer. Since Reggie has been living in the apartment behind you for more than a year, he must have been part of your involuntary audience. This means Reggie had numerous opportunities to hear your songs and you can prove access.

Sally and Reggie can probably be persuaded by a stern letter from your lawyer that it would be *much* better if they came up with an entirely new melody for "Six-Pack Sally" and left your melody to you. You're going to need it, since one of the producers who heard your demo of "My Sweet Susie" thinks your song is just right for his new act, a singing hunk named Bobby Joe Jones with big blue eyes and a motorized pelvis who makes mamas swoon and daddies wonder where their teenage daughters are.

Q. Your band is in the studio recording a scathing indictment of life in the media age called "Media-crity" when Tyrone the bass player pulls out a tape of "samples" taken from radio and television programs of his, and your, childhood. Tyrone thinks you should use his tape as a background track for your demo to add "atmosphere." On his tape are the Monkees singing a line from "Daydream Believer"; a sound bite from the chorus of "Feelings"; a piece of Sammy Davis, Jr.'s, rendition of "Candy Man"; Daffy Duck's distinctive laugh, Bugs Bunny saying "What's up, Doc?"; signature melody lines from the theme songs of *Dragnet, Mr. Ed,* and *The Jetsons;* a short piece of dialogue between Marcia and Greg Brady; Archie Bunker calling his son-in-law "Meathead!"; and Ed McMahon saying, "Heeere's Johnny!" You and the other band members agree that Tyrone's tape underscores the mediocrity of American media, but you're worried that you could somehow get into trouble for "borrowing" all the little bits of banality Tyrone has collected. Is it infringement?

A. Yes. Several kinds, in fact. The copyrights in popular songs are typically protected fiercely, and your use of the signature melody lines from the songs and television themes Tyrone recorded could easily generate several copyright infringement lawsuits from the publishers that own the copyrights in those songs. It's probable that not every one of these six publishers would sue, but if one lawsuit is a grave misfortune, more than one is a catastrophe. Even so, maybe you'll get lucky and no one will actually file suit. Sometimes publishers who object to infringements of their copyrights offer to settle out of court if the infringers will assign 50 percent or 75 percent or 100 percent of the copyrights in the infringing songs to them. That's only about 600 percent of "Media-crity" that will be owned by people other than you.

But there are a lot of *other* people who are going to call their lawyers when they hear your song. They probably won't sue for *copyright* infringement, but they're trouble just the same. Warner Brothers is going to be very unhappy that you have used the distinctive voices of Daffy Duck and Bugs Bunny without permission. They will probably threaten to sue you for unfair competition and trademark infringement, since their characters represent them to the public and your use of those characters' voices implies that your recording of your song may somehow be connected with or sponsored by Warner Brothers.

The owners of *The Brady Bunch*, *All in the Family*, and *The Tonight Show* probably won't sue you for copyright infringement, since your use of snippets of those shows in your recording does not add up to "substantial similarity" and is, as far as the copyrights in the shows go, probably fair use. The bad news is that the owners of the shows may threaten to sue you for unfair competition and trademark infringement, for the same reasons that Warner Brothers can. And the *entertainers* whose voices you used may sue you for infringing their right of publicity, since you're trading off their fame when you use pieces of their performances. No matter how short these clips are, they depend for their effect on the recognizability of the voices of the entertainers involved—which is the same as saying you're using their fame without their permission.

As a practical matter, however, because demo recordings are not ordinarily broadcast, you may never attract the attention or raise the ire of any of these people. However, if your song depends for its punch on the samples Tyrone assembled from his record collection and old shows on cable TV, no publisher will want to sign it. If your band gets lucky and lands a record deal, your producer, if he's a good one, will know that cutting "Media-crity" for your first album with Tyrone's samples intact may mean that there won't be a second one, unless, of course, you can afford to hold up production of your album while a law firm you hire for $150 an hour "clears" each sample, or contacts each copyright and trademark owner and actor's representative for permission, which may not be granted, to use the sampled segments. Or maybe your producer is not so clever about the legalities of sampling and you ship the master for your album to the record company without clearing the samples. In that case, the release of your album will be held up while lawyers for the record company determine whether there is anything in the "Media-crity" cut that will result in a suit against the record company. Make no mistake, the record company, no matter how much you like its A&R guy, is not necessarily looking out for your interests. On your record company's Scale of Concern money occupies the number one slot, followed closely by whether *it* can be sued for something you do. You and the other members of your band all fall far down the Scale of Concern, somewhere in the much-ignored Concern for Fellow Human Beings area.

By now you've probably decided it would be easier just to tell Tyrone that his tape won't cut it—or, rather, that you won't cut your song with his tape. Tell Tyrone that although you appreciate his idea and admire his dedication, you want to be remembered for your music, not because you were litigated out of existence for copyright and trademark infringement. Sampling is really safe only if the sounds you take from other sources are so brief that they cannot be identified as being a distinctive guitar riff or horn solo or vocalization from a certain artist *or* are electronically altered to the point that they're not recognizable as having come from any particular source. In other words, to eliminate the threat of lawsuits, you must take only minuscule slices of other people's records, television shows, etc., or turn the samples you take into something so different from what they were originally that they're not identifiable.

If your samples are longer than a note or two and are recognizable for what they are and where they came from, you must get permission to use them from the copyright owners, trademark owners, and entertainers involved. This is a difficult, tedious, and sometimes impossible process, since there's no requirement that the people contacted by you or your lawyer grant you the permissions you want, even if you offer to pay for the privilege of using pieces of their songs or shows or performances.

A Short Survey of the Delights of Copyright Litigation

People who believe their copyrights have been infringed often have no idea how complicated copyright infringement lawsuits are, and have exaggerated ideas about how much money they can recover if they bring suit against the suspected infringers. Unfortunately, the unwarranted contemplation of the large amounts of money one feels certain one will be awarded is often the most satisfying stage of a copyright infringement suit. As with most civil litigation, copyright infringement suits are more fun for plaintiffs to think about than participate in. For defendants, lawsuits are no fun at all.

Every ancient mapmaker knew that his very own country lay at the center of the world, but most were confused as to what was over the horizon. They prudently decided that what they didn't know could hurt them and often marked these vast "terra incognita" areas with the warning *Heere Bee Dragons* to warn explorers of the perils there. If you've never been involved in a civil lawsuit, this is a wise attitude to cultivate toward suing and being sued, because today in the United States the dragons are called Litigants and Lawyers.

This doesn't mean there are no issues worth going to court

over. Regrettably, litigation is sometimes the only way to settle a dispute or pursue that elusive goal, justice. However, litigation should be viewed as a last resort, especially with regard to business disputes of any sort. In civilized countries, if your neighbor offends you, you do not engage him and his clan in a feud. Rather, you file your complaint in a court of law and let a judge decide the dispute. Unfortunately, the U.S. judicial system is so complex that a lawsuit can leave you as bloodied as a fistfight; even if you win you're bruised by the experience.

If you decide to sue someone, the first thing you must do is find a lawyer to represent you. In Great Britain, lawyers are classified as barristers, that is, lawyers who represent clients in court, or solicitors, lawyers who counsel clients concerning every sort of legal matter, including lawsuits, but who do not represent clients in court. In the United States, there is no such formal division among lawyers, but most lawyers consider themselves either primarily counselors or litigators. If you have an established relationship with a lawyer you trust, it's probably a good idea to take your lawsuit first to that lawyer for evaluation and advice, just as you would first consult your family physician for possible referral to a specialist.

Litigators are attorneys whose specialty is representing clients in lawsuits. For that reason, litigators may not always be the best source for objective advice on whether to sue, since their judgment in evaluating possible solutions to your problem may be overly influenced by the remedy they know best—litigation. In addition, a good evaluation of whether to bring suit in a suspected case of copyright infringement involves a careful analysis of the question whether the suspect actions actually constitute copyright infringement. Only a lawyer who is well versed in copyright law can reliably make this evaluation, since lawyers who are not thoroughly familiar with the issues involved in copyright infringement cases, however well-meaning they may be, are often poor judges of copyright infringement.

Responsible lawyers will not bring frivolous suits on your behalf. A lawyer has an ethical duty to determine that any lawsuit he or she files for you is founded on a reasonable interpretation of the law and that your allegations are based on fact, not on unfounded claims. However, no lawyer can guarantee the outcome of any suit; the best your lawyer can do is predict your chances of prevailing, based on his or her interpretation of the copyright statute and the precedents set by court decisions in similar cases.

Remember, your lawsuit is brought in *your* name, not in your lawyer's. Your lawyer is only a skilled agent acting on your behalf; it's *your* testimony that will be required, and you who stand to gain from any judgment in your favor. And it is *you* who will be bankrolling all the work your attorney must perform to represent you adequately.

Lawyers' fees run from a low of around $75 per hour to $300 or more per hour in some cities. What your lawsuit will cost, in attorneys' fees and expenses such as court filing fees, costs of court reporters for depositions, and expert witness fees, depends mostly on how complicated the issues in your case are, how many people are involved, how well financed they are, how vigorously they defend against your claims, and whether the suit must be brought in another city or can be brought where you live. It can cost several thousand dollars to bring even a relatively uncomplicated suit to the point of trial. Complicated lawsuits involving multiple plaintiffs and/or defendants are a litigator's dream; despite your lawyer's best efforts to bring such a suit to a quick resolution, the legal work involved may produce fat fees for several years.

Sometimes lawyers are willing to represent plaintiffs who have valid copyright infringement claims on a "contingency fee" basis. This means that the lawyer agrees to accept a large percentage, ordinarily one-third, of any amount the court eventually awards the plaintiff (in lieu of charging an hourly fee for work performed during the lawsuit). If the court rules in favor of the defendant, the plaintiff receives no award of damages and the plaintiff's lawyer receives nothing.

Although this may sound like a "free" lawsuit for the plaintiff, it's not. The plaintiff must cover all the expenses of the suit, such as the fees of court reporters and expert witnesses.

You must have a really convincing case against your defendant to persuade a qualified lawyer to take your suit on a contingency fee basis, because a lawyer who works on this basis is, in effect, sharing with you the risk that you'll lose the suit. Before accepting your case on a contingency fee basis, a lawyer will look long and hard at the amount of legal work involved, the amount of damages that will probably be awarded, and the likelihood that you can win the suit, because a lawyer who agrees to represent you on this basis may earn nothing in return for years of work if the court rules against you. In other words, one-third of nothing is still nothing.

And though most clients who have been through an expensive lawsuit would hesitate to admit it, there's nothing unfair about a lawyer's charging for his or her work. If anything is unfair about a lawsuit, it is the fact that circumstances compel you to be involved in one in the first place. All your lawyer can do is use every tactic at his or her disposal to get you out of it as quickly as possible.

If more people had fewer assumptions about lawsuits and the judicial process, the public image of lawyers as a group would be better. Clients somehow believe in their hearts that their lawyers can control the outcomes of lawsuits, and they very often become disenchanted with their own lawyers, as well as the lawyers of their adversaries, if they lose their suits. Judges decide cases based on laws passed by legislators who were elected by *you*. Lawyers are like guides through what is today in the United States often a legal jungle; they're stuck with the laws and the judges they encounter and must do their best to guide you through the difficult litigation process, but cannot change the basic rules by which the litigation must be conducted.

Nevertheless, clients often think all a lawyer has to do is reach into the bottom drawer of his or her desk, fill out a form marked "Lawsuit," file it at the courthouse, and—voilà!—the worthless human being who has just been labeled "the Defendant" will be hauled away to a dungeon under the courthouse that very afternoon by two or more burly federal marshals.

Unfortunately, it doesn't happen that way. You may know that your defendant is dead wrong and is a sneaky, dishonest person besides, and the defendant may know it, too. But before any *court* knows it, you have to *prove* it, while simultaneously fighting the defendant's best efforts to avoid admitting any wrongdoing. That's why your lawyer will plot your lawsuit like a chess game and view the trial as a battle.

Copyright litigation is a long process, and in real life most of it takes place before the trial. The first thing your lawyer will do after investigating the facts surrounding your grievance and the law that applies to it is draft what's called your "complaint." A complaint is a carefully worded document that sets out the facts of your dispute, relates them to the law, tells how the defendant has transgressed your rights under the law, and asks for certain "relief" from and on account of the defendant's transgressions. Such relief may take the form of an injunction (an order from the court directing the defendant to do something or to stop doing something) or an award of damages (money to compensate you for your losses or to punish the defendant).

Plaintiffs should know that lawyers always ask for more than they have any hope of actually receiving. Those "Million-Dollar Lawsuit" headlines you see may result, long after the newsprint has faded, in actual awards of only a few thousand dollars, which may be barely enough to cover the legal fees of the plaintiff.

The lawsuit officially begins when your complaint is filed with the court. After the defendant is formally notified of the suit, he or she has a specified period within which to file an "answer" with the court that responds to each allegation, giving the defendant's side of the matter.

In many suits, before and sometimes after the answer is filed, the defendant will file various motions objecting to one or another important procedural aspect of the lawsuit in an effort to have the case dismissed, or at least to delay it. Your lawyer must file a response challenging any such motion and must support your position with a written "brief," a short statement of the law and facts relating to the issue raised in the defendant's motion meant to educate the judge and persuade him or her that the defendant's motion should not be granted. These motions, all duly supported by well-researched and carefully written briefs, can continue for a very long time.

Meanwhile, another interesting and, for the lawyers, often lucrative part of the lawsuit is going on. This is "discovery," the minuet between the parties to the suit by which each "discovers" from the other as many facts as possible related to the lawsuit. Discovery tools include interrogatories (written questions), requests for production of documents (written requests for pertinent paperwork), and depositions (oral testimony taken out of court, but under oath and recorded by a court reporter). Discovery can also take forever.

Once the complaint and answer have been filed, all the motions have been made, answered, and ruled on by the court, and discovery is complete, the case can be set for trial. Both your lawyer and the defendant's lawyer will pore over the facts they've gathered, assess the strengths of their arguments, and map out their plans to present those facts and arguments in court before the judge. (Copyright infringement suits are ordinarily tried before a judge rather than a jury.)

A very large percentage of lawsuits are settled just before trial, sometimes literally in the hallway outside the courtroom just before the proceedings are to begin. Copyright infringement suits are no exception to this rule. This is because no one, least of all lawyers, wants to go through a trial if an acceptable settlement is possible. Even more persuasive is the attitude of most judges, who actively encourage settlements to reduce their heavy workload, to save taxpayers' money, and to clear perpetually clogged court dockets.

A settlement agreement between the litigants usually eliminates the possibility that the lawsuit isn't over even after the fat lady sings. Many losing litigants can find reasons to appeal the judgments entered against them by their trial courts. Sometimes they appeal up the ladder of courts more than once, on one ground or another, until all the people involved in the original lawsuit feel that they have unwittingly wandered into Charles Dickens's famous never-ending fictional lawsuit, *Jarndyce v. Jarndyce*.

The only thing worse than being a plaintiff in a lawsuit is being a defendant. A plaintiff at least has the choice of filing the suit or not and chooses, to some extent, when and where the suit is filed and what issues are involved. A defendant has none of these choices. In a suit brought on meritorious grounds, a plaintiff has some justifiable hope of winning the suit and collecting an award of damages and, possibly, of the attorneys' fees and costs incurred in pursuing the suit. The best most defendants can hope for is to have the court rule in their favor, in which case they pay their own often enormous legal fees and go home. (No lawyer ever represents a *defendant* on a contingency fee basis.)

At worst, a defendant is held to have transgressed the rights of the plaintiff, is ordered to pay the plaintiff money damages, is enjoined from further conduct of the sort the plaintiff sought to have stopped, and has to pay the plaintiff's legal fees in addition to his or her own legal fees. Sometimes plaintiffs come out ahead in lawsuits; defendants almost never do, even if judgment is in their favor.

Our judicial system is, in theory, one of the best ever invented. In practice, it often leaves a great deal to be desired. Some disputes cannot be settled out of court and must be litigated to avoid injustice, but too often litigation is commenced because someone is trying to prove a point or holds a grudge or gets greedy. Many frivolous copyright infringement suits are brought because plaintiffs simply don't understand enough about copyright law to realize that they have no valid basis to bring a suit. These lawsuits make even lawyers tired.

It's important to be right, but what you really should aim for is to be right *out* of court. That calls for careful choices in your business relationships, careful attention to the rights of others, and a careful lawyer who counsels you on ways to avoid disputes before they ripen into that bitter fruit, a lawsuit.

4

Copyright in the Marketplace

The law automatically grants you a copyright when you write a song, but there's nothing automatic about earning money from it. The entire recording industry is founded on copyrights; this includes both song copyrights and sound recording copyrights, but a good argument can be made that of the two varieties of copyrights, song copyrights are more important to the industry, since nothing happens until someone writes a song. Everyone who works in the recording industry would be unemployed if copyright law did not exist; without copyrights no one's work would produce any money, and the recording industry is about money, not art. The best songwriters and performers are artists, but even they write their songs and make their records for money as well as for love.

All of this means that if you hope to write songs for money, you must understand something about the way song copyrights are exploited. (This "exploitation" does not have the negative connotations that word usually entails. This is exploitation in the sense that a gardener exploits the earth to produce vegetables. A songwriter who wants to earn a living from his or her songs tries to exploit them by turning them into royalty checks.) Unless you're unusually precocious, you'll need to depend on music publishers to help you exploit your songs, and they'll want a piece of the action. This is fair, because without music publishers, most songwriters' gold records would still exist only in their larval stage, in the form of dusty demo tapes in a box in the hall closet.

Before you start trying to find a publisher, you need to know how music publishing agreements work so that you'll be able to evaluate whether an offer you receive is a good one. One of the main things you need to understand is how music publishers gain rights in the songs they publish.

As you've learned, if you write a song you own the copyright in it by operation of federal law, simply because you have created the song. This ownership occurs immediately and automatically. You don't have to notify any government agency that you've written a song and created a copyright, and you don't have to register a copyright to own it. There are three ways by which ownership of all or part of a song copyright can be transferred from a songwriter to someone else: "assignment," "license," and "work-for-hire."

Music publishers want to own the copyrights in the songs they publish. The customary method of transferring copyrights from songwriters to publishers is "assignment." (Assignments of copyright ownership are also called "transfers" of copyright.) An assignment of a song copyright is like a sale; it's the transfer of ownership of the copyright from the songwriter to the publisher, made in return for the promises the publisher makes in the music publishing agreement, most of which have to do with what portion of the royalties produced by the song the publisher will pay the songwriter, and how often. The copyright statute requires that any transfer of copyright ownership be made in a written document signed by the person assigning the ownership of the copyright. No verbal transfer of copyright ownership is possible. Anyone who acquires any right of copyright by assignment can, in turn, sell that right to someone else unless the written assignment document provides otherwise.

It's possible to transfer ownership of copyright to a publisher for less than the entire duration of copyright. Such transfers are often negotiated by songwriters (or their lawyers) who have enough clout to insist on assigning their songs to publishers for only a few years, after which ownership of the copyrights reverts to the songwriters. Usually these transfers provide that if the publishers manage to get the songs recorded, the assignments are made effective for the full term of copyright. (We will discuss these "reversion clauses" at greater length later.)

The second major way in which rights in copyrights pass from a copyright owner to someone else is the "license." A license is simply a permission granted by a copyright owner to allow someone to use or exploit a copyright in a certain way for a specified period. If an assignment of copyright is like a sale of the copyright, a copyright license is like a lease. Copyright licenses may be exclusive (that is, the only person who is permitted to exercise the right granted by the copyright owner is the person to whom the exclusive license is granted) or nonexclusive (that is, more than one person is allowed, by means of separate nonexclusive licenses, to exercise the right granted by the license). Like assignments of copyright ownership, exclusive copyright licenses must be in writing to be legally effective. (Nonexclusive copyright licenses do not have to be in writing. You can say, "O.K., Edgar, you can use my song for your TV commercial if you want, but I may also let my neighbor use it to advertise his pizza parlor.")

Like assignments of copyright ownership, copyright licenses may be granted for the full term of copyright or for shorter periods, as the copyright owner chooses. However, unlike transfers of copyright, which always specify the length of the transfer of ownership, some copyright licenses are "terminable at will" by the copyright owners who grant them. That is, unless a period is specified in a written license during which the "licensee" (the person who is granted the license) is permitted to exercise the right granted, the copyright owner (the "licensor") may terminate the license whenever he or she chooses. ("My neighbor doesn't like your using my song for your TV commercial. Since he paid me two hundred fifty dollars, I'm going to have to ask you to stop using it. Don't whine, Edgar. It's unbecoming in a man your age.")

As a practical matter, song copyright licenses come into play more in the lives of music publishers than in the business affairs of songwriters, since publishers rather than songwriters are typically responsible for exploiting songs. There are as many kinds of licenses as there are uses for songs. As you learned in Chapter One, the right to record a song and release it in the form of phonorecords is called a "mechanical license." The right to synchronize a song with visual images (as in a television show or movie) is called a "synch license." The right to prepare and sell sheet music for a song or to include it in written form in a songbook is called a "print license." These licenses, as well as others, are granted by music publishers, who negotiate (except in the case of some mechanical licenses, where the rate is set by law) fair prices for the rights granted to the licensees, based on how famous the licensed song is and how big the use is. (Do you want to use a Simon and Garfunkel hit as the soundtrack for your big-budget movie or do you want to use an obscure song recorded once by a now-forgotten fifties girl group as the overture for the play you wrote for your little-theater troupe?) Sometimes customary rates guide a publisher in negotiations for licenses. Sometimes the only standard that applies is *What will the traffic bear?*

Although most music publishing agreements provide that the songwriter transfers ownership of the *entire* song copyright to the music publisher, the law views copyright as an infinitely divisible set of rights. Grasping this concept is important to an understanding of copyright. Think of it this way: Any copyright is like a pie that can be sliced into as many large or small pieces as the size of the pie allows. If you've cooked up a song, you can assign the whole pie to a music publisher in return for an advance payment of some of the royalties you expect your song to earn and your publisher's promise to pay you specified percentages of the revenues it will produce. Your publisher, who becomes the copyright owner, can then slice off small permissions, called licenses, allowing others to use your song for certain purposes. There's one important difference between copyrights and pies, however. Anyone to whom you give a piece of pie will eat it; anyone who buys a piece of a copyright can use it and sell or license it to someone else, who can then also use it, but the original slice of copyright is never consumed by anyone who acquires it. Your copyright is, for a while, an inexhaustible resource; it does not disappear until it falls into the public domain at the end of the copyright term.

The third method by which copyright ownership comes to rest with someone other than the songwriter is almost never properly used between songwriters and publishers. This is the much feared, widely misunderstood, and sometimes misused "work-for-hire." "Work-for-hire" is the term used to describe a copyright created by an author who is a full-time employee as a part of his or her job. In such circumstances, the *employer* owns the copyright from the inception of the work and is considered, for copyright purposes, the author of the work.

The concept of work-for-hire almost always makes songwriters' hair stand on end because it seems unfair to them, but in the right situation there's nothing unfair about it. If you work as a staff composer for an ad agency or a jingle production company, you trade the creative output of your fertile imagination for a paycheck and leave the job of selling the music you create to your employer. Any music you compose or lyrics you write in the course of fulfilling your obligations to your employer are "works-for-hire" and belong—lock, stock, words, and music— to the people who hired you. You have no ownership in the copyrights in these products of your imagination, no control over how they are used (even if you object to the use of a jingle you wrote as the campaign song for a politician you dislike, you can't do anything about it), and no share in the revenues they produce, even if they're substantial. Your employer has taken the risk of setting up in business to exploit what you create. Your only reward is your paycheck and whatever you can learn on the job. This variety of work-for-hire occurs at the intersection of capitalism and copyright and is the first of the sets of circumstances enumerated in the copyright statute in which the work-for-hire concept applies.

Besides the situation of a full-time employee who creates copyrightable works as a part of his or her job, the copyright statute specifies nine other situations in which works-for-hire can result from the work of independent contractors (freelancers) whose works are created outside the confines of a full-time job. Only two of the nine work-for-hire situations enumerated in the copyright statute have any possible application to the professional life of a songwriter. They are:

- A contribution to a "collective work" (such as a song written for an album recorded to commemorate an historical event)
- A part of a motion picture or audiovisual work (such as a piece of music designed to become part or all of a movie soundtrack)

If a musical composition created by an independent contractor is specifically commissioned for one of these purposes *and* the person who commissions the work and the creator of the work both sign a written document that states that the work is agreed to be a work-for-hire, the composition is considered a work-for-hire. No work created under other circumstances can qualify as a work-for-hire.

This means, of course, that the work-for-hire concept has almost no application in situations ordinarily encountered by songwriters, who are among the most independent of independent contractors and who seldom run into people willing to commission them to write songs for either of these two narrow purposes. Once in a while a music publisher who's short on scruples will try to insert a work-for-hire provision into a songwriting agreement. The legal effect of such an attempt is uncertain, but you don't want to wait until the effect of work-for-hire provisions in music publishing agreements is a settled point of law to know what to do. Since anyone who tries to turn an ordinary publishing agreement into a work-for-hire agreement must use specific work-for-hire language to have any chance of success, all that's necessary is that you—or better still, your lawyer—carefully examine *any* agreement relating to a song you write to ensure that no work-for-hire language is buried in an innocuous-looking paragraph.

You may be asking yourself what difference it would make to sign a work-for-hire agreement if most ordinary publishing agreements provide that ownership of the song copyright is transferred to the publisher anyway. Well, there are several big differences between having someone acquire the copyright in a song you write as a work-for-hire and having someone acquire it through an assignment. The law treats work-for-hire copyrights very differently from those created under ordinary circumstances. Even if you were paid the same royalties for uses of your work-for-hire copyright that you would earn under an ordinary publishing agreement, your rights in your song would be seriously diminished.

The duration of work-for-hire copyrights is, usually, shorter. Copyright protection for a musical composition created as a work-for-hire will endure seventy-five years; for a work created under ordinary circumstances, protection endures through the life of the songwriter and for fifty years thereafter.

This is a big difference. But the biggest difference between a work-for-hire copyright and a copyright transferred to a music publisher under an ordinary music publishing agreement is that, believe it or not, with an ordinary copyright transfer you get a second bite of the apple after thirty-five years. That is, you can legally have second thoughts about having signed your copyright over to a publisher and decide to undo the assignment. There's a good reason why this is so.

Our current copyright statute was drafted to allow authors who sell or license their copyrights for less than those copyrights later prove to be worth to recover their copyrights at about the halfway point of copyright protection. This is called the "termination-of-transfers" provision of the statute. Authors who exercise their right to terminate assignments or licenses then become, once more, the owners of the copyrights they created and can further exploit those copyrights by selling or licensing them again. Or at least they *will* be able to. The termination-of-transfers provision of the new copyright statute that applies to copyrights created on or after January 1, 1978, is only exercisable thirty-five years into the terms of those copyrights. This means that beginning in 2013, U.S. songwriters will begin to take steps to recover ownership of copyrights they assigned in 1978 to music publishers. (Songwriters who transferred the copyrights in their songs to someone else before that year can also terminate those transfers, after fifty-six years of copyright protection. Unless you're old enough to have written songs before 1978, you can ignore this provision of the copyright statute.)

Some songs, including hits, are dead at age four or five and have long been decently buried by age thirty-five, but others become standards and are worth much more at thirty-five than they were when freshly hatched. Think, for example, of "September Song," which was a smash for Willie Nelson (and its writer and publisher) many years after it was first recorded. If you think you might write a few deathless songs, pay some attention to the short course in terminations of copyright transfers that appears at the end of this chapter, and photocopy and *use* the "Notice to My Heirs and Executors" (which is reproduced in the Appendixes of this book). Even if you don't like to think about being thirty-five years older, when you get there you may be glad to have the information about assignments of your songs that this form will preserve; if you don't live thirty-five years more, your heirs will be happy that they had a progenitor who knew the value of a copyright.

As a songwriter, most of the money you earn from your songs will come to you in the form of either mechanical royalties, paid by record companies for the privilege of recording and selling your songs, or performance royalties, paid by radio and television stations that broadcast recordings of your songs and clubs and other entities where your songs may be performed. Half of the mechanical and performance royalties your songs earn belongs to your music publisher, and the other half goes to you. Your share of mechanical royalties will be paid to you through your publisher; your share of performance royalties will be paid directly to you by BMI or ASCAP or SESAC.

There are three other primary sources of earnings besides U.S. mechanical and performance royalties. Print licenses, issued by your publisher to one of several U.S. sheet music companies to allow the publication of your song in sheet music form, can produce substantial revenues for the right song. Synchronization (or "synch") licenses are granted to allow the use of your song in movies or television shows; the right song in the right movie can earn $25,000 or more.

Foreign royalties are payments that result from the use outside the United States of your songs in one of the ways discussed above; generally these monies are collected by foreign subpublishers under agreements with your publisher. Foreign royalties are simply (primarily) mechanical and performance royalties produced in other countries; however, publishing agreements treat them as a separate category of revenue from U.S. mechanical and performance royalties because they're collected separately and differently. Because lots of recording artists whose stars have dimmed in the United States (or were never brighter than refrigerator lightbulbs) are popular in Japan or Sweden, foreign royalties can exceed U.S. royalties.

A lot of things must happen before checks for any of these royalties land in your mailbox, however. First you write a song, of course. Then you record a demo of it so that a publisher can determine whether the song is a good one. These two steps are relatively easy compared to the third step in making money from songwriting—convincing a publisher to sign your song. As hard as it is to write a good song, it's often even more difficult to "sell" it once it's written. Maybe you really *are* the next Billy Joel, but you and your songs are going to have to persuade a publisher of the fact before those songs ever ride the airways.

A persuaded publisher will offer you a "single song agreement." This is a written contract that gives the publisher the right to publish your song and collect royalties from any exploitation of it. If you've had several cuts and the publisher thinks you have a future as a songwriter, you may be offered an "exclusive publishing agreement," which signs all the songs you create during a specified period. After you have a real track record as a songwriter, and especially if you're also a performer with a record contract, you may be able to talk a publisher into a "copublishing agreement," an exclusive publishing agreement in which your publisher agrees to own less than the entire song copyright, to take less than the publisher's customary share (half) of the royalties produced by your song, and to treat you like a publisher, at least to the extent of paying you part of the royalties otherwise due your publisher.

For now, you really don't need to worry about anything but learning the standard provisions of a single song agreement, because the other sorts of publishing agreements are really only expanded versions of a single song agreement, and anyway, you're going to take *any* agreement a publisher offers you right down the street to your lawyer's office (or maybe to a songwriters' organization, as we will discuss later) for review before you sign it. If your song is good enough to interest a publisher, it's valuable enough to protect. Luckily for you, learning how a single song agreement works isn't hard to do, and you don't really have to remember everything you learn (that's what you'll pay your lawyer for—lawyers are paid to remember stuff that would only get in the way of the hit songs forming themselves in the crinkles of your brain).

All single song agreements are not the same. Single song agreements are called by different names, their provisions are not always arranged in the same order, and they don't all include the same provisions. Some are more fair to the songwriter than others. However, although each music publishing company uses its own particular version of the single song agreement, all single song agreements share certain characteristics. These characteristic provisions are what makes any single song agreement function as it is intended to function, that is, to transfer from the writer to the publisher, under specified conditions, certain rights in the song copyright and to the revenues the song produces.

A tour of the major provisions of a standard single song agreement would include stops at the following paragraphs:

• **The "grant-of-rights" clause:** This is often the first full paragraph in a single song agreement and always falls near the top of the first page, after the language that names the parties to the agreement the "Composer" and the "Publisher" and specifies the song that is the subject of the agreement (referred to thereafter as the "Composition"). It contains the language that formally transfers ownership of the U.S. and foreign copyrights in your song to your publisher. This transfer language is always as broad as possible to give the publisher every possible present and future right to the song, throughout the world and, sometimes (in our space age), "throughout the universe." (After all, lots of things can happen during the term of a copyright. Think of all the changes in the world since, for instance, Fats Waller wrote "Ain't Misbehavin'.")

Under the current U.S. copyright statute, no transfer of copyright ownership is effective unless it is evidenced by a written document signed by the owner of the rights conveyed. This means it's impossible to sell or give your copyright to anyone verbally and that the grant-of-rights paragraph is the heart of any music publishing agreement. One fairly standard grant-of-rights paragraph reads:

Composer hereby sells, assigns, transfers, and delivers to Publisher, its successors and assigns, all right, title, and interest, of every kind and nature, in and to said unpublished Composition, including the lyrics, music, and title thereof, and all copyrights, and the right to secure copyrights, and in any works derived therefrom, throughout the entire world and any and all other rights that Composer now has or to which Composer may become entitled under existing or subsequently-enacted federal, state, or foreign laws, statutes, or regulations, including, without limitation, the following rights: to reproduce the Composition in copies or phonorecords, to prepare derivative works based upon the Composition, to distribute copies or phonorecords of the Composition, and to perform or display the Composition publicly.

Sometimes songwriters limit this very broad transfer by persuading publishers to include somewhere in their single song agreements what is called a "reversion clause." Usually a reversion clause simply states that if the publisher does not produce a commercially released cut of the song (that is, it doesn't count if the publisher's brother-in-law's band cuts the song and "releases" 400 cassette copies of the recording by selling tapes at club dates) within a specified number of years (usually between two and ten), ownership of the copyright will "revert," or return, to the songwriter. Negotiating a provision of this sort is an extremely good idea, since reversion clauses make publishers *do* something in return for the transfer of ownership of songwriters' copyrights to them. Some publishing agreements do provide that "Publisher agrees to exert reasonable effort to commercially exploit the Composition in accordance with its customary business practices," but language of this sort is too vague to really compel any specific action from a publisher. A publisher who acquires a song copyright under an agreement that includes a reversion clause will pay attention to that song, since the copyright in it will be lost if the demo for the song doesn't regularly see daylight. Otherwise, it may languish in the publisher's file room.

If you (or your lawyer) ask that a reversion clause be included in a single song agreement, ask that the reversion be made automatic after a certain period. Reversion clauses that require the songwriter to do something to trigger the reversion are cumbersome and unnecessarily complicated. An "automatic" reversion clause would read something like this:

> If by the fifth anniversary of the date of execution [signing] of this Agreement a sound recording of the Composition has not been made and released through commercial channels by a recording artist (other than the Composer) who records for a major record company or for an independent record company distributed by a major record company, this Agreement shall terminate and all rights of any and every nature in and to the Composition and in and to any and all copyrights secured therefor in the United States and throughout the world shall automatically re-vest in and become the property of the Composer.

• **The royalties provision:** This paragraph is usually a very long one and ordinarily contains a string of subparagraphs, each of which deals with a certain category of royalty. The royalties paragraph is the provision in which the publisher promises to pay the songwriter certain specified percentages of any revenues created by any exploitation of the song. In most cases, the split is 50/50 for all categories of royalties. Print royalties are, however, quite commonly divided differently, with the songwriter receiving only 10 to 15 percent of the revenues from the various print licenses the publisher grants to companies that produce and sell sheet music. Other than remembering that the industry standard for ordinary publishing agreements is a 50/50 split for most royalty categories, you don't really need to remember more, since that lawyer we talked about a few paragraphs ago will remember these details for you.

• **The royalties statement and payment paragraph:** This is the provision of the agreement that specifies when the publisher will account to the songwriter for the royalties collected during the immediately preceding accounting period and pay the songwriter his or her share of those royalties. Usually publishers pay songwriters every six months, within forty-five or sixty days of the end of the accounting period. (For instance, a publisher would pay its songwriters by August 15 or 30 of every year for the January-through-June accounting period.) Sometimes publishers pay songwriters quarterly, but not often, and most publishers will not agree to pay one songwriter more often than it pays its other songwriters, since any such variance from a publisher's usual payment schedule would create bookkeeping problems for the publisher.

Songwriters often complain because publishers hold songwriters' royalties as long as the provisions of their publishing agreements allow. Royalties earned in November but not collected by the publisher until January may not be paid to the songwriter until August 30—sixty days after the end of the January-through-June accounting period. This is money that could be sitting as comfortably in the songwriter's checking account, available to pay bills, as in the publisher's bank account, earning interest for the publisher. But that is not, alas, the way things work. Once in a while a publisher will agree to make an advance payment of royalties to a songwriter when the publisher knows there is money on the way ("pipeline money") for some exploitation of that songwriter's song. But a publisher has no obligation to give a songwriter an advance or make royalty payments any more often than the single song agreement provides. That's what contracts do—specify the obligations of the parties. Any more lenient treatment from a publisher is a favor to the songwriter and, for some good reasons that have to do with a publisher's need to run the publishing company in an orderly fashion, can't be depended on.

The royalties provision of a single song agreement provides that any advance payments of royalties ("advances") the publisher has made will be "recouped" (recovered) by the publisher from revenues created by the song before any payment of royalties is made to the songwriter. The same goes for money spent to record demos. Your publisher may give you $250 when you sign a single song agreement, but you should remember that this is actually *your* money.

Music publishing agreements always include a provision that royalty statements are "binding" on a songwriter (that is, cannot be objected to as inaccurate) after a specified period (often two years). This limits the period during which a songwriter can discover any underpayment by the publisher. Ordinarily any lawsuit must be commenced within the specified period and is barred thereafter. To allow a songwriter (or the songwriter's lawyer or accountant) to determine whether a publisher has been fiddling with the books related to that songwriter's songs, most provisions of this sort end by stating the conditions under which the songwriter is allowed to examine the publisher's books. This is called the "audit provision" and is an important right, although it may never come into play in the life of most songwriters. Unless this right is given a songwriter in a publishing agreement, he or she may have to go to court to compel the publisher who is suspected of malfeasance to make its records available for examination.

If you know and trust the publisher whose agreement you sign, you may believe that the audit provision, among other provisions, is unnecessary. However, consider the fact that your friendly neighborhood publishing company may sell its entire catalog to a bigger publisher at some point during the life of your copyrights. This sort of sale happens every day in the music industry. If your publisher is sold, you may find that your copyright is owned by a company you don't like run by people you don't like. In such a situation, you'll need all the safeguards your single song agreement gives you, even though you may initially have regarded them as excess baggage.

- **The "warranty clause":** This provision is found in every music publishing agreement. It's like a big suitcase, because it has every possible protection for the publisher stuffed into it. In it the composer warrants, covenants, and represents that the Composition is the Composer's original unpublished work and that no part thereof infringes upon the title or the literary or musical property rights or the copyright in any other work nor unfairly competes with any person or entity; that the Composer is the sole author, composer, and owner thereof and of all the rights therein, and that prior to executing this Agreement, the Composer has not sold, assigned, transferred, pledged, or mortgaged any right, title, or interest in the Composition, the copyright therein, or in any of the rights herein conveyed; that the Composer has not made or entered into any other contract or contracts affecting the Composition or any right, title, or interest therein, or in the copyright rights therein, and that no person, firm, or corporation other than the Composer claims, or has claimed, any right, title, or interest in or to the Composition, and that the Composer has full right, power, and authority to enter into this Agreement and make all of the grants, promises, and convenants herein contained.

If you think it's a little scary to make such broad promises about a song you write, you're right. But scarier still is another provision found in every single song agreement. This is:

• **The "indemnity" provision:** This provision, in conjunction with the warranty clause just discussed, makes the songwriter responsible, legally and financially, for claims of copyright infringement made against the song transferred to the publisher in the single song agreement. The loaded language in indemnity provisions is relatively short:

The Composer hereby indemnifies, saves, and holds the Publisher and its successors and assigns harmless from any and all liability, claims, demands, loss, and damage (including reasonable attorneys' fees and court costs) arising out of or connected with any breach or default by the Composer hereunder or any claim or action by a third party that is inconsistent with any of the warranties, representations, or agreements made by the Composer in this Agreement and which results in a judgment in a court of competent jurisdiction or settlement entered into with the Composer's prior written consent, which such consent shall not be unreasonably withheld.

Usually there is also a sentence (or two or three, since lawyers like to say things more than once—this is what your dad called the "belt-and-suspenders approach") that provides that the publisher may withhold a songwriter's royalties until any claim of copyright infringement or other breach of all the things that the songwriter warranted wouldn't happen is settled. In terms of simple math, this means that one hit song that earns big bucks by stealing the melody from another song equals no royalties for the publisher and a big hole in the wallet of the songwriter who said the song was original. Or, as *many* dads have said, "Son, the big print giveth and the fine print taketh away."

A word about publishers. Publishers of every stripe have made songwriters rich. Little publishing companies can do it as well as big ones if they have the know-how, a good song to pitch, and a little luck. And despite songwriters' suspicions, most music publishers are honest. Ask around about any publisher that offers you a contract. Find out whether your would-be publisher has a history of cuts and hits. Pay attention to the musical judgment, or lack thereof, of the people you meet on the publisher's staff—they must to be able to *hear* a hit before they can persuade anyone else that your song is one. Call up everyone you know in the music industry and ask about the publisher's reputation for honesty and paying songwriters on time. Once you've determined that a particular publisher is competent, you can take the agreement to a lawyer. Songwriters often sign single song agreements with several publishers before being offered an exclusive publishing agreement. This is good, because it gives a songwriter a

chance to look at the performance of several publishers before getting involved in a long-term relationship with one of
them.

You probably have a headache by now. This is normal and
natural. Only lawyers can read this stuff for very long without
getting a migraine, and after a few years it affects even them.
(There are only twelve lawyers in the continental United
States who do not keep at least one pair of reading glasses in
their desk drawers.) Lucky for you that this discussion is almost
over.

We've been examining the provisions included in most
single song agreements. There are others, but they're less important and have mostly to do with legal formalities, such as
in what state a suit would be filed if the songwriter decides to
sue the publisher, or vice versa. The provisions we have examined, although not unusually harsh toward the songwriter,
were taken from a single song agreement drafted for a publisher, which means it was drafted in favor of the publisher in
every place where it was possible to put a little English on a
standard provision and give the publisher more control. In the
Appendixes of this book there is a single song agreement
(called a Popular Songwriters Contract) that has been developed over the years by a national songwriters' organization,
The Songwriters Guild of America. Read it to find out what
people who have songwriters' interests at heart think a single
song agreement should say. As a practical matter, you're probably not going to be able to persuade most publishers to use
the Songwriters Guild contract because it's more favorable to
your interests as a songwriter than makes most publishers
comfortable. However, you can use it as a standard by which
to judge contracts that are offered to you and, if you join the
Guild, you can get advice from trained Guild staff members
about the provisions of those agreements. The Guild's advice
may not be as extensive as your very own lawyer's, but it is reliable and less expensive. The Guild's offices are listed in the
Resources section of this book. Other songwriters' organiza-

tions may also offer similar advice. (Check it out. Songwriters banding together to stick up for themselves! The underclass revolts against the Establishment! Unfair publishing practices disappear in the face of organized resistance! Who says songwriters are naive?)

The management of this book apologizes for the boring nature of this chapter. It's hard to make this stuff less hardcore than it is. But in a way this chapter is an object lesson for you, because it emphasizes that music publishers take your songs so seriously that they surround themselves with bulletproof contracts when dealing with songwriters, whose only weapons are their pens (and their lawyers). If a publisher thinks your song is valuable enough to nail down north, south, east, and west, shouldn't you take it just as seriously? Nobody knows how valuable a new song copyright is. It's worthless (as a source of income) until somebody turns it into a record or a television theme song or, even, a movie (think of "The Gambler," written by Don Schlitz and made famous by Kenny Rogers).

An unexploited copyright is like a seed that can grow into a money tree. A good copyright can transform your professional life into an actual career and your finances into something to brag about. And although you may put your blood, sweat, and tears into a song, it's free to write. If you live in the United States, you're free to write just about whatever you want, thanks to the First Amendment. Think of it. You can turn your own freedom of expression into freedom from having to work at a real job ever again.

If you're a songwriter, you ought to view the entire music industry as a complex and carefully designed system that exists to send you money in the mail. Think of that the next time you're intimidated by some record company executive in a $500 suit. She may lose that big job tomorrow; without the gig, that executive is just an *empty* suit. You, however, can *always* write songs. And it will always be true that one of them may be a hit. Don't just sit there. Where's your guitar?

Recapture of Copyrights: Sell Them Now, Own Them Later—Legally

In 1976, the United States got a new copyright law, the first entirely new U.S. copyright law since 1909. Two provisions of the new copyright law, which became effective January 1, 1978, are of potentially great benefit to copyright owners, since they allow, under certain circumstances, the *termination* of previous transfers of copyright. A "transfer" of copyright is an assignment or sale of the copyright to someone else. These provisions allow a creator of a copyright to make a sale of the copyright and later *cancel*, or terminate, that sale and regain, or "recapture," ownership of the copyright. The termination-of-transfers provisions of the new law are somewhat complicated, but any songwriter owes it to himself or herself—and his or her heirs—to learn a little about the new provisions and how they work.

There are two groups of copyrights that are affected by the new termination-of-transfers provisions. Section 203 of the new copyright law provides that transfers of copyright made on or after January 1, 1978, by the songwriter may be terminated thirty-five to forty years after the transfer. Section 304(c) of the new copyright law provides that transfers of copyright made by the songwriter or certain members of the songwriter's family before January 1, 1978, may be terminated after fifty-six years from the date copyright protection was first secured. The right to terminate a transfer is statutory; this means you can't waive this right or bargain it away.

When you (or certain of your heirs) exercise the right to terminate a transfer, on the date that the termination is effective you (or they) regain ownership of all the rights of copyright (with some limitations in specific situations) that were originally sold or otherwise conveyed to someone else. You (or your family) then own those rights for the remainder of the term of copyright (until fifty years after your death or the death of your last surviving cowriter for songs created on or after January 1,

1978, and for nineteen more years for songs that have been protected by copyright for fifty-six years), or the copyright may be sold or licensed again. It's important to remember, however, that only U.S. copyright rights may be regained; the U.S. copyright law is only effective in the United States and its termination-of-transfers provisions affect only U.S. copyrights. Further, the termination-of-transfers provisions do not apply to copyrights that were created as works-for-hire.

The new copyright law sets out specific procedures that must be followed by anyone who seeks to terminate a transfer of copyright. Written notices of intent to terminate must be given, *by and to* the proper people, during specified periods in advance of termination. These notices will be ineffective to accomplish termination if they are given too soon or too late, or by or to the wrong people.

The termination of copyright transfers is a complicated area of the law that confuses even lawyers. This means that the termination of a copyright transfer is *not* a do-it-yourself job. If a song copyright is valuable enough, decades after its creation, to make its ownership desirable, it's valuable enough to justify paying a copyright lawyer to help regain that ownership. However, before a lawyer can help you or your family regain ownership of a copyright, you or your heirs must first remember that such a procedure is possible and, second, you must be able to supply that lawyer with sufficient information about the original transfer of the copyright to enable him or her to carry out the termination. This means you should keep accurate records of every assignment of any copyright you create. Keeping records concerning the assignments of your copyrights does not have to be time-consuming. The best way to keep the records you need is to set aside an evening once every year (the day before your birthday?) to compile records that could result in increased old-age income for you or enhanced income for your spouse, children, and grandchildren after your death.

A form for recording important information about the copyrights you create and assign to someone else appears in the

Appendixes of this book. Make a supply of clear photocopies of the form, called "Notice to My Heirs and Executors." Fill out one of these forms for each assignment you make of a song copyright and attach to the filled-out form a copy of the assignment document (which may be named a "Single Song Agreement" or something similar or may be titled simply "Assignment of Copyright"), along with a copy of the copyright registration certificate, if you have one, or of the lead sheet for the song itself.

Put the records concerning all transfers of copyright made during any given year in a folder marked "Copyright Transfers—1995" (etc.). Keep these records with your other important personal papers; tell your spouse, your adult children, the executor of your will, and your lawyer you're keeping such records and why.

The termination-of-transfers provisions of the new copyright act were included because Congress wanted to give songwriters and other creators and their families the chance to regain ownership of copyrights that grow to be valuable after they are originally sold. In the case of terminations made after fifty-six years of copyright protection, Congress wanted to give them the benefit of the nineteen-year extension period it tacked onto the end of the copyright terms in existence when the new law was passed. The copyright law is our government's way of rewarding and encouraging creativity in our society; the termination-of-transfers provisions of the new copyright law can help you make sure that your successful songs benefit you and your heirs as well as your publisher.

III

THE BUSINESS
OF MAKING MUSIC

5

Partnership Law for Musicians

Although making music is an art, making a living from it is a business. The music business is glamorous only on its surface. Underneath that shining surface is a cold, hard heart that will break yours unless you learn enough to watch your back and where you step. As a general rule, the parts of the business side of music that you most need to understand are those that are closest to you. And your closest relationships will be with the other members of your band. In fact, many partnerships are closer, more intense relationships than most marriages. That's why you need a working knowledge of partnership law before you get "married" to the boys in the band and certainly before you "divorce" them.

Lots of performing groups don't understand that they are partnerships. They think that because they're musicians who name themselves something unserious like The Mad Bombers and because they have never signed any written partnership agreement, they somehow are immune to the boring dictates of business law that apply to more ordinary businesses. What they don't understand is that their state's partnership statute hovers over everyone within the boundaries of their state and descends to envelop anyone whose actions trigger its provisions, whether or not the people affected notice that they have become bound by them. If you're stopped for speeding, you can't avoid a ticket by telling the police officer you didn't know you were driving over the speed limit; neither will ignorance of partnership law prevent its governing some aspects of your relationship with the other members of your band, if your activities bring you within its scope.

This means first that you should be extremely careful in choosing your partners—musical ability is *not* enough—because that guy snoring in the seat beside you in the back of the band van on a road trip can make or break you financially as well as musically. He can obligate you to pay for things he buys and create liability for you by the things he does and stop you from doing something you really want to do, for a good reason or a bad one or just because he feels like it. He can also tie you up in court for years by claiming that when you asked him to leave the group you didn't treat him fairly or by acting so badly himself that *you* have to sue *him*.

Second, you should take care that you do not stumble into a partnership you don't really want to be in. This can happen more easily than you may think. Let's suppose you and your old friend Sam have been playing and singing and writing songs since high school. You like Sam and she likes you and you decide that now that you're both living in your hometown again, you should start a band. Sam brings her friend Johnny to your first practice session, since you need a drummer, and you persuade a guitarist you know named Vanessa to play lead for the new group. Nobody even thinks about any more permanent business relationship than a pickup band until Sam gets the group a gig at a fraternity party at the local college. The Greeks love you.

Before you know it, you're hot on the frat house and deb party circuit. You buy some sound equipment and sign an agreement with a booking agent. You hire a publicist and pay to print flyers advertising your upcoming dates. You publish a newsletter for your fans and sell sweatshirts with your name on them. You hire a recording studio and record an album so that you can sell cassettes during the breaks in your performances. You think of trying to find a manager and consider shopping a tape of original songs that you and Johnny and Sam wrote to publishers and record companies.

Then one day you realize that you're a part of a four-way marriage and wonder whether you really want to be married to Johnny and Vanessa. Sam is O.K. as a partner, but the other two members of the band can be jerks. Johnny thinks he's another Casanova and never makes it back onstage on time after the break between sets because he's always trying to wow some sorority girl with his bogus stories of having been a Guardian Angel. Vanessa is nice enough until she has a couple of beers and then she gets belligerent; once you even had to hustle her out the back door of a frat house after she told the president of the fraternity that he and his "brothers" were all "rich little white boys" who couldn't dance and didn't understand rock and roll.

You and Sam ask her brother, who is a third-year law student, just what your obligation is to Johnny and Vanessa. You are chagrined to hear that even though you and Sam have never signed any partnership agreement with Johnny and Vanessa, they are your partners because you're engaged in a business with them and share with them the profits from your performances. You didn't realize you could become someone's partner so easily—almost by accident. Even though you can't figure out how you ended up with these two bozos, you *certainly* can't imagine spending the rest of your career playing with them. Sam's brother tells you that extricating yourselves from the partnership could be messy and will certainly be complicated. Somehow you thought music was supposed to be more fun.

Partnership law is state law; that is, there is no federal statute that governs partnerships and their activities. Partnership statutes vary from state to state, but most states have adopted some version of a model law called the Uniform Partnership Act. The Uniform Partnership Act defines a partnership as "an association of two or more persons [who] carry on as co-owners a business for profit." If the members of a group have no written partnership agreement, but meet the criteria for a partnership (that is, they have associated themselves in a band as co-owners for the purpose of profiting from it), their state's partnership statute makes certain presumptions about their activities.

In the case of a performing group, your state's partnership statute assumes:

- That each group member has an equal say about how the business of the band will be conducted and that a vote of a majority of the band members will determine any decision of the partnership
- That each group member owns an equal share of band assets, which include physical assets, such as sound equipment or a van for road tours, and intangible property, such as the name of the group and the right to profit from contracts the group enters into
- That each group member is entitled to an equal share of profits the group earns and must bear an equal share of any financial losses it incurs
- That each group member is responsible for the actions of his or her partners while those partners are conducting group business—for instance, if a band member falls asleep while driving the group from one engagement to another, he and the other members of the group are equally responsible for the costs of repairing the barn he runs into and replacing the chickens that were in it

Now, these presumptions can be varied and, to some extent, avoided by including contravening provisions in a written partnership agreement. That's one reason a written partnership agreement is so important—if you don't decide for yourself how your partnership is to be conducted, the partnership statute in the state where you live may determine for you, without your consent, some things you would really rather decide for yourself. Like just what share of the money the group makes from a club date your worthless keyboard player is entitled to receive. (Even though he drank too much the night before you left and didn't make it to the airport on time to catch the plane, he's entitled to an equal share of the profits from the date because he's a partner in your band.) Or whether your egomaniac lead guitar player can leave your group and perform with his *new* band under the same name that you and he and the other members of your band used before he decided to leave (believe it or not, he may have the right to do just that because, as a partner in your group, he's an equal owner of the name). Or whether your lead singer can charge five hundred dollars' worth of new stage clothes to the band because he thinks he looks better in blue. (Since he's a partner, he can obligate the band for a debt he incurs if his purchase is, arguably, made to advance the group's business interests.)

There are several other very good reasons to enter into a written partnership agreement.

One advantage of a written agreement of any sort is that it reduces to writing the understanding that exists between the "parties" to the agreement (not *that* kind of party—the "parties" to an agreement are the people or companies who sign it). This is an important advantage, since dishonest people sometimes use the fact that an agreement isn't written down to try to finagle a better deal for themselves than was actually agreed to, and even honest people have been known to have bad memories.

Getting your group's partnership agreement in writing is even more important than writing down some other, short-term contracts that bands enter into, such as contracts for club dates. This is because if you're a professional entertainer and play with a group, your partnership agreement governs the whole of your primary business relationship and endures as long as your band does. It's a road map for conducting your partnership because it sets out the rules by which you and your partners have agreed to play. It can also ensure that you're all treated fairly and help you avoid time-consuming and counterproductive disputes.

But a partnership agreement will also have several important applications *after* your band breaks up. (Considering the high mortality rate of even successful groups, planning for the possible breakup of your band is only realistic.) In fact, in some respects, a band partnership agreement is remarkably like a prenuptial agreement—one of those documents couples sign before they get married so that everyone will know who's entitled to what if there's a divorce. This is because even though a written partnership agreement is an important management tool for the business of the band during the life of the partnership, it can be even more important when the group splits up. If you've ever watched any prime-time soap operas, you know that the time to sign a prenuptial agreement is *before* the wedding. The same is true for partnership agreements—the time to sign one is while you and your partners are still happy with one another, because once you aren't, no one is likely to be objective enough to negotiate fair terms for the breakup, especially if any money is involved.

(Of course, maybe you'll be lucky and won't make enough money to fight over. You won't need a written partnership agreement then because no one ever fights over an empty pocketbook and your state's partnership statute already tells you what you'll have to do about your partnership debts. The trouble is, any good band can become wealthy nearly overnight, no matter how broke they were beforehand. Even though the odds of becoming The Beatles are small, if you're in the music business, one of the things that keeps life interesting is the actual possibility of sudden wealth.)

Another very important reason to write down your group's partnership agreement is that unless you agree to the contrary in writing, when one of the members of your group leaves or is asked to leave by the other members, your partnership terminates immediately. This is because partnership law defines a partnership as an association of *particular* people. If one member of the partnership is no longer a part of it, its membership has changed and the partnership is, therefore, at an end. The termination of your partnership has serious legal implications. The most difficult result of the end of a partnership is that the partners must clear up all the debts of the former partnership, even if they have to sell off partnership assets or borrow money personally to do so. If any partnership money is left over after the debts of the partnership are cleared up, that money must be "distributed," or divided among the partners.

After the partnership has been dissolved and the people to whom the partnership owed money have been paid, the partner who is leaving can take off for parts unknown and the remaining partners can form a *new* partnership. This new partnership will not be a continuation of the old one but instead will be like a new baby—that is, an entirely new entity under the law. It will not own any of the assets of the old partnership unless the old partnership sold those assets to the old partners and the old partners contributed them to the new partnership. Neither will it have any of the obligations of the old partnership; either any debts or liabilities of the old partnership will have been paid off when the old partnership was dissolved or the old partners will have personally taken them over.

If you think this sounds like a long rigamarole to go through just because somebody in your group decides to make pop music history without the encumbrance of partners, you're right. But it's the way the law says things must be handled, and you really have no choice but to jump through all the hoops the law specifies if you find that your partnership is ending.

Unless, that is, you've had the foresight to enter into a written agreement with your partners that includes that very important provision of a band partnership agreement called the "leaving-member clause." If you have one of these handy provisions, your existing partnership can continue with the minimum of trauma and paperwork, even if one of your partners resigns from it.

Generally, a leaving-member clause provides that a group

member who wants to resign as a partner must give the other partners advance notice of his or her intention, that the existing partnership will continue after the exit of the resigning partner, and that the partnership will pay an amount equal to the value of the resigning partner's share of the partnership assets to him or her (often in installment payments over a specified period), and the appropriate share of royalties (from previously recorded records and other sources of revenue) when the partnership receives them.

Sometimes there is also a provision that limits the ability of the leaving member to work as a musician and performer after leaving. This sort of provision is designed to discourage defections from the band, but this is America, where slavery is against the law, so there's really no way to prevent a group member from leaving if he or she really wants to go. However, although a partner may be able to get out of the partnership, he or she is not magically released from other agreements the partners may have signed, such as tour contracts and recording agreements. The partnership agreement governs only the relationships between the partners, and a provision allowing one partner to leave the partnership does not affect any obligation that partner may have to a third party, such as a concert promoter or a record company.

Leaving-member provisions typically include half a page or so of dense language specifying how the assets of the partnership are to be "valued" so that the resigning partner may be paid for his or her share of the assets of the partnership. This language may seem unnecessarily complex to a band that earns $300 a night max and doesn't *have* any assets, but it will make a lot of sense to any group that becomes prosperous overnight when it starts climbing the record charts.

There are several important questions that you and the other members of your group should ask yourselves *before* you attempt to put your partnership arrangement in writing. One of them is: *Who will be your partners?*

Should every member of your group be a partner? Should the

three members of the band who founded it be the partners and the other two musicians you want to add to the group be simply employees of the band rather than partners? There is some advantage to this sort of arrangement. It recognizes that some members of a group may have been more instrumental in its formation and in setting its artistic direction and business goals than others. It also allows for recognition of the greater contribution of one or more group members. If you're the lead singer of your group and the songwriter who furnishes all the group's material, you may justly feel that you're more important to the success of the band than another member of the band who is only an average guitar player and has never written a decent song.

A corollary of the question *Who is a partner?* is the issue of what vote each member of the group has in making business and artistic decisions. Many partners agree among themselves to give equal votes to each partner; others decide that, for whatever reason, it's more equitable if one or more partners have a greater say.

An associated question concerns the division of band profits. For the same reasons that some partners' votes may carry more weight than others, group members whose contributions are very valuable to the success of the group may receive a greater share of the profits the group earns. Sometimes both of these situations occur. For instance, if the lead singer of a band was the founder of the band, writes all the songs the band performs, and has singlehandedly set its artistic direction, her vote may count double what the votes of the three other band members count *and* she may receive a double share of the band's profits. This is all a matter of negotiation among partners; although state partnership statutes presume that each partner has an equal vote and is entitled to an equal share of partnership profits, you and your partners may establish any arrangement you believe is fair when you reduce your agreement to writing.

Another question you and the other members of your group will want to ask yourselves is *Who will be responsible for managing the business affairs of the group?* Most partnership agreements provide that every partner has an equal vote in making business decisions and divide responsibility for the chores surrounding the management of the partnership equally among the partners. However, it's also quite common for partnership agreements to designate one partner as the "managing partner" and to assign to that partner primary responsibility for directing certain areas of the group's business. Although there's always enough work to go around for *all* the members of a band that cannot yet afford to hire a manager, it might be a good plan to officially delegate the task of keeping the band's business straight to one of your partners. If this is a significant amount of work, you can pay your managing partner a small salary on top of his or her share of profits or increase that share by 5 or 10 percent during the period he or she is your managing partner.

What is *not* included in your partnership is as important as what is included. Another decision you and your partners should reach before you write down your partnership agreement is whether income produced by songs written by group members is included in the "partnership income" that you hope will someday be sufficient to buy you all cars that don't leak oil. In other words, do you own part of the publishing for the song your lead singer and bass player wrote just because you and they are partners in the same band? As a general rule, the income earned by a songwriter's compositions belongs only to that songwriter (and his or her publisher) and is not included in the definition of "partnership income." However, this can be a touchy issue for the members of a group, who may have a certain proprietary feeling toward "their" songs, even if those songs were written by only one or two members. Because song copyrights last a lot longer than most bands and because it's usually not really fair to include the publishing income from songs in the partnership kitty, this issue should be discussed and resolved before anybody calls a lawyer for an appointment to discuss a partnership agreement.

You may have noticed that a lawyer has crept into this discussion. Even though lawyers do, unfortunately, sometimes have a way of intruding where they're not wanted, this one belongs here. That's because a partnership agreement, especially one that will determine the division of income that could amount to millions of dollars over the life of a hit album, is not a do-it-yourself project, no matter how good a grade you got in your college "Introduction to Business Law" course. Remember, a band partnership agreement can be one of the most important documents you ever sign, far more important than any apartment lease or management or booking agreement or, even, recording contract. Those agreements, even though they're very important, are over after a specified number of years. Your partnership agreement can conceivably endure for as long as you live and may have important effects even after you die (it may provide, for instance, that your share of income from the records your band made while you were alive will be paid to your heirs after you aren't). A partnership agreement you write yourself is like an airplane you build in your basement—it might fly, but you won't know whether some important part has been left out until it crashes and burns.

As with every other situation described in this book for which you need a lawyer's advice, the kind of lawyer you need to write (or, as lawyers say, "draft," as in "draw up") your band partnership agreement is *not* your cousin the criminal lawyer or the divorce lawyer you hired to get you out of your impetuous marriage to that blackjack dealer you met in Las Vegas. You need a *music* lawyer to draft your partnership agreement, one who knows that the considerations inherent in a band partnership agreement are different from those connected with, for example, a real estate partnership agreement. A band partnership agreement is very specialized and should include some provisions that are not found in most ordinary partnership agreements.

Your lawyer will probably want to meet with all the members of your group who will be partners and will begin the meeting with a string of questions that must be answered before any partnership agreement can be drafted. Some of these questions are discussed above. In addition, any good music lawyer will also ask several others, such as:

- How will you decide when the partners should put money in the partnership kitty, and who decides when the partnership spends its money?
- What happens if one of the partners gets sick for a while or is permanently disabled—will the other partners buy out that partner's interest in the partnership, and, if so, how long does the sick or disabled partner have to be unable to work before they do so?
- How can you get rid of a partner who stops holding up his or her end of things—do all the other partners have to vote to replace such a partner or is a majority vote enough?
- How will you decide whether to add a new partner, and, if you do, will the new partner have the same vote and receive the same share of profits as the original partners?

Your lawyer will also insist that you include a provision in your partnership agreement that protects the most valuable asset of your group—its name. Protecting your band's name is, in fact, one of the very best reasons for writing down your partnership agreement. Your name is the way people ask for tickets to your shows and the way they will find your albums if you ever get a record deal. Without that name to identify your performances and your recordings, you won't sell many tickets and you won't sell many records.

Your band name is a trademark, and under U.S. trademark law (which we will discuss at length in the next two chapters), trademarks are owned by the first person, or persons, to use them. This means that if you and the other four members of your group perform and record under the name Blitz for a few years, you each have individually gained equal ownership rights in that name. This is not a problem if your band stays together as long as The Grateful Dead, but it can be a big problem if you split up, or even if *some* of the members of the group leave. This is because if you all go your separate ways, *everybody* has an equal right to continue to use the name Blitz, in the absence of a written agreement that defines what happens in such a situation.

Picture this. You form a new band with some of your buddies and bill yourselves as Blitz because you were the lead singer and lead guitar player for the original band and there is a certain reputation attached to that name. Your bass player, meanwhile, also forms a new group called Blitz and feels justified in doing so because, in his view, *he* was responsible for the success of the original band. Clubs don't know who they're booking when they book a group named Blitz. Fans of the old band feel cheated when they show up to hear your new band or your former bass player's new group because they want the old Blitz, not a *piece* of it plus some new people they don't expect to see onstage. Then you hear that the other two members of the old band are thinking of suing both you and the bass player because *they* have hired a new lead singer and bass player and formed a new band and *they* want to use the name Blitz.

What happens in a situation like this? Well, there are several possible outcomes. Somebody could sue somebody else, ask the court for the exclusive right to use the name Blitz, and get it. Or the court could rule that *all* the members of the original band have the right to use the name, since each acquired an equal right in the name by performing under it. Or the court could rule that *nobody* should use the name because the recordings of the original band are still being sold and consumers won't know whose records they're buying if new groups use the same name. Any of these rulings could result, depending on how much the judge involved knows about trademark law and what he or she had for breakfast. Whatever the court's ruling, the losing litigants may appeal, leading to another long and expensive round of legal proceedings.

There isn't much case law on this question because one of

two things usually happens before or when the question arises. The first is that any group that has a big enough name to fight over probably also has or has had a recording contract, and the record company insisted when the recording agreement was signed that the group enter into a written partnership agreement with a satisfactory provision protecting the name of the group and the record company's investment in it. The other thing that happens is that when a band that has not entered into a written partnership agreement splits up and somebody decides to sue somebody else, the would-be litigants are sternly lectured by their lawyers on the enormous costs of engaging in such litigation and are urged to settle out of court like good boys and girls. If they do, no written court opinion makes it into the law books to set precedents for future cases of the same sort.

The best way to avoid this sort of expensive and nonproductive custody fight over your group name is to agree, *before* anybody leaves your group or is asked to leave or dies or is disabled, who owns your name and what happens when the membership of the group changes or the group is dissolved. The only really effective way to do this is with a provision in a written partnership agreement that deals with all the contingencies that may occur during what you hope will be the long, profitable life of the band. And the best provision of this sort probably will say that the name of your band is an asset of the group, not a personal asset of the members of your group, that if a member of the group leaves for any reason or is asked to leave, ownership of the name of the group remains with the band, and that a leaving member has no further interest in the name or control over it, other than receiving a proportionate share of income created by his or her services, including money from recordings, merchandising and sponsorship agreements, etc., made before his or her departure. In addition, it will provide that if the group breaks up entirely, none of the former members of the band is entitled to use the name unless he or she buys the name from the partnership.

Or you can provide that if your band disbands, the name of

the group will become the property of the lead singer, who thought of it and used it first. This solution is particularly appropriate, of course, in the case of a band that bills itself as Vito and the Choirboys, since no band with another lead singer could legally use the name (to find out why, read the next chapter), and it's unlikely that the Choirboys, without Vito, would sell as many tickets or records.

Your lawyer will also advise you regarding the partnership statute in your state (remember, every state has a *different* partnership statute) and will brief you on how partnerships pay taxes (essentially, the partnership does not pay federal income taxes on its profits, which are paid to the partners as individual income and then taxed). Your lawyer can also tell you whether there are any state or local filings your partnership must attend to, such as a state "assumed name" filing or registration of your new partnership in some county government office.

You should also know that although there are other forms for doing business besides partnerships, in most instances none of them is the right solution for a band just beginning to make waves in the music industry. Most bands that aren't partnerships do business as corporations.

In the exceedingly dull treatises on corporation law that lawyers read at night before going to sleep (a guaranteed effect), corporations are called "artificial persons." This term refers to the fact that the law views a corporation as an entity separate from any of the people who set it up. In fact, except for walking around and eating lunch and having a beer after work, a corporation can do just about anything a real person can do, including entering into contracts, owning property, and bringing lawsuits.

The biggest advantage of the corporation form is that it limits the liability of corporation owners to the investment they have in their corporation. It's like this: if your band is incorporated and, because of the negligence of your sound man, a piece of falling sound equipment injures someone in the audience at a club date, that injured person can reach only what the *corpora-*

tion owns in collecting any judgment awarded to compensate him or her for your negligence. If your corporation becomes liable for a judgment big enough to entirely consume its assets, you may lose whatever you have invested in it when the person who sues your corporation comes to collect the judgment, *but*, under ordinary circumstances, because your corporation is a legal entity separate from you the individual, your personal bank account is *not* available to pay any such judgment. This is not what happens with partnerships. If your partnership owes anyone anything for any reason, that person can sue you *personally*, if necessary, to collect what he or she is due, and a big enough judgment can bankrupt you.

If your present assets amount only to the proverbial two nickels to rub together, the ability a corporation gives you to protect your assets from court judgments and creditors may not seem important. This is one of the main reasons that most bands start out as partnerships and become corporations only when the partners earn enough money to make protecting it seem important. This is, in fact, a good solution to the question of business organization for bands, because a partnership can be quickly converted to a corporation by any good attorney.

Another form of corporation sometimes used by bands is owned by a backer rather than by the band members themselves. There's nothing fishy about such a corporation, but there are some serious questions that you should consider before becoming part of one. If you're a partner in a band or a shareholder in a band that has incorporated, you're an owner of your business and have some control over the business life of your band. As a partner or a shareholder, you also share in any profits of the band. It may be that neither of these circumstances will exist if your band is backed by a corporation owned by an investor.

Often when an investor backs a band, the band members are employees of a corporation formed by the investor. This means that the investor, rather than the band members, runs the show. From the viewpoint of the band, this is both good and bad. The investor pays the corporation's bills and takes care of all the business concerns of the band, but the band members themselves, who are employees of the investor's corporation and often may be replaced almost at will by the investor, may have little say over their professional lives as long as they work for the corporation. If the band lands a record deal, the corporation owns the recording contract. The proceeds from the band's performances are paid to the corporation. The band's name is owned by the corporation. The corporation also probably owns the band's sound equipment and stage costumes and, maybe, its instruments.

If you're a part of a band employed by an investor's corporation you will be assured of a weekly paycheck, which may or may not be big enough to make you happy but will certainly not equal what you would have earned if you were a partner or one of the owners of the incorporated band. But as important as money is, it's only money. The most valuable thing you can lose if you become an interchangeable part employed by a backer's corporation is control over your career as a performer. Do you really want a rich dentist or real estate executive who dreams of being a music industry mogul to run your professional life? There's nothing illegal or unethical about the investor corporation business form for bands, but many experienced music industry professionals would tell you it's an unwise arrangement, at least for anyone who has any talent. If you're not the next Springsteen, a weekly paycheck may be the best you can do. If you believe you might be, though, think twice before you hand over control of your life as a musician to anybody. In fact, because investor corporations can take many forms, some of which are more desirable arrangements than the sort described above, it's important to get independent legal advice about the structure of any such deal in order to evaluate its likely effect on your career.

The Name Game

As long as you can't look at a CD or a cassette and *see* what it *sounds* like, trademarks will continue to be almost as important to the music business as copyrights. In the recording industry, the music sells the album, but the trademark lets you *find* the record you want to buy. Consequently, trademark infringement lawsuits are a very serious matter for anyone unlucky enough to be either a plaintiff or a defendant in one. If you read this chapter, however, you'll know how to avoid the problem of trademark infringement and the misfortune of trademark infringement lawsuits.

A trademark is a word, phrase, sound, or symbol that represents in the marketplace the commercial reputation of a product or service. (Lawyers use capital letters to indicate the precise verbal content of trademarks; in this chapter and the next one we'll do the same with all trademarks and with all titles, slogans, and names used like trademarks.) The most important trademarks in the music industry are the names of bands, individual performers, and record companies. These names come to *mean* something to the consumer; when you ask for the latest GUNS N' ROSES album, you won't be satisfied by *Tony Bennett's Greatest Hits*, and when you check the newest ALLIGATOR RECORDS releases, you're not looking for WINDHAM HILL.

Every record or concert ticket sold, in the United States and elsewhere, is marketed in conjunction with one or more trademarks and is bought because those trademarks guide the consumer to that particular record or ticket. Consequently, trademark owners are usually quick to act against anyone who infringes their valuable marks. That means that a very efficient way to get yourself sued is to adopt a trademark that already belongs to someone else.

Because copyright does not protect song titles, many music industry professionals incorrectly assume that there is no protection available for *any* name. Often trademark disputes arise because trademarks are chosen solely on the basis of their artistic merit and the image they will create in the media, with no attention to the possibility that the new trademark will infringe an established one. Whether you *knew* that by using your new mark you were infringing someone else's rights is immaterial; ignorance of trademark law will not save you from an infringement lawsuit if you step on the toes of a trademark owner who is determined to protect an established mark.

Imagine this scenario: After a lot of hard work and three years of playing small clubs, your band, THE BOOMERS, gets some attention from a major record label, which offers you a recording contract. For the first time since you and the other members of the band quit your day jobs, you have the chance to make big money from your music. Your mom is happy, your manager is happy, your creditors are happy.

Then, the day after you hear that the first single released from your new album will be number seven with a bullet on next week's *Billboard* chart, your manager calls to tell you that you and the other members of your band and the record company have been sued in federal court for trademark infringement by some band in Los Angeles that has performed for seven years under the name THE BOOMERS and owns a federal trademark registration for that name. The Los Angeles BOOMERS are asking for damages, the profits from your album, and an injunction that would force your record company to freeze distribution of the single and pull all previously distributed records off record store shelves. They also want to stop you from performing or releasing records under the only name by which you have ever been known as a band.

The record company is unhappy. Your manager is unhappy. Your lawyer, however, is *not* unhappy; he's going to bill you $200 an hour to get you out of your goof.

The saddest news of all comes when your lawyer tells you that because they have been using their name four years longer than you have used yours, the best thing to do is to bite the bullet and settle with the Los Angeles band, abandon the name you only thought you owned, and begin to build a following for your band under a *new* name. Your reputation as a rocker will be erased! Your flicker of success will be snuffed out! Your emergence as a pop music legend will be stymied! You'll have to go back to your job as a computer programmer! There is no joy in Mudville.

None of this had to happen. Trademark disputes can almost always be avoided by paying attention at the right time to a few simple considerations.

In the United States, trademark rights are acquired by *use* of the trademark; trademark registration only enhances the rights trademark owners gain by using their trademarks. This means that the first person to use a trademark acquires rights in that trademark superior to those of anyone who later uses the same mark, roughly commensurate with the geographic scope and variety of commercial uses of the mark. That is, a band with a major-label recording contract that tours and sells tickets, records, and T-shirts throughout the United States has a much stronger claim to its name and is much better able to halt anyone else's use of its name (for a band, records, or promotional clothing) anywhere in the United States than a teenage garage band that has never played outside its hometown or released any records other than the eleven homemade tapes it sold last weekend.

Trademark infringement occurs when someone chooses a

name for a new product or service that is similar to a name that has been used longer for the same product or service, *if* the new name is similar *enough* to the established one to cause consumers to confuse the two. Infringing similarity between two trademarks is said to result in "likelihood of confusion"; that is, consumers are likely to confuse the new name with the older, established trademark because of the similarities between them.

The similarity between marks is gauged by what is called the "sight, sound, and meaning test"; the new name is compared to the established mark for similarities of appearance, sound, and meaning. If the marks are so similar that the average buyer is likely to confuse the products or services the marks name, or to believe they're somehow related, the new name infringes the older mark.

The first way to avoid infringing an established trademark is to consciously avoid choosing a name identical or similar to another trademark that somebody is already using for a band or any music-related product or service. More than a few trademark infringement lawsuits have been filed because someone who heard a good name decided that if a name had worked before, it would work again. And don't get clever and think that changing a few letters in the name or spelling it differently or even combining it with other words will eliminate the problem, because, as you'll see, it's just not that simple.

A few examples of "confusing similarity" will give you an idea of the degree of similarity between trademarks that constitutes infringement.

The appearance of a trademark is very important in gauging infringement. Naming your band JINXS (pronounced "jinks") will get you into trouble with the well-known group INXS (pronounced "in excess"). Even though the two names have very different meanings and don't sound alike when spoken, their appearance in print, and on album covers, would be very close. Further, INXS is an unusual name and the band that owns it is famous; it's very dangerous to get too close to unusual trademarks that name famous products or services because the "name recognition" of famous marks is so high that people are likely to mistake similar marks for the famous ones.

In fact, some trademarks are *so* famous that anyone who uses them for *any* product or service will incur the wrath of whole platoons of trademark lawyers. That's why you can't call your band THE PEPSIS or THE OREOS or THE XEROX MACHINES; if you do, Pepsi or Nabisco or Xerox is going to send you a nasty document known as a "cease and desist letter" telling you that you are "diluting" its famous trademark and demanding that you immediately *cease* any use of the infringing mark and *desist* from any further use of it. (An example of one of these poison-pen (cease and desist) letters is reproduced in the Appendixes of this book to give you an idea what awful things they threaten.) The next step after a cease and desist letter is a lawsuit in federal court, which you will lose.

The way a trademark sounds when spoken is a very important factor in evaluating infringement. A recording artist who performs and releases albums as LA DONNA is going to hear from the lawyers for MADONNA, even if she is a sixty-year-old black gospel singer who can't dance and never made a video. And even if ANDY TRAVIS *is* his real name, he can't perform under that name without encountering some strong opposition from RANDY TRAVIS. Soundalike names, especially in an industry that depends on radio for a large part of its revenues, always create problems; even if the new name looks different from the established trademark in *Billboard,* if it sounds the same on the air, the new name has to go.

The meanings of trademarks can create problems in ways that sometimes surprise their owners. We already have RHINO RECORDS, ALLIGATOR RECORDS, FLYING FISH RECORDS, and SPARROW RECORDS. That means that HIPPO RECORDS, CROCODILE RECORDS, BIG FISH RECORDS, and WREN RECORDS are out of the question; these names don't sound the same as the names of the actual record companies, or look the same in print, but their meanings are close enough for infringement.

Think you've got it? Maybe not. It's important to remember

that trademark infringement can jump product or service categories. If the product or service named by the new trademark is similar or even *related* to that named by the established mark, infringement can result.

For example, PEARL manufactures drums, not guitars, but anyone who tries to name a new line of electric guitars PEARL will encounter serious opposition from the drum manufacturer. Because PEARL is so well known as a manufacturer of drums, consumers could easily assume that PEARL guitars were simply a new product from the makers of PEARL drums. Drums and guitars are very different products, but trademark law thinks they are both simply "musical instruments" and would allow the Pearl Corporation to win a trademark infringement suit.

The same is true for *kinds* of music; trademark law classifies rock, rap, hip hop, jazz, rhythm and blues, country, and classical music in the same category. All music is "similar" to all other music, at least in the eyes of the trademark lawyers. A new gospel group that named itself THE EURYTHMICS would get into trouble just as quickly as any pop group that adopted the name. Consumers might not confuse the *music* of the identically named bands, but they could confuse the names in ads for concert tickets, club appearances, and record stores. And record store buyers, music columnists, radio stations, and owners of clubs and concert halls would have a hard time distinguishing the "Sweet Dreams" EURYTHMICS from the brand-new, same-name gospel group on their orders from record distributors, in their columns, on their playlists, and in their bookings.

So far we've looked at trademark infringement only as a way of getting into trouble with names. Trademark law is really only the little brother of a broader area of law called "the law of unfair competition," which includes several other ways to be sued in federal court that are similar to trademark infringement. Anyone who writes songs, names a band, or chooses a professional name needs to learn enough about unfair competition law to avoid running afoul of it. Luckily, that isn't hard to do.

As you've seen, no copyright protection is available for titles. The same is true for slogans and the names of literary characters. Under the right conditions, however, you can get into serious trouble for failing to respect the *trademark value* of titles, catchy popular sayings, and characters' names. When a title, slogan, or name becomes famous and is widely recognized as having come from a *particular* song, comic strip, or television show, it has turned into something very much like a trademark, even if no products or services are sold under it.

The owners of any song, book, or movie that has achieved a widespread reputation have valid legal rights in that reputation, whether it is embodied in a title, slogan, or character's name. It only makes sense that the law should protect that good reputation from imitators who want a free ride on it. Anything else would be unfair. Our system of free enterprise encourages competition, but our laws also allow competitors to sue to stop *unfair* competition.

Consider, for instance, Michael Jackson's THRILLER album and tour. There is no *copyright* protection for the song title THRILLER, but the album sold more copies than most recording artists can hope to sell in a lifetime and the tour was an American media event. As a result, that title has achieved trademark significance or, as lawyers say, "secondary meaning" and has become so linked with Michael Jackson that, for some years at least, nobody in this country will be able to name a band, book, song, or movie THRILLER without creating an association, intentional or otherwise, with him.

While books, movies, and comic strips are protected by copyright, the *names* of characters from them are not. However, like song titles and slogans, these characters can earn trademark status if the book or movie or comic strip they live in becomes very famous. The best recent example of this in the music industry is the record company once called LUKE SKYYWALKER RECORDS. LucasFilms, Ltd., objected strongly, by means of a lawsuit, to the use of the name of one of the main characters in its *Star Wars* movies by a record company completely unrelated to it. The court agreed with LucasFilms; LUKE SKYYWALKER

RECORDS is now named something else. Similarly, a band named DICK TRACY won't be for long, because of both the famous old comic strip *and* the recent Warren Beatty movie. Ditto for a group that names itself BATMAN or SUPERMAN or TEENAGE MUTANT NINJA TURTLES.

You must remember, though, that fame is fleeting, even for ninja turtles. As the popularity of a song, book, or movie fades, its owners have fewer rights in its name and in the names of characters and slogans from it, but its fame must have died to nothing more than a spark of recognition before the risk of an unfair competition suit is eliminated. Generally, when a song title, slogan, or character's name has more nostalgia value than current popularity, it is becoming fair game for a rock band searching for a *nom de guerre*. It may be that nobody will sue you if you name your band KRAZY KAT, after the famous comic strip character created in 1910. The artist who drew the KRAZY KAT strip is dead and can't create any more comics; his famous character has lost its currency and has now become merely a faint figure on the wallpaper of American popular culture, only dimly remembered as having originated with him. But be careful, because famous old characters have a way of reviving themselves. A band named LITTLE TRAMP in 1978 might have escaped a complaint for trademark infringement, but the same band in 1986 could have run afoul of the IBM Corporation and the Charlie Chaplin estate, which licensed the famous Charlie Chaplin "little tramp" character for use in IBM's ads.

If you think none of this stuff concerns you, think of it this way: nobody ever fights over an unsuccessful project. If you never get a record deal and never make any money from your songs, you may escape the notice of anyone who could sue you for trademark infringement or unfair competition (or both, since these claims have a way of cropping up together in complaints filed by plaintiffs). But if you're chasing gold records and hope to catch one, remember that you'll look like a more attractive defendant just as soon as you have some money.

People with money also make better plaintiffs, both because

they can afford to sue and because they want to protect the goose that laid the golden egg. This means that the more famous the trademark, the more vigilant its owners will be to halt any infringement; under U.S. law, they can actually *lose* their rights in their mark if they don't enforce them. And the bigger the song, movie, or book, the more determined its owners will be to protect their valuable rights in its title or in characters' names or slogans. In other words, don't step on the toes of anyone who is big enough and rich enough to squash you.

Pop Quiz

You've already had one pop quiz, but that was several chapters ago, some of you haven't been paying attention, and, anyway, it was about copyright law. This one tests what you've learned so far about trademarks.

Q. You and your buddies decide that the perfect name for your classic rock band is THE MUSTANGS. You book yourselves as part of a nostalgia-group tour your booker is organizing. Your act plays in Peoria. You are also a smash in Louisville, Buffalo, Wichita, and the Catskills. The fans in Baltimore like you, too, but you don't think the federal marshal there does, since he serves you with a temporary injunction from a New York federal court ordering you to stop selling your popular T-shirts, emblazoned with THE MUSTANGS and the familiar Ford Mustang running-horse logo. It seems that Ford objects to your use of its name and logo, even for your services as a band. Ford has sued you for trademark infringement and unfair competition and has asked the court to stop you permanently from using the name THE MUSTANGS and any version of its famous logo. You are outraged. Playing nostalgic rock music has nothing to do with manufacturing and selling sports cars. And the word "mustang" is just a name for any small wild horse—how can Ford stop you from using it? You think the judge was wrong to grant the temporary restraining order and that he will see his error just as soon as your lawyer makes your case at the preliminary injunction hearing.

Is it infringement?

A. Alas, yes. The reason THE MUSTANGS works for your band and your music is that MUSTANG is the famous name of a famous automobile that calls to mind a particular slice of American life in the sixties and seventies. All you were trying to do by using the MUSTANG name and logo was to evoke that era; unfortunately, you accomplished your goal by using someone else's trademarks. The New York judge will grant the preliminary injunction, and, if you're foolish enough to fight Ford, will find you guilty of trademark infringement, because what you have been doing is "diluting" Ford's famous trademarks by using them and, perhaps, falsely suggesting that there is some connection between your band and the automaker. You have also been pocketing the tidy profits from sales of your popular MUSTANG T-shirts, but you'll have to give those profits to Ford, along with all the shirts you have on hand, which Ford will destroy. Think about changing your name to THE RE-TREADS.

Q. Nobody will give you a record deal, so you decide to release and distribute your own album, a collection of country music standards. Because the songs you record have all been hits by various country music stars, you title the album COUNTRY MUSIC CLASSICS and list the titles of the songs on the album. You also tell the graphic designer who creates the album artwork to put the following copy on the front of the album in large type: "Favorite country songs originally recorded by CONWAY TWITTY, CHARLIE PRIDE, WILLIE NELSON, WAYLON JENNINGS, JOHNNY CASH, ROY CLARK, FERLIN HUSKY, and MARTY ROBBINS." In small type at the bottom of the album cover, you add "As interpreted by Charlie Smith." Your cousin Susie, who is a dental assistant by day but a law student by night, says you could get into a lot of trouble for what you think is a very clever marketing idea.

Is it infringement?

A. Sorry, Charlie. You're going to keep a bunch of music lawyers employed for a while, but you won't like what they'll be doing with their time, because they'll be trying to figure out who on earth Charlie Smith is and where he can be found, in order to sue him for unfair competition. Your clever idea is, in fact, a blatant effort to trade on the fame of the country music stars who made the songs on your album famous, and it won't fly in any court in the country. Your tricky album cover copy falsely indicates to all but the most careful consumer that your album includes recordings by the famous stars you list. Most country music fans would rather hear Charlie Pride than Charlie Smith, but that doesn't mean you can use Mr. Pride's name to sell your records. Better ditch that album cover artwork and go back to the drawing board to come up with a nice cover that reads COUNTRY CLASSICS BY CHARLIE SMITH. You may not sell as many copies of your album, but think of the money you'll save in legal fees.

Q. Your lead singer is a Native American, so you decide to call your band POWWOW. A duo called TOM TOM (both members of the duo are named Tom) that plays in some of the clubs you do sends you a hot letter telling you that you are infringing its trademark rights.

Is it infringement?

A. Probably not. Both POWWOW and TOM TOM are phrases associated in the popular imagination with Native Americans, and both are double words, but the two names don't really sound alike or look alike in print or have the same meaning, so there is no infringement. Further, since, as you discover, TOM TOM has been using its name only six months, it is in no position to challenge your use of your name, since you have been using POWWOW for more than a year and a half in six states.

That means the complaint from TOM TOM is meaningless, since you have rights in your name superior to those it has in its name. If the names *were* confusingly similar, you could even demand that TOM TOM stop infringing *your* trademark rights. You tell TOM TOM to get lost. Then you tell the trademark lawyer who gave you all this information to start the process of registering your band name in the U.S. Patent and Trademark Office. Since you have used your name in interstate commerce, you're eligible for federal registration, which is, your lawyer says, the best protection against pesky infringement claims. (More about trademark registration in the next chapter.)

Q. You are an Elvis impersonator whose stage name is ELVIS JONES. You save your money from your job at the Country Club Lounge in Columbus, Ohio, and drive to Memphis to see the home of your idol, Elvis Presley. You are so overcome with emotion after visiting Graceland that you stay up all night in your Memphis motel room, writing songs. When you return to Columbus you record your new songs and assemble them into a cassette album to sell at your club dates. In view of the inspiration for your songs and the place where they were written, you call the album GRACELAND. After you've spent your savings to have 3,000 cassette copies of your album manufactured, you begin to worry that Paul Simon, or his lawyers, will object to the title of your album, since it is the same title Mr. Simon chose for his very famous 1986 album.

Then you remember that the Paul Simon GRACELAND album consisted of songs in a variety of styles and included African singers and instruments. You figure that your album is nothing like the Simon album, since yours includes only Elvis-style ballads and rockabilly songs and the most exotic instrument on it is a steel guitar.

Is it infringement?

A. Probably, in a strict sense. You shouldn't have named your album GRACELAND; that name is "used up" for *any* album for many years to come. It makes no difference that your album includes songs in different styles from those on the Paul Simon album; what you did is still unfair competition and is actionable under the law. As a practical matter, though, you probably aren't going to be sued by Mr. Simon's record company for unfair competition because you aren't in any position to give his album any competition at all, unfair or otherwise. It would be a different story if you had major-label distribution for your album, but if that were the case, somebody would have nixed the GRACELAND name for your album before you had 3,000 copies made of it. You gotta figure this stuff out, Elvis, or you'll never make it out of Columbus.

Now that you know *what* you're not supposed to do, you need to know *how* not to do it. This means knowing which names are unavailable for use before you mistakenly choose them and rashly use them.

The only way to safely choose a name is to have a trademark search done. A trademark search is a survey of data on existing trademarks performed by a company whose gigantic computers can regurgitate information on trademarks similar to the one you want to use.

It works like this: If you want to call your band FALLEN ANGELS, the search service computer will produce a printed search report that includes data on bands named THE ANGELS, DARK ANGELS, THE FOUR ANGELS, GUARDIAN ANGELS, PLAYING THE ANGLES, THE BANGLES, and FALLEN WOMEN. Since none of these marks is close enough to FALLEN ANGELS to be likely to cause consumer confusion, the trademark attorney who commissions the search on your behalf will write an opinion letter based on this search telling you that FALLEN ANGELS appears to be available for your use. The search report will also include information on existing trademarks in use for other products or services related in some way to music, the music industry, or the entertainment industry, like brand names for musical instruments or the names of record albums or concert tours or video production companies.

The trademark search service will charge about three hundred dollars to produce a search report on trademarks similar to the mark you want to use. Your lawyer will charge you about the same amount to write an opinion letter interpreting the data in the search report and evaluating the chance that you will be sued if you decide to use your proposed mark. (An actual trademark search opinion letter is reproduced in the Appendixes of this book to show you what one looks like.)

This may seem like a lot of trouble and expense to guard against something that may never happen anyway, but, of course, *that is the idea.* You want to eliminate every possibility that anyone will object to your use of your name, because if they do, their objections will first take the form of a cease and desist letter and then, assuming you are too fond of your name to cease and desist using it immediately, will be stated at great length and in complete detail in the lawsuit filed against you to *compel* you to stop using it.

In case you forgot already, a trademark infringement lawsuit is no laughing matter. At best, you will spend a lot of money defending your right to continue to use your mark and win the suit, provided, of course, that the plaintiff has a weak case. At worst, you will spend a lot of money defending your right to continue to use your name and *lose* the suit, which means paying a lot or a little to the plaintiff and starting all over again under a new name.

As a practical matter, though, things may never get this far. You and the other band members may decide to abandon the name that's responsible for landing you in a lawsuit and file for bankruptcy. Really. It has happened more than once to nice guys like you who just wanted to make some money making music.

And bear in mind that while it's possible to be sued for infringement *before* you have any money, it's just as likely that you won't be sued until you do. In other words, just as soon as you look like what lawyers call a "deep pocket defendant," everybody and his brother will carefully examine the question *Don't I have some reason to sue those rich guys?*

Even if you win a suit like this, you will have had to spend a lot of time that could have been used to record a new album and a lot of money that could have been used for stage clothes, new instruments, and better hotel rooms on the road, and you will have gained *nothing* but the right to continue using the name by which the whole world knows you already anyway.

There's a clause in every recording contract that says, in effect, that your name doesn't infringe anyone else's name, and that if it does you will "hold" the record company "harmless" from any resulting damages. This means that you will pick up the tab (yours *and* your record company's) for any lawsuit, settlement paid, or judgment awarded as a result of your infringement of someone else's mark. The only thing worse than having to abandon the name your record company thought would sell thousands of albums because you find you can't warrant that you own it is having to abandon the name because you and the record company have been sued, at your expense, by the people whose trademark you have been infringing.

How do you win the name game? Even if you don't really have the money, hire a trademark lawyer to conduct a trademark search when you name your band or choose a professional name to make sure that the name you choose is available for use. A trademark search is cheap insurance. And make a real effort to stay away from other people's famous titles, slogans, and characters' names. You can't get away with hitching a ride on their fame, anyway; if you're smart, you won't even try.

7

Naming Names

The wheels of American commerce would grind to a halt without trademarks, since trademarks distinguish the products of one manufacturer from the similar products of another. This is as true for record companies as for toothpaste manufacturers. No one walks into a record store and asks simply to buy "a record." More so than with most other products, records and tapes and concert tickets are requested and sold by name—the names, that is, of the performers.

In fact, a band's name (its trademark) is arguably more valuable than its musical ability. Not convinced? Think about it this way: although your musical ability will create the demand for your records and concerts, it's your name that will guide your fans to *your* records and *your* shows and their money to *your* pockets. Every single person who buys your albums will find them in a record store bin behind a divider imprinted with your name. And every single one of the people who buy tickets to your concerts will say something like: "Give me two tickets to the DANCEARAMA concert" before sliding a couple of twenty-dollar bills across the counter to the ticket agent.

It takes talent, guts, and a lot of hard work and luck to create your own unique identity in the music marketplace. But hard work and talent aren't enough. At every stage of your metamorphosis from opening act to main attraction, you must protect your identity from the imitators who try to hitch a ride on every rising star. Otherwise, nobody will ever stand in line for tickets to hear you play, because no one will know who you are or why you're different from the thousands of other bands born in U.S. garages every year.

Choosing the *right* name is critically important to the success of your band because in order to own your name exclusively, you must create a name that can be protected from trademark infringers. This is important both now and later. Before your name has become a household word, you need to make sure that you're the only band using it in order to ensure that whatever reputation you're able to build is yours alone, unencumbered by the good or bad music of any competitor with a similar name. When you've become famous, you'll have even more reason to want to stop trademark infringers, because by then your band's name may represent hundreds of thousands of dollars of record and ticket sales every year.

The most important step in protecting your trademark is registering it, because trademark registration makes stopping infringers much easier. There are two sorts of trademark registration: federal trademark registration, which is not easy to obtain but which offers significant benefits to the owners of registered marks, and state trademark registration, which is easy to obtain but confers fewer benefits. Most trademark owners want to register their marks federally, that is, with the U.S. Patent and Trademark Office, because federal trademark law gives federal trademark registrants much more clout than is available under any state trademark law. Because federal registration is the goal you should aim for, when we discuss "trademark registration," we'll be referring to federal trademark registration.

You already know how to avoid the headaches that can result if you step on someone else's trademark; you also need to know how to protect your *own* name. If you become a successful band, or even if you don't, you need to be able to protect your trademark against the encroachments of trademark infringers, who come in several distressing varieties. There is the innocent infringer, the band from Cleveland that hit on your name by accident, performs under it in clubs, and presents a big problem to you and your booker, who keeps encountering club managers who never want to book your band again because the *other* band couldn't sing and couldn't play when it was last in Columbus or Louisville or Indianapolis. Just as dangerous is the band that adopts your name and becomes more famous than you. How are you going to convince fans, club owners, or record companies that you own your name and that the *other* band is infringing *your* rights, rather than the reverse? Then there are the true trademark villains, the T-shirt pirates who show up outside every venue where famous bands play to sell counterfeit shirts to fans; they'll pocket everything they can earn from the popularity of *your* name, and they're hard to stop because they're fast and sneaky and move around a lot.

Protecting your trademark usually means threatening to sue infringers. If you've registered your trademark, a nasty letter from your lawyer is probably going to stop every sort of infringer except truly determined T-shirt pirates, because most lawyers will advise a client who receives a cease and desist letter from the owner of a federally registered trademark to find another name—this afternoon. Further, your federal registration means that your mark will start turning up in the trademark searches other people commission. That is, any band that commissions a search for a name similar to yours will find out that your name is definitely unavailable and will choose instead a name that won't become the subject of a trademark infringement lawsuit. In other words, registering your trademark will actually have the result of *diminishing* the possibility that you'll have to go to court to protect your ownership of your name. Anyone who has ever been involved in any kind of lawsuit will tell you that this is a very big advantage.

If you do have to sue to protect your trademark and you have registered it, you can recover the profits of the infringer, the costs of bringing the infringement suit, attorneys' fees (sometimes), and up to triple the amount of damages the infringer caused you. T-shirt pirates and other real evildoers (as opposed to ordinary infringers who somehow blunder into infringing your trademark) may also be subject to criminal penalties for ripping off a registered trademark.

But trademark registration is not as easy as copyright registration. When you apply to register the name of your band, you are, in effect, asking an agency of the federal government to give you a nationwide monopoly on that name. Filing a registration application with the Trademark Office sets in motion a complicated process called the "examination" of your application. Your application must prove you're entitled to receive a registration; to do this it has to comply with requirements set out in the U.S. trademark statute, in trademark court decisions, and in regulations of the Trademark Office. The toughest of these are the restrictions on trademark registrability set out in the trademark statute. They're the only ones you really need to know about. The others will be the concern of the lawyer who prepares and files your registration application; however, since your lawyer can only work with the name *you* choose, the rules that govern which names are eligible for registration are really more your concern than your lawyer's. Ignorance of these rules is *not* bliss, since you're most likely to bump up against these restrictions on trademark registrability only after you've begun to use a mark that proves to be unregistrable. Consider this dilemma from the perspective of a band.

Let's suppose you're forming a new group with your brother and three cousins. Before you can commence your brilliant career, you have to choose a name. You have a beer together one evening after rehearsal and each of you comes up with a name you like. The favorites are:

BAND IN BOSTON (your cousins live in a suburb of Boston and you and your brother are in college there)

BREAD AND ROSES (proposed by your cousin the history ma-

jor, who knows that "Bread and roses!" was the cry of striking nineteenth-century Massachusetts millworkers)

THE WALTONS (Walton is your shared surname)

HARVARD DRINKING SQUAD (you and your brother, who also
goes to Harvard, think this one is hilarious)

F.U.C.T. (the name proposed by your cousin Isaac, who is a
little strange)

Because you know your band could spend the proceeds from
its first gold record defending against a lawsuit for trademark infringement if it adopts the *wrong* name, you consult your
friendly neighborhood trademark lawyer, Fred, who used to beat
you up for your lunch money when you were a kid. You are
amazed when Fred tells you that *none* of the five names you like
is a keeper. You ask in an indignant tone just why he is so eager
to see you discard the five great names you culled from hundreds of possibilities when you expected him to recommend a
trademark search for one of them. Fred puts his feet on his desk
and explains that although it *is* extremely important to make
sure the name you adopt for your band is available for use, you'd
be wasting your money on a search for any of your five proposed
names, because they are *all* unregistrable.

You ask Fred what he means by "unregistrable." He says the
Trademark Office will deny federal registration to some trademarks because of certain characteristics of the marks themselves. Then Fred demolishes your list of hit band names one by
one.

It seems that BAND IN BOSTON is what's known as a "descriptive" mark. That is, it *says* what it *is,* according to Fred.
You tell him that if he had any sense of humor he would recognize it as a pun—"banned in Boston." Fred says it's immaterial
whether or not he has a sense of humor because the Trademark
Office does not; it is, in fact, very literal-minded and would not
grant a registration to a Boston band for the name BAND IN

BOSTON because doing so would prevent any other "band in Boston" from using those words to describe itself. Further, says Fred, any trademark that uses a geographic term is suspect as far as the Trademark Office is concerned because, for example, the Trademark Office can't go around giving one restaurant the exclusive right to use NEW ENGLAND FISH HOUSE or OLDE VIRGINIA HOME COOKING or RIO GRANDE CHILI PARLOR because there is more than one fish house in New England, more than one homestyle restaurant in Virginia, and more than one chili parlor on the Rio Grande.

You're not sure you understand what Texas chili has to do with a band in Boston, but you think Fred knows his stuff, so you ask him why BREAD AND ROSES won't work.

Fred says BREAD AND ROSES is not only unregistrable, it is also downright dangerous to use. You make a rude noise and ask Fred if he is a total ignoramus, since he seems not to know that "Bread and roses!" was the cry of striking nineteenth-century Massachusetts millworkers. (You're not so sure yourself, since it's your cousin who's the history major, not you.) Fred says it wouldn't matter if "bread and roses" were the favorite saying of the president of the United States, since, as a band name, it is confusingly similar to a trademark Fred is sure must be registered already—GUNS N' ROSES—and the Trademark Office will not grant a registration to any trademark that is confusingly similar to a previously registered mark used for the same goods or services. Fred tells you that besides being unregistrable because of its confusing similarity to GUNS N' ROSES, BREAD AND ROSES would also subject you to a lawsuit for trademark infringement from GUNS N' ROSES. You mumble that you don't see what's so similar about BREAD AND ROSES and GUNS N' ROSES, but you secretly think Fred makes sense.

Fred says THE WALTONS will be denied registration because it's the surname of every member of the band and is, therefore, another kind of descriptive trademark. Fred says that the Trademark Office does not register surname marks until those trademarks are famous. He explains that because there are thousands of Waltons in the United States, the name THE WALTONS could refer to any of the other Waltons, and would not function as a trademark, that is, would not point to you and your brother and cousins as the particular source for your musical entertainment services, until you had made such a name for yourself that no one thought of anyone but you when they heard or read the name THE WALTONS.

You tell Fred that you intend to become famous pretty quickly and can wait for trademark registration, but he shakes his head and says that as soon as you become famous enough as THE WALTONS to qualify for trademark registration, you will come to the attention of the producers of the television show THE WALTONS, who will sue you for trademark infringement and unfair competition. You tell him he's been watching too many reruns, that the television show THE WALTONS was canceled years ago. Fred says he *has* been watching reruns, and so have millions of other people every day all over the country, and when they hear the name THE WALTONS they still think of John-Boy and Jim-Bob and the others, not of you and your brother and cousins. He tells you this means you and your kin can use THE WALTONS on your mailboxes, but not as the name of a band.

Fred is just as negative about the name HARVARD DRINKING SQUAD, which he does *not* think hilarious. He says the name is unregistrable for two reasons. He tells you that the first thing the Trademark Office will ask if you apply to register this name is whether you are Harvard University or have permission from Harvard to use its name as a part of your band's name. Since neither of these two prerequisites for registration is likely to come to pass, Fred says you would be denied registration because the Trademark Office cannot register a mark that falsely suggests a connection with the institution.

He goes on to say that the Trademark Office would also consider HARVARD DRINKING SQUAD unregistrable because the name would have the tendency to tarnish the dignity of the august university, another rule about trademark registration that you had no idea existed.

As for the name F.U.C.T., which Fred, who has grown more genteel over the years, is careful to pronounce "eff-you-see-tee," Fred says there is even *less* chance that it will be registered, since the Trademark Office is prohibited by the trademark statute from granting registration to marks that are blatantly off-color. You tell Fred to loosen up, that none of your friends would think F.U.C.T. was so bad. Fred reminds you that the Trademark Office is considerably stuffier than your buddies and is generally not able to be jollied into disregarding its many rules governing the registration of trademarks, which you mutter must be written down in a book the size of Wyoming. Fred reminds you that it doesn't much matter what you think, because the Trademark Office is the government and you are not, and unless you want to put your nearly completed degree in political science to work to start an alternative government, a step that has been known to get people shot for treason, you'll have to cope with U.S. law as it exists.

You ask Fred what his hourly fee is for being a wet blanket. He says he charges much less than the other lawyers in his firm—only $150 per hour. You tell him $150 is fine because that's just about how much lunch money he stole from you during 1978 and 1979. You eat an apple off Fred's desk as you leave. You hope it was his lunch.

The following week, you and the band have Fred search the name EARTH 2 MARS. It appears that no one has beat you to it and that the name is yours to use. You also apply for federal trademark registration the week your band debuts in a "battle-of-the-bands" showcase, because you believe Fred when he says coming up with a registrable and protectable trademark is not an easy thing to do.

The moral of this little tale is that, in addition to determining that your new trademark will not infringe an established mark, it's also important to consider whether the name you choose will be eligible for federal trademark registration. In fact, choosing a registrable trademark should be your first concern, since an unregistrable trademark may also be much harder to protect; that is, you may have a harder time preventing others from using or imitating it.

The federal trademark statute governs the sorts of trademarks to which the Trademark Office may grant registration. There are nine reasons the Trademark Office will reject your application to register the name (or logo) of your band; all of them have to do with the inherent characteristics of your trademark. They are:

1. The name or logo does not function as a trademark, that is, does not act in the marketplace to identify the source of your services as a band.

This restriction is often cited when someone tries to register a symbol that decorates a product without actually acting as a "brand name" for it. Bands are most likely to encounter this restriction with applications to register their logos if they are used more as ornaments than trademarks. For example, a band called THE PTERODACTYLS may use a drawing of the flying dinosaur in the background of its album cover art; the Trademark Office will consider this a nontrademark use of the mark and will not grant THE PTERODACTYLS' application to register their logo. If the band uses its pterodactyl logo on T-shirts, caps, and tour jackets and sells these items at its performances, the Trademark Office will register the logo for clothing. Using the logo in association with the name THE PTERODACTYLS in ads for the band's concerts would enable the band to register the logo for entertainment services.

2. The name (or logo) is immoral, deceptive, or scandalous.

Usually, bands and performers have to worry mostly about the "immoral" and "scandalous" parts of this restriction. Some names that are slightly risqué will be granted registration, but a name that is truly offensive will not. Before you cry "First Amendment" and "government censorship," bear in mind that the Trademark Office will not, no matter how much it hates your band name, tell you not to *use* it; your government just draws the line at *registering* any "immoral, deceptive, or scandalous" name. But maybe you don't want to choose a really offensive name for your band, anyway, because many clubs and concert halls and radio stations will hesitate to use your name if it is really smelly, and it *is* possible that someone at your eventual record label will object to it, although record labels are not known for their sensitivity and politeness. To be rejected for registration on this ground, a name has to be blatant. Usually double entendres, obscure sexual slang, and all but the most shockingly vicious phrases or symbols will pass muster with the trademark examiner, even though it is the examiner's job to review your application and try diligently to figure out why *not* to grant it.

The "deceptive" part of this restriction is usually not much of a problem for bands unless the band is already going to be in hot water with somebody anyway. For instance, if you get the bright idea to call your band SONS OF METALLICA because you think you sound like METALLICA, the Trademark Office will deny your application to register that name on the ground that, because you have no connection whatsoever with METALLICA, your name is "deceptive" (and maybe on some other grounds that we discuss below). But by the time this rejection reaches you, it will have to be forwarded to the dungeon of some federal courthouse, where you will be residing for the heinous crime of trademark infringement, courtesy of the able lawyers for METALLICA.

(Not really. Trademark infringement is a "civil" offense, which means that infringers are sued in civil courts, not brought up on criminal charges by the D.A. Infringers pay for their transgressions in dollars, not days in jail. Which is funny, if you think about it, because if someone breaks into your apartment and steals your guitar, he can be imprisoned; but if he infringes your hard-won trademark, which is like stealing your reputation, he won't go to jail, even though his infringement of your trademark may have cost you a lot more than your guitar was worth.)

3. The name (or logo) disparages or falsely suggests a connection with persons, institutions, beliefs, or national symbols or brings them into contempt or disrepute.

This restriction is similar to the "immoral, deceptive, or scandalous" restriction. If you'll recall, this is the reason EARTH 2 MARS was not named HARVARD DRINKING SQUAD.

For example, if you want to call your band TRICKY DICK in honor of the only U.S. president ever to resign from office, that's your business, but the Trademark Office may deny your application to register that name on the ground that it disparages Richard Nixon. It doesn't matter that TRICKY DICK is merely a nickname for Richard Nixon. It doesn't even matter that he is now deceased. And your arguments that Mr. Nixon's reputation would be hard to hurt aren't going to make the slightest difference to the Trademark Office.

Applications to register names that suggest nonexistent connections with particular well-known institutions will also be denied. For instance, the Trademark Office would not grant a registration to a band called THE F.B.I.; call your band G-MEN, though, and you may be able to register the name. Ditto for SEARS AND ROEBUCK and TEXAS MARSHALS—neither of these names is registrable because they belong to Sears and the Texas Marshals; call your band MALE ORDER or FRONTIER JUSTICE, however, and you, too, can be the proud owner of a registered trademark.

And no matter how clever and ironic *you* think it is, the Trademark Office will refuse to register any name or logo that disparages any belief or national symbol.

If you are a group of Jewish cantors who sing traditional Jewish songs at wedding receptions you may be able to call yourselves STARS OF DAVID and convince the Trademark Office to register the name, since your use of it would not be disparaging. However, you won't be able to register that name for any rock or metal band or register the familiar six-pointed Star of David as a part of a band logo without running into some trouble from the Trademark Office, which could reasonably interpret your use of the name or symbol as disparaging.

The same goes for crucifixes; Madonna may wear them as jewelry and decorate her videos with them, but she would have a hard time registering one as a trademark. Any attempt to register any name or symbol that the adherents of any religion hold dear will encounter the same obstacle.

This is the rule for Eastern religions as well as more familiar Western belief systems; for instance, four fat boys who try to register the name THE BUDDHAS for their rap group will be chased ignominiously from the imposing premises of the Trademark Office after a stern lecture from His Highness the Trademark Commissioner on respecting other people's religious beliefs, despite their piteous pleas that they meant no disrespect.

All this is also true for "national symbols." If you try to register as your band trademark a logo depicting Uncle Sam wearing red lipstick and rouge, white theatrical makeup, and blue eyeshadow, the Trademark Office will turn you down, even if your only goal in turning Uncle Sam into a female impersonator was to make him look like you and the other members of your pretty-boy band, because your manner of using this famous American symbol will be interpreted by the Trademark Office as bringing it into "contempt or disrepute."

4. The name (or logo) consists of or simulates the flag, coat of arms, or other insignia of the United States or of a state, municipality, or foreign nation.

The American flag, for instance, belongs equally to every American citizen. Since trademark registration gives the registrant the exclusive right to use the registered mark, the trademark statute prohibits the registration of any mark that consists of the American flag. This doesn't mean you can't *use* the American flag as a part of your logo, you just can't *register* your flag logo as a trademark. If your logo includes the American flag only as a small part of a larger design, you may be able to register the entire design by disclaiming any exclusive right in the flag portion of it.

The same goes for other official symbols from just about

everywhere. A reggae group called THE BAHAMIANS cannot register the Bahamian flag. Neither can a cowboy band called THE LONE-STAR BAND register the state flag of Texas as its logo.

5. The name (or logo) is the name, portrait, or signature of a living person who has not given consent to the use of the name, portrait, or signature as a trademark or of a deceased president of the United States during the life of his widow, unless she has given her similar consent.

This is an easy one to understand. How would you feel if you woke up one morning and found that the Trademark Office had given somebody else the exclusive right to use *your* name for a band without your permission? You'd be steamed, right? Well, everybody feels the same way, which is why you have to prove to the Trademark Office that any living person after whom you name your band consents to that use before you can register his or her name as the name under which you perform.

You can call your jazz group JELLY ROLL after the great Jelly Roll Morton or name your singing duo GILBERT AND SULLIVAN after the famous English composers of comic operas or perform under the stage name LUDWIG VAN BEETHOVEN after the famous classical composer because all these musical gentlemen are now playing harps under long-term engagement.

(A caveat, however. Be very careful about adopting the name or even the nickname of any famous figure who died after, say, 1900. There is something called the "right of publicity" that famous people acquire with their fame, and sometimes it can be inherited. Basically the "right of publicity" is a celebrity's right to be the only person who profits from the use of his or her famous name. This means you should be very careful about naming your act after any celebrity of this century, alive *or* dead. This is all you need to know about the "right of publicity" until you yourself are a celebrity, at which time some sharp entertainment lawyer who went to school for about twenty years but would rather be a rock singer will be glad to tell you more.)

Remember that this restriction applies *even* if you are one of the band members. Honest. Without Tom Petty's and Bob Seger's permission, TOM PETTY AND THE HEARTBREAKERS would have to register its name as THE HEARTBREAKERS, and BOB SEGER AND THE SILVER BULLET BAND would become just THE SILVER BULLET BAND.

So much for living people. The dead presidents restriction is sort of a leftover from when companies were likely to name their products after popular politicians in an effort to appeal to the people who made the politicians popular—you know, "TEDDY ROOSEVELT MOUSTACHE WAX." This restriction is of less concern to performers than many of the others in the Trademark Office's long list of types of unregistrable marks, but it could play a role in your choice of a name for your band. For instance, you could not have registered the name JFK during the lifetime of Jacqueline Kennedy Onassis without her permission. The trademark statute doesn't say what happens if the dead president is female; presumably, her widower would have to consent to any use of her name. Apparently the men (they *were* men) who wrote our trademark statute back in the forties thought that the possibility of a woman being elected president was so slender as to be nonexistent, so they specifically worded the statute in terms of deceased *male* presidents.

6. The name (or logo) is confusingly similar to a trademark that is already registered with the U.S. Patent and Trademark Office for a band or performing group.

The test the Trademark Office uses to determine whether your mark is "confusingly similar" to a registered mark is the same "sight, sound, and meaning" test used by judges in trademark infringement suits to determine whether the plaintiff does indeed have grounds to complain about the defendant's use of its name, but the only thing the Trademark Office will do to you if you adopt a name that's too close to a registered trademark is deny your application to register your name. It remains the job of the owner of the registered mark to sue you.

7. The name (or logo) is merely descriptive or is deceptively misdescriptive of the services to which it is applied.

This restriction is the main reason Fred nixed BAND IN BOSTON. The trademark statute prohibits the registration of marks that are "merely descriptive" (also known as "generic marks") because it would be unfair to give one person the exclusive right to use what are essentially ordinary words used in an ordinary way for services or products that those words simply describe. In other words, if a mark describes what it names, the mark is unregistrable. Some examples will help you understand.

You can't register BLUES BAND as the name for a blues band or RAPPERS for a rap group or SINGING FEMMES for your girl group. (The Trademark Office translates foreign words to determine whether they're descriptive, so using a word from another language won't get you around this restriction. Neither will misspelling words.) BLUES BABIES and RAP IT UP and FEMMES FATALES might work, however, because they don't so immediately convey the nature of what they name.

Marketing people hate this restriction, since they often think the best names describe what they name. It's easy to see that this is not so. Actually, the best trademarks suggest what they name without describing what they name. That is, at least a small leap of the imagination is required to connect them with the products or services they name.

In fact, the most protectable marks are *completely* arbitrary, with no relation at all to what they name. Think of R.E.M., GENESIS, NED'S ATOMIC DUSTBIN, NIRVANA, PEARL JAM, and NINE INCH NAILS; these names, by themselves, don't tell you anything about what they name. But you remember them. And they are registrable and protectable. Ever since bands starting naming themselves THREE DOG NIGHT, JEFFERSON AIRPLANE, STRAWBERRY ALARM CLOCK, and THE GRATEFUL DEAD, the trend has been toward names for rock groups that don't mean *anything* in particular. Somebody should write a dissertation on them: "Existential Alienation Among Young People in the Last Quarter of the Twentieth Century as Evidenced by Absurdist Names for Musical Performing Groups." Anyway, stick with the trend and you'll be able to register your mark. And protect it.

The "deceptively misdescriptive" half of this restriction is akin to some of the other restrictions mentioned above, which are designed to discourage the adoption of misleading or distasteful marks by denying them registration. A "deceptively misdescriptive" mark is a name that describes what it names, but *falsely*. The restriction against registering deceptively misdescriptive marks is intended primarily to discourage manufacturers from choosing misleading names like LEATHERCRAFT for a new line of vinyl sofas or SILKSHIRT for polyester blouses, but it should not be disregarded in choosing the name of a band. This restriction is most likely to be of concern with ironic band names; in other words, you may get the joke in your new name, but the Trademark Office will not be persuaded to register it by the mere fact that the name is funny if it transgresses one of the trademark statute's nine restrictions on registrability. For example, THE ZITHER ORCHESTRA, used for a band that never saw a zither, may not be registrable, no matter how much fans of the band like the name for its wackiness.

8. The name is primarily geographically descriptive or is geographically deceptively misdescriptive of the services it names.

If the name of a product or service includes an actual geographic term, such as a place name, the name of a river, mountain, etc., that either tells where the product or service comes from or suggests falsely that it comes from a place that it doesn't, the name will run afoul of this restriction when its owners try to register it in the U.S. Trademark Office. The general rule has been that if the trademark examiner could find the geographic term in an atlas or gazetteer, registration would be denied to the mark that contained it.

The reasoning behind the first part of this restriction is that if a product comes from the geographic region named in the mark, registration for one mark that includes a geographic term that is equally applicable to all products of the same sort produced in that region would unfairly deny other manufacturers the right to use the term to describe their products. For example, TENNESSEE SIPPIN' WHISKEY for a whiskey distilled in

Tennessee would be unregistrable because there is more than one whiskey distilled in Tennessee and the phrase "Tennessee sippin' whiskey" applies equally to every such product. The reason for the second part of the restriction, that registration will be denied to any mark that suggests a nonexistent geographic origin, is similar. If the whiskey was *not* distilled in Tennessee, the name TENNESSEE SIPPIN' WHISKEY would be "geographically deceptively misdescriptive," because it would lead consumers to a false conclusion about the origins of the whiskey. This restriction has more application to manufacturers of cheese and wine and other products tied to certain regions than it does to people who make music, but it can have an effect on innocent musicians like you who didn't even know it existed.

Translated into music industry terms, this restriction means you have to be careful about using the name of a state, city, or region in your band name, even if you do expect to become your hometown's big contribution to American music. Rock bands and other sorts of pop groups are not immune, but country bands are particularly prone to name themselves after the landscape; THE TENNESSEANS, THE ROCKY MOUNTAIN BOYS, THE MISSOURI JUG BAND, and KENTUCKY BLUE GRASS are all going to be turned down by the Trademark Office if they try to register their names. (At least until they become as famous as ALABAMA or KANSAS, that is. When a very famous band name, even one that the Trademark Office otherwise considers unregistrable, comes to signify *only* the group it names to the public, it becomes registrable because, in effect, its fame enables it to escape the anonymity inherent in a geographic name and function as a trademark.)

If you use a geographic term in your name but have no connection to that place or region, the Trademark Office could refuse to register your name because it is "geographically deceptively misdescriptive," but, as a practical matter, probably will not cite this as a reason for refusing registration. If your band is not based in the city, state, or region you use in your name, that use of that geographic name is not a description but becomes merely an allusion. The more fanciful the use of the geographic term the better. For example, THE KENTUCKY HEADHUNTERS is a registered trademark because Kentucky is a state notably devoid of headhunters and because the band that owns the name is not based there. In other words, the name is arbitrary.

Bear in mind that the restriction on registration of geographic marks applies to graphic representations of a state or country in band logos, too. If your entire logo is the map of a state or some other recognizable representation of a piece of the world, the Trademark Office will deny it registration.

9. The name is primarily a surname.

Personal names are not considered distinctive enough, when used as trademarks, to point, in and of themselves, to a particular source for a product or service. This is another way of saying that they're "descriptive." Think of it this way: there are a zillion people in the United States named Smith; the source of SMITH'S SHOE POLISH could be any of them. Until SMITH'S SHOE POLISH becomes so well known that it transcends the anonymity inherent in most surname trademarks, *all* the Smiths in the country could market shoe polish under their shared surname without infringing each other's trademarks rights. In other words, surname marks do not work as trademarks until they have achieved something called "secondary meaning," which is a term trademark lawyers use to mean "Everybody knows *that* trademark because it's famous."

There are, obviously, a lot of famous surname trademarks; many of them have been registered in the U.S. Trademark Office. Think of WATERMAN fountain pens, CAMPBELL'S soups, WILSON sporting goods, or the DOLBY noise reduction system. These marks are registered because they achieved fame enough to function as trademarks.

What all this stuff means to you is that using your last name as the name of your band isn't a great idea. If you do, you'll have some trouble registering your band name until you are pretty well known, a state the Trademark Office is usually willing to presume has occurred only after you have been performing under that name for *five years* in interstate commerce, and *then* only with some extra persuasion from your trademark lawyer. The same goes for band names made up of the last names of the band members. We all know that CROSBY, STILLS, NASH AND YOUNG, HALL AND OATES, BON JOVI, and WILSON PHILLIPS have done all right with their surname marks, but did you ever hear of a band named SMITH, JONES, AND BROWN? They weren't good enough to escape the anonymity of their surname trademark and had to give up performing and go back to school.

Now that you have memorized the Nine Deadly Sins of Trademark Selection, it must be said that there are exceptions to these restrictions. The Trademark Office is not as consistent as you might believe; there are some exceptions to these restrictions that are so complicated, you don't want to even try to understand them. Let your trademark lawyer worry about the fickleness of the government; your job is to make sure that you choose a name that can be registered, because many unregistrable marks are also all but unprotectable. That is, if you adopt an unregistrable mark, it may be next to impossible to prevent someone else from using your name, depending on the grounds on which the Trademark Office denies registration.

Consult this list of restrictions *before* you choose a band or stage name. Then get a lawyer to commission a trademark search. And then, because every trademark wants to be registered as soon as possible after it is born, register your trademark, even if you have to use the money you were saving for a new keyboard to pay for it.

(If you hire an artist to create your logo, which is a separate trademark from the word or words you choose for your name, or art for T-shirts you'll sell, you need to own the copyright in the logo or T-shirt art. Use the Designer's Agreement and Assignment of Copyright in the Appendixes of this book to transfer the copyright from the graphic designer to you, the individual performer, or to you and the other members of your band, a partnership. If you've forgotten, you can review what you need to know about copyright transfers in Chapter Four and find out everything you need to know about band partnerships in Chapter Five.)

Although trademark registration is important, it does not *create* your rights in your trademark. In the United States, trademark rights are gained by *use* of the trademark in the marketplace. Since a trademark is simply the word or symbol that embodies the commercial reputation of a product or service, there *are* no rights in a trademark without actual use of the word or symbol in commerce, because a product or service that is unavailable to consumers has, as yet, no commercial reputation.

Until recently a new band had to begin to use its name before it could apply for trademark registration to protect that name. Because the U.S. Trademark Office is a federal agency, that use had to be in interstate commerce, the sort of commerce that the federal government is empowered to regulate. Fortunately, a change in the U.S. trademark statute has made adopting and registering a trademark much easier. Since November 16, 1989, it has been possible to apply for registration of your band name before you begin to use it. This puts American performers on a more even footing with those in most European countries, where it has been possible for some time to reserve a trademark before using it. The new U.S. law stops short of allowing outright reservations of trademarks, but it does give trademark owners some similar advantages for the first time.

One very good reason to apply for registration of your trademark before you begin using it in interstate commerce is that an "intent-to-use" application, when it finally ripens into a federal registration, has the effect of enlarging your rights in your trademark in a surprising way. If it were not an important part of the newest version of the U.S. trademark statute, it might be fraud, but there it is, a provision that says that if you file an application to register your mark now and don't use the mark in interstate commerce (across state lines) until, say, nine months from now, upon registration your rights in the mark are deemed to have begun *on the date you filed your appli-*

cation rather than on the date you really began to use the mark.

In effect, this sort of registration has the effect of "backdating" your rights, which means that you will, by virtue of your registration, be able to scoop anyone who begins to use the same name after you file for registration, even if he or she uses the mark before you actually begin to use it. In other words, you can get priority of use by registering your mark. This can be *very* important in standoffs between two trademark owners who each argue that they got to the trademark first. If you're thinking this sounds like blue smoke and mirrors, you're right, but since the hocus-pocus benefits you, take advantage of it.

Of course, you can still file to register your mark *after* you have begun to use it in interstate commerce, just like always. This is now called a "use" application.

Trademark registration will cost you a $245 filing fee plus whatever your lawyer charges to prepare your application, which usually runs about $450. The Trademark Office divides all the products and services in the world into forty-two classifications; the classification of greatest interest to bands is Class 41, "Education and Entertainment Services" (you render "entertainment services" when you perform). Many bands also register their trademarks in Class 9, "Scientific Apparatus" (believe it or not, this is the class that includes records and tapes) and Class 25, "Clothing" (for T-shirts you sell at your concerts and to members of your fan club). Registering your trademark in all three classes strengthens your rights in your mark considerably, but a Class 41 registration is the most important, so if you can't afford to file three registration applications, file in Class 41 first and worry about the other two classes when you get a record deal and make some money.

It's *possible* to file your trademark registration application yourself. In fact, the Trademark Office offers a booklet called "Basic Facts About Trademarks" that includes all the information necessary to prepare an acceptable application and all the required forms, plus instructions for filling them out. A notation on the application form included in the booklet says the form should require no more than fifteen minutes to fill out; this is probably correct. Unfortunately, the time it takes to fill out the form isn't the problem. The really tough part of applying for registration is knowing *which* blanks to fill in, *what* to write in them, *what* you must file besides the basic application form, and *when*.

Trademark law is a pretty esoteric area of the law. There really are some important things about applying for registration that require the help of a *trademark* lawyer, not your sister's boyfriend the personal injury lawyer. If you file incorrectly, the Trademark Office will return your application. Even if your do-it-yourself application provides enough information in the proper form to make it past the first level of review and is not returned to you, chances are good that you will get a long communiqué from the trademark examining attorney assigned to your file citing a string of reasons why your application has been rejected. You will have six months to respond, making your best case for registration. As a practical matter, you probably will be ill equipped to respond adequately, and your filing fee and a lot of time will have been wasted.

Once you've begun to use it, you own your trademark roughly to the extent you make use of it, both with regard to the geographic area and the areas of commerce in which you use it. You own a song copyright until you sell it or it expires, but you can lose your rights in your trademark by not using it. If you intentionally abandon use of your trademark for at least two years, it becomes available for use by anyone else. In other words, when it comes to your trademark, you "use it or lose it."

If you think someone is infringing your trademark, ask a trademark lawyer to help you evaluate the situation. Trademark law is like a maze, and for a reliable opinion, you really do need a lawyer with considerable trademark experience.

IV

LAWYERS AND OTHER STRANGERS

8

Booking Agents and Managers

Very few people who make it in the music business arrive at stardom alone. Most performers who achieve any success *and keep it* do so with the help of a coterie of other music industry professionals who furnish advice as well as services. This team usually consists of at least a booking agent, a personal manager, and a lawyer—who may join your team in that order or may show up in some other sequence.

In the best situation, the efforts of each member of this team are enhanced by the efforts of the others. In the worst case, the members of a performer's professional team spend their time collecting commissions from the performer and dodging each other's calls. This is actually rational behavior from people who are supposed to cooperate but find that they can't. Since some of the members of a team that doesn't work out will be *out* of work soon, it is understandable that they want to collect whatever commissions they can before they find pink slips in the mail. However, none of this should make you happy, because you may be the one paying for this infighting with your hard-earned money and, maybe, your hard-won career.

It stands to reason, then, that you should pick your team with as much care as you use in choosing members of your band. Before you can make wise choices, you need to understand what each team member does and know something about evaluating the capabilities of each. This chapter talks about the two music industry professionals you're likely to encounter first in your career in music, your booking agent and your personal manager, and tells you what to look for and what to watch out for, which are two entirely different, important things.

If you perform regularly, the first sort of advisor who will want to jump on your bandwagon may be a booking agent, also called a "booker." A booking agency (also called a "talent agency") secures employment, usually in the form of contracts for live performances, for its clients.

Booking agents are energetic animals, but they are cold-blooded. They peddle meat—the clients they represent. Your booking agent's only concerns are getting you and your band to show up at that club or concert date and collecting the money you're paid for your services so that he or she can collect a commission. Your booker may buy you a beer once in a while, but almost any booking agent is going to be your friend only as long as you can draw a crowd or as long as your booking agreement lasts, whichever comes first. This is merely capitalism in action. Your booking agent runs a business, not a charity. If he or she can't book you into dates, you won't produce any commissions and someone will show up at the booking agency and start repossessing typewriters and telephones.

This may change after you've built a reputation. Name acts get special treatment from everyone who is due a piece of the action, whatever anyone tells you otherwise. But it's unlikely that, as novice performers, your band will earn large enough fees for performing to command more attention from a booking agent than is strictly produced by his or her self-interest. Until you become a big enough act to be coddled ("Bongo, my boy, how *are* you? Get Mr. Jones a chair, Igor"), your booker will view you as mere cannon fodder, useful primarily for young agents in the office to practice on and as a possible source for part of the overhead of running the agency.

Most booking agents live on the phone and can tell you at

any given point in the day what time it is in any U.S. time zone. They trade in promises. They promise a club owner in St. Louis or Milwaukee or Atlanta that your band is the hottest act since The Rolling Stones and that you will show up to sing and play on a given date. In return, the club owner promises to provide certain facilities for your performance and to pay a certain sum for your services, part of which will be collected in advance by the booking agent. These promises are embodied in a performance engagement contract. Because a performance engagement contract promises that *you*, not your booker, will perform on a certain date, you must either sign the agreement yourself or give your booking agent the authority to sign for you. (When you get one, your manager will probably approve performance dates and sign such contracts on your behalf.)

Established performers usually require their booking agents to clear any bookings with them or their personal managers before accepting the engagements. However, performers in the early stages of their careers often allow their bookers to sign performance engagement contracts on their behalf, taking into consideration any previously agreed guidelines ("I won't even get out of bed for less than five hundred dollars, Benny!") and the constraints of the performer's calendar ("I'm going to be hiding out at my parents' lake house writing songs the first two weeks of April, Benny"). This is where the "agency" part of a booking agent's duties comes into play. An agent is someone whom you have authorized to act on your behalf. Most booking agents are authorized by their clients to solicit and accept offers to perform, to collect the revenues produced by such performances, and to keep a commission of 10 to 15 or even 20 percent. These authorizations are made in the booking agreement.

How do you find a booker? The same way you get to Carnegie Hall—"practice, practice, practice." If your band pays enough attention to its music so that you're able to book yourselves regularly into clubs in your area, you can build a respectable press kit from reviews of these performances. Then take or send your press kit to several booking agents with an invitation to come out for your next date. If you're good enough, a little of this sort of promotion will result in the offer of a booking agreement.

Ask other acts and club owners for the names of booking agents who might be appropriate *for you.* Look for an agent who has experience and success at booking other performers at *your* level of the music business food chain. Success in booking Billy Joel is no big deal; booking The Fine Young Cannibals into any club that seats more than eleven people may be harder. Look in *The Yellow Pages of Rock!* or *The Recording Industry Source Book* for names of bookers in your region. Your booking agency doesn't have to operate in the city where you live, but because it's important that you meet regularly with the agents assigned to you in order to maintain a good working relationship with them, it's a good idea to find an agency within reach.

Before you sign with any booking agent, consider whether that agency is really the one you want. Does the agency represent metal acts or bluegrass bands or gospel singers? Does it book acts into the sorts of venues you need? Is the agency big enough to do the job? Is it too big to pay attention to you and your career? How enthusiastic are the agents who work there— does anybody love your music? Do the agents have any good ideas about developing your career—maybe the agency represents a headline act you could open for? Do they have enough clout to get A&R people to your shows occasionally? Are they more concerned with preserving their good relationships with the venues into which they book acts than representing their clients' best interests? Do you like them?

Don't consider signing with an agent about whom you have too little information. It's much better to book yourself a while longer than to sign with the wrong booker. In the early days of your career, an agency relationship can make or break you. Your agent will be handling what you hope will be a lot of money for you and will be, in a very real sense, setting the direction of your career by the venues into which he or she books you. It's important to approach this relationship carefully.

Agents are salespeople. They have to be able to persuade club owners and venue managers to book their acts or they won't be in business for long. Consequently, booking agents are among the most charming people in the recording industry. This charm can work against you as well as to your benefit. Some agents extrapolate their charm into prevarication; they will say anything to get through the next thirty seconds, regardless of the facts that their exaggerations will come to light and the people on the receiving end of their tall tales will be angry at having been misled. Remember that when a booking agent promises you the moon by tomorrow, he or she may really mean that a small asteroid is being shipped to you by freighter. Agents who exaggerate in this way don't call this lying, they call it hype, and they think everybody does it. Since enthusiasm is a large part of an agent's job description, the best approach to dealing with one is to get it in writing and believe it when you see it.

Which brings us to the working diagram for the agent/performer relationship—the booking agreement. These agreements vary widely. For the most part, California and New York talent agency agreements are fairer than those of booking agents based in other states. This is because the activities of talent agents who operate in those states are strictly regulated by state law. The American Federation of Musicians (AFM) and the American Federation of Television and Radio Artists (AFTRA) also recognize certain agents who agree to abide by rules set forth by these unions; AFM or AFTRA members can be subjected to disciplinary action by the unions if they agree to be represented by an agent who is not recognized ("franchised") by the unions. In many of the states between New York and California, where the law is less specifically concerned with talent agents and the unions have less influence, there are more "creative" booking agencies. These agencies will offer prospective acts agreements that are as close to contracts for indentured servitude as the agents think they can get away with.

Unless you're dealing with a New York or California agent

who is franchised by the unions and you're very sure you're signing *only* a form booking agreement that has been negotiated on
behalf of all musicians and performers by the unions, get a
lawyer to review any booking agreement before you sign it. Like
almost any sort of music industry agreement, a booking agreement can be significantly improved by a music lawyer who
knows what's going on. If you think you can do this yourself,
you *deserve* to be an indentured servant.

Signing a booking agreement is not as important an event
in the life of a performer as signing a recording agreement, but
it can have a very large *negative* effect. That is, sign the wrong
booking agreement and you'll have plenty of time to regret
your action. (Marry in haste, repent at leisure.) You'll have to
get a lawyer anyway, of course, but only after you bump into
some of the hard facts hidden in the provisions of your
booker's "standard" agreement. ("Don't worry, Bongo—*everybody* signs it.")

If you think you won't need a lawyer until somebody offers
you a record deal, consider a troublesome little animal called
the "365-day return-booking clause" found in some booking
agreements. One of these clauses reads: "The Performer agrees
that all individual Performance Engagement Contracts have a
365-day return-booking clause which is enforceable for all jobs
booked during the term of this agreement whether the performance dates fall within the term of this agreement or after."
Each individual performance engagement contract this booking
agent signs for his client provides that:

The Performer and the Employer agree that the Agent has
rendered a valuable service to each of them, and therefore
agree and guarantee to the Agent that if the Performer accepts employment from the Employer within twelve (12)
months from the play date of this Performance Engagement
Contract, that the Performer and the Employer will negotiate any such employment through the Agent. In the event a
job is not negotiated through the Agent, then it shall be the

sole responsibility of the Performer to pay the Agent the usual and normal commission on the revenues produced by said employment.

In plain English, the provision in the booking agreement, when coupled with the 365-day return-booking clause in every performance engagement contract, means this: any performer represented by this booking agent would owe the agent a commission on every date he or she played in any venue into which the agent booked the performer during the three-year term of the booking agreement, even if the agent did not negotiate the performance engagement contract, for a period of one year after the last date the performer played that venue. Watch out for clauses of this sort; any such language should send you to a lawyer for advice on its effect and for evaluation of whatever else may be lurking in the booking agreement.

Booking agents routinely (and fairly) collect commissions on dates booked before the expiration of a booking agreement that are played after it expires, but return-booking clauses can have the effect of prolonging an act's entanglement with a booker well into everybody's old age. If Benny the Booker books The Yetis into Club Fred for a November 15 date, even though his contract with the band will have expired on the preceding January 15, The Yetis will owe him a commission on the money they earn for a return engagement at Club Fred on November 14 of the *following* year—*twenty-two months* after the expiration of the booking agreement.

The worst thing about this is that by the time of their second Club Fred date The Yetis may have signed with a *second* booking agent, who may also expect to collect a cut of the revenues from the date. Double commissions can wipe out a band's profits in a hurry—they can even make it more practical to stay at home rather than play a date that will leave the band digging in its empty pockets for booking commissions. But avoiding the clubs and venues where it has made its small reputation may deprive a band of most of its audience. Performers who sign a booking agreement that includes a return-booking clause may find themselves robbed of either their spotlight or their earnings.

Most booking agreements are "exclusive" agreements; that is, you can't use any other booking agent during the term of the agreement. This does not work the other way, of course. Booking agents can and do represent more than one act. The following language specifying the duties of a booking agent is fairly typical of that found in booking agreements.

> Agent agrees to use reasonable efforts in the performance of the following duties: assisting Artist in obtaining and obtaining offers of and negotiating engagements for Artist; advising, aiding, counseling, and guiding Artist with respect to Artist's professional career in connection with bookings and personal appearances; promoting and publicizing Artist's name and talents; carrying on business correspondence in Artist's behalf relating to Artist's professional career in connection with booking engagements and personal appearances, including radio and television appearances, motion pictures, and all phases of the entertainment business; and cooperating with duly authorized representatives of Artist in the performance of such duties.

If you think these promises by the booking agent sound a little vague, you're right. But that has more to do with what booking agents *do* than with anything else. Unless he or she fails to secure any bookings at all, it's hard to prove that an agent is not doing what agents are supposed to do. This means that you can't really rely on the language of your booking agreement to compel performance from your booking agent and must, as a practical matter, instead rely on the good faith of the booker and on his or her desire to do whatever is necessary to earn commissions on your bookings.

Most booking agreements endure for three to five years. Five years is as good as forever in the life of a performer—it can be the difference between "up and coming" and "over the hill."

You don't *have* five years to waste. This fact alone should make you cautious in signing any booking agreement. And it should make you think about getting a lawyer, who will certainly try to limit the term of your agreement to one or two years or, at least, negotiate an escape clause for you that allows you options to leave at certain intervals if the agency has not sufficiently increased your income during the preceding period. As with all agreements related to your services as a performer (or as a songwriter), your goal should be to be tied up in the relationship only so long as the relationship is working. In the case of a booking agency, "working" means you're being booked into the sorts of venues you want and your income is increasing.

Monies due performers for engagements are commonly collected by booking agents, who turn them over to their client acts after deducting their percentage fees. So that everyone will know what the booker is due a piece *of*, any booking agreement will carefully define which of the performer's earnings are to be commissioned by the agent. One typical booking agreement includes the following provision to specify the commission payable to the booking agent and to define what sources of the performer's income are included in the definition of commissionable income.

(a) In consideration of the services to be rendered by Agent hereunder, Artist agrees to pay to Agent commissions equal to fifteen per cent (15%) of the monies or other considerations received directly or indirectly by Artist for each engagement for which commissions are payable hereunder. In no event, however, shall the payment of any such commissions result in the retention by Artist for any engagement of monies or other consideration in an amount less than the applicable minimum scale of the AFM or of any local thereof having jurisdiction over such engagement. In no event shall the payment of any such commissions result in the receipt by Agent for any engagement of commissions, fees, or other consideration, directly or indirectly, from any person or persons, including the Artist, which in aggregate exceed the commission provided for in this agreement. Any commission, fee, or other consideration received by Agent from any source other than Artist, directly or indirectly, on account of, as a result of, or in connection with supplying the services of Artist shall be reported to Artist and the amount thereof shall be deducted from the commissions payable by the Artist hereunder.

(b) Commissions shall in each instance become due and payable to Agent immediately following the receipt of the corresponding monies by Artist or by anyone acting on Artist's behalf.

(c) No commission shall be payable on account of any engagement for which Artist is not paid regardless of the reasons for such nonpayment.

(d) Agent's commission shall be payable on all monies or other consideration received by Artist pursuant to contracts for engagements negotiated or entered into during the term of this agreement and, if specifically agreed to by Artist by initialing the margin hereof, to contracts for engagements in existence at the commencement of the term hereof (excluding, however, any engagements with regard to which Artist has a prior obligation to pay commissions to another agent), and to any modifications, extensions, and renewals thereof or substitutions therefor, regardless of when Artist shall receive such monies or other considerations.

(e) In addition, Artist shall reimburse Agent for any sums advanced by Agent to Artist and for any expenses incurred and paid by Agent in connection with Artist's professional career; provided that Agent first obtains Artist's approval before incurring any expense of an unusual or extraordinary nature.

Sometimes musicians, being musicians, figure that signing agreements is no big deal—that they can simply sue to get out of the contracts they sign if they become unhappy with the people on the other end of them. This is a very dangerous notion. First of all, you can't sue someone just because you feel like it. If you try, your lawyer will tell you to sit down, quit waving your contract, and say slowly and clearly what exactly it is that the other party to the contract has done to breach that contract.

Then your lawyer will give you the third degree. "Has the other party failed to do something promised in the contract? Has that person done something that is prohibited by the contract? Which provision of your contract leads you to believe that you have grounds to sue? Are you aware that your failure to live up to the promises you made in paragraphs 7 through 9 would allow the other party to your contract to retaliate with a countersuit against you if you file suit? Have you considered the implications of paragraph 12 of the agreement, which requires you to give written notice of any claimed breach and allow the other party to the agreement to try to 'cure' the default that you claim has occurred? Do you understand that paragraph 13 of the agreement requires that you bring your suit in the courts of Peoria, Illinois, where the other contracting party maintains its home office? Do you realize that you could become liable for the attorney fees of the person you want to sue if you bring suit and lose?" Your lawyer will end this distressing discussion with the question all lawyers ask all clients before they lift their expensive fountain pens to begin work: "How do you expect to pay my fees?"

Get the picture? Not a pretty sight, is it? But it is realistic. It may be that the first lawyer you hate if you decide to bring suit is your own, because he or she may have to tell you some home truths about the agreement you signed so cavalierly years ago when you still thought you were bulletproof.

Even if you can find a reason to sue and can afford it, and even if you win your suit, you may not get what you want. Judges don't give plaintiffs what they ask for just because they ask. And there are many more likely results of a lawsuit involving a contract than that the contract is declared null and void.

One of the most common remedies judges use when someone is unhappy with a contract is "reformation"; this means the judge orders the contract to be altered in some way to cure the inequity the plaintiff complains about. Another result is that the defendant is ordered to pay the plaintiff money damages to compensate the plaintiff for whatever the defendant did wrong. A third remedy is "specific performance," which is the name for what a court orders when it requires the defendant to do what he or she promised to do in the contract. Each of these remedies can give plaintiffs some relief in situations that have become uncomfortable, but none of them gives a plaintiff what he or she may really want, which is never to have to lay eyes on the defendant again. The law respects the right of adults to enter into contracts, presumes that people mean what they agree to in contracts, and hesitates to allow one party to a contract to change his or her mind and back out of an enforceable agreement. If the law takes seriously your power to enter binding agreements, shouldn't you?

One of the more important agreements you'll enter into during your career is your first management agreement. Every management agreement you enter into is important, of course, but your relationship with your first manager is critically important because it will shape one of the "launching" relationships that will define your career.

It must be said that, for most of the rest of this chapter, we will be talking about *personal* managers, as opposed to *business* managers. This is because you'll need a personal manager long before you'll earn enough to need a business manager and because you probably will be choosing a personal manager armed only with what you can learn from musician gossip and this chapter. You should acquire a personal manager about the time you first start making small waves in the music industry.

No business manager will knock on your door until you have earned enough income to manage. Most business managers charge 5 percent to manage the income of their clients; until you're making major money, 5 percent of your income probably won't be enough to keep a business manager in No. 2 pencils. Until you sign a record deal, your best solution probably is to consult an accountant for a briefing on how to set up your books and keep the proper financial records. You can then keep your own checkbook and tax records and let your accountant prepare your tax returns. Or you can hire a bookkeeper a few hours a week to handle your day-to-day financial affairs, such as making deposits, keeping your checkbook balanced, and paying bills, and save your accountant for important questions and tax preparation. Bookkeepers are not hard to find and charge between ten and twenty-five dollars per hour. Most accountants can recommend several reliable ones. When your income becomes large enough to justify the services and the fees of a business manager, ask your lawyer (you'll have one by then) to recommend three who have good track records and good reputations.

The other important thing you need to know now about handling your relationships with the people who handle your finances is that you must be extremely careful in choosing whom to entrust with your financial life and in deciding what responsibilities to hand over to someone else. For example, it's almost always a bad idea to give anyone else the power to sign your checks. Sign your checks yourself, even if they're written out by someone else, at least until you've worked with a bookkeeper, accountant, or, later, business manager long enough to trust him or her completely. Get references for anyone who could steal more than paper clips from you. When you have only a little money, it's important to be careful with it *because* you have only a little. When you're earning a lot, you should be more cautious because there's more at stake. The moment you lose faith in your bookkeeper, accountant, or business manager, get another.

Finding a personal manager is more difficult. Finding the right manager is like finding the right mate—you may know the right person when you see him or her, but there's no way to know where to look. The best approach is to look like a hit act.

If you're not talented or expect to create a career in music by dreaming about it, no manager worth his or her salt will want to represent you. If you are talented and work at your career, you won't have to look for a personal manager because a manager will find *you*. Although the most direct route to hooking up with the right manager is an indirect one, when would-be managers start pressing their business cards into your hand you need to know how to choose one.

The functions of a personal manager are varied. A personal manager acts as both a buffer and a liaison between the artist he or she represents and a host of other people with whom the artist has business dealings, including the artist's booking agent, lawyer, business manager, tour promoter, investor (if any), and record company. A manager's job is a difficult one. Managers are "fiduciaries," that is, they occupy powerful positions of trust with regard to their dealings with their clients and have a special obligation to refrain from turning that trust to their own advantage as they perform their duties. Your personal manager will probably guide your career more than any other advisor, and will work closely with you on everything from your stage clothes to the songs you perform. The provision of one fairly ordinary management agreement that specifies the duties of the manager reads as follows:

Services: Manager agrees to use Manager's best efforts to perform the following services on behalf of Artist:

(a) To represent Artist and act as Artist's advisor in all business negotiations and matters of policy relating to Artist's entertainment and literary career;

(b) To supervise Artist's engagements and to consult with employers to ensure, to the best of Manager's ability, the proper use of Artist's services;

(c) To advise and counsel Artist concerning Artist's employment, publicity, wardrobe, public relations and advertising, proper presentation of artistic talents, selection of literary, artistic, and musical material, and theatrical and/or booking agencies, and all other matters relating to Artist's professional activities and career, including but not limited to motion pictures, legitimate stage productions, concerts, personal appearances, television, radio, recordings, merchandising, literary endeavors, and other entertainment activities in related fields; and

(d) To be available to Artist for consultation and the rendering of Manager's services hereunder at reasonable times at Manager's office.

As you can see, the duties of a manager, at least as specified in most management agreements, are both very broad and nearly as vague as those of a booking agent. In some respects, they overlap with the duties of a booking agent. In practice, however, booking agents and managers have distinct and separate areas of activity and don't step on each other's toes. In fact, most managers act as chief executive officers for their clients— that is, to some extent, they supervise and direct the activities of the other members of their clients' teams of professionals, including those of booking agents.

Not everyone who wants to be a manager has what it takes, and music lawyers derive a fair portion of their income from trying to get their clients out of management agreements—just as often because they're with the wrong managers as because the agreements are unfair. This means you must know what to look for in a manager. Avoid any wannabe manager who displays more than one of the following Five Warning Signals of Negative Capability.

The First Negative Capability: The manager doesn't understand your music. The primary task of any manager is to shape and develop the career of his or her client, creating in the process income for the performer and commissions for the manager. Since tours sell records and records create an audience that will buy tickets to tour dates, this usually means your manager will chiefly be concerned with getting you a record deal and seeing that you keep it. You won't get a record deal unless your music is good enough and focused enough and popular enough to attract the attention of a record company. And you won't have a *career*, as opposed to a record deal that fizzles after the first album, unless you maintain good relations with your record company. This only results from records that sell, which means you have to pick the right songs to record and the right producer and get enough publicity by playing the right venues and having the right public image, and develop your craft as an artist and, preferably, a songwriter. Your manager will be worthless as an advisor at every stage of this juggling act unless he or she understands the kind of music you make and knows how to sell it.

The Second Negative Capability: The manager is inexperienced. No amount of understanding of your music will make a manager worth a vinyl 45 unless he or she knows how to help you build a career. You yourself will have to create the initial interest in your act, by the originality and appeal of your music and the panache with which you perform it, but you need someone whose experience is wider than yours and whose judgment is more informed to help you take that spark of record company interest and turn it into a recording budget and a touring schedule. This means you want a manager who is *not* depending entirely on on-the-job training. Look for a manager who knows the ropes and, in turn, is known by some music publishers, music lawyers, booking agents, and record company A&R people. However, you don't necessarily have to hold out for a big-time manager with lots of experience. Unless you've been able to create remarkable record company interest in your act by yourself, this sort of manager is simply going to be too busy frying bigger fish to consider representing you. The best method for evaluating a prospective manager may be to weigh his or her experience against the knowledge, hustle, and congeniality he or she displays. Superior performance in the last three categories can offset some lack of experience.

A subcategory of inexperienced manager is the "brother-in-law manager," that is, a relative who wants to manage your career. Music history is well populated with brother-in-law managers who worked tirelessly to promote their acts, sitting up late at night to sew sequins on stage clothing, taking part-time jobs to survive before fame and money arrived, and hocking their houses to buy new instruments for their talented relatives. These faithful folks exist, but the only conclusion that can be safely drawn from their existence is that their relatives were lucky. More common is the brother-in-law manager who must be gotten rid of a few years into the talented relative's brilliant career because of bad advice or an overgrown ego or sticky fingers. It seems to be a rule of physics that a large percentage of relationships between performers and their brother-in-law managers end as spectacular disasters, usually with very bad vibes between the parties and sometimes complete with lengthy lawsuits.

Love your brother-in-law—just don't let him manage your career, even without a commission. Bad advice is no better because it is free. Your personal relationship with your relative will be polluted by the difficulties that exist in every professional relationship, and your feelings for a family member will make it difficult to fire him, even if it becomes obvious that you need to. In short, if you wouldn't hire someone if he or she were *not* related to you, you shouldn't hire that person at all.

The Third Negative Capability: The manager lacks objectivity. You want a manager, not a fan. Although cordiality is essential to an effective manager/performer relationship and friendship is both possible and desirable, your manager does not have to be your best friend to do the job. In fact, if your manager loses the ability to look hard at you and your music and make the difficult artistic and business decisions that are a part of marketing any act successfully, your manager will become useless to you because you will have lost one of the main things you need from a manager—constructive criticism. If your manager can't work up the nerve to tell you candidly that your new song is interesting but about four minutes too long for radio air-play and, therefore, unsuitable material for a first album, you'll find out the hard way, from the record company. And if your manager likes your road manager too well to make the hard decision to hire a better one, your career will suffer.

The Fourth Negative Capability: The manager lacks drive. Pop music managers are nocturnal creatures. They have to head out to the clubs when most of the other people on their block are looking for their nightshirts. But they also have to be up early enough for morning meetings and important phone calls and lunches with People in the Industry. If a manager doesn't have enough energy and drive to juggle all these necessary evils for you and, maybe, for a few other clients, regardless of whether you have begun to make any money, he or she doesn't have the vision, determination, and gumption the managers of successful acts must have. Lots of managers work out of their homes. Some of them are young. A few are too old to be surprised by the music industry anymore (although managers who are good at what they do usually move on to other, less demanding music industry jobs before their hearing is ruined by too many nights in clubs). None of these things matters if the other characteristics of a successful manager—experience and drive—are present. In other words, you should look at a manager's performance, past and present, to evaluate his or her usefulness to you.

The Fifth Negative Capability: The manager is too busy. Your manager must have enough time to give your career the attention it deserves. After all, you'll look to your manager for guidance or, at least, a second opinion, on almost every area of your professional life. You need your manager's attention and advice *when you need it*—next week may be too late. There are two situations when a manager may be too busy. An established manager may be too occupied with the affairs of other, more successful, clients to take your phone calls and spend the necessary time with you in strategic planning sessions. A novice manager who has to work a day job to support himself or herself may be able to attend to your career only in off hours. Neither arrangement is likely to catapult you into stardom. Sometimes the careers of talented musicians limp along for years with no real success because nobody, including the musicians, ever puts real time and effort into them. Insist that anyone who wants to be your manager be capable of really doing the job. Don't settle for being somebody's third priority.

One question performers often ask is *When do I need a manager?* The answer is not as simple as the question. Sometimes performers, especially bands, get the cart before the horse; they think they need a manager (and a lawyer and a record deal and a tour bus) before they have really jelled as performers. Even if you can persuade a talented manager to listen to your tape or come out to hear you play, nothing will come of the connection unless it's obvious that you're no longer merely a musical apprentice. The best time to get a manager is that magic day when you're in full control of your musical and vocal talents, display them to advantage in your performances, and have worked at your music long enough to know what it is and where it's going. A competent manager can then help you turn your potential into a paying career. A manager who is willing to work with an act before the act is earning any noticeable money is more likely to have his or her client's best interests at heart than one who somehow never noticed the act before it landed a record deal, but a manager who is willing to work with the act before it knows where it's going won't be a manager long.

Personal management agreements come in all shapes and lengths. Many are short letter agreements, which are just as binding as any agreement in another format, even though they seem friendlier and the word "whereas" occurs in them less often. Others are written in a formal legal style and go on for page after page. All management agreements submitted to new clients by managers are written to the advantage of the managers. This doesn't necessarily mean that these agreements are overreaching, but it does mean that any client who does not take such an unnegotiated agreement to his or her lawyer before signing it is foolish.

Every personal management agreement will contain some provision similar to the following one:

> *Engagement:* Artist hereby engages Manager, and Manager hereby accepts such engagement, as Artist's sole and exclusive personal manager in the entertainment, amusement, music, recording, and literary fields, throughout the world, for the Term and under the terms and conditions of this agreement.

This short paragraph contains a lot. All management agreements, like all booking agreements, are "exclusive" as far as the artist is concerned. That is, the manager may have other clients, but the artist may not have other managers. This provision includes in the scope of varieties of activities in which the manager will be involved every sort of employment you as a performer are likely to engage in—"throughout the world"—unless you have to go back to being a housepainter to pay the rent. This, of course, when read with another provision later in the agreement, allows the manager to commission your income from everything *but* housepainting.

Most managers will want to commission every dollar a group earns, but there are exceptions to this. If you're an established actor who aspires to a recording career, you should expect your manager to forgo a commission on your earnings as an actor. The same is true for established songwriters; many management agreements with songwriters who want careers as performers specifically exclude from the definition of commissionable "gross income" money earned by the songwriter/performer through writing or publishing songs. (Lots of successful songwriters publish their own compositions.) This exclusion, of course, can represent a large savings to the artist, especially if the artist writes one or more hit songs while signed to the manager. This alone is an exceedingly good reason to hire a lawyer to negotiate on your behalf when you're asked to sign a management agreement. A skilled lawyer will try to limit the bite the manager takes out of your income and will know that there are certain categories of income (such as recording costs, producer's fees, tour support money, and some other costs of doing business) that are almost never commissionable by a manager.

Your lawyer will also try to limit the period during which the manager can bite. It's fair for a manager to collect a commission on income that he or she arguably had a role in creating, but you'll think kinder thoughts about your first manager if you don't have to hand over 15 percent of the revenues from the fifth album, recorded this year, under a recording agreement that manager negotiated seven years ago. This will be especially true after you've taken a second manager and must also pay him or her a commission on your earnings. If you're not careful in signing agreements that provide for this sort of perpetual payment, you may soon feel that 150 percent of your income is promised to a horde of former associates and that you're really working to put *their* children through college rather than for your own benefit. The best preventive measure against this is one medium-sized, well-informed lawyer, sworn to protect your interests and to fend off the attempts of others to reduce you to involuntary servitude. Your lawyer will try to get your manager's lawyer to agree to a time limit or some diminishing payment scale for the commissions to be paid to the manager after the expiration of the management agreement. You'll eventually get to put your first manager's 15 percent in your pocket and may, in time, come to feel kindly enough toward the manager who first believed in you to send a ham at Christmas.

Another good reason to hire a lawyer to haggle with your manager's lawyer over the provisions of the management agreement is the duration, or "term," of the agreement. Although most management agreements provide for a term of three to five years, some management agreements lock the artist into a relationship with a manager for four or five or six years, with no hope of parole. These agreements are remarkably like indentured servitude agreements. (Involuntary servitude is slavery; indentured servitude is an agreement to serve someone for a period of years, usually in return for passage to America and room and board. Both are now outlawed but occasionally still crop up in the music industry.) The first thing any music lawyer will do with one of them is pencil in a few escape hatches to allow the artist to terminate the agreement if the relationship does not prove to be a good one; the second thing the lawyer will do is tell the manager's lawyer that the artist will walk if those escape hatches are not included. The smart artist will, in this case, take the lawyer's advice. But artists who won't get married because "marriage is too confining" will sign management agreements that set up a management relationship, which is remarkably close to marriage, without providing any mechanism for divorce. Or, rather, they provide that the manager can divorce the artist but not vice versa. Go figure.

The best management agreements allow both the manager and the artist a way out at several points during the agreement. The exits for the manager are usually in the form of "options"; that is, the manager may, at certain specified intervals, exercise an option to extend the term of the agreement for an additional period, usually a year. The manager may decline to represent the artist any longer merely by choosing not to exercise an option. For the artist, the exits usually take the form of the right to terminate the agreement at certain intervals if the artist's income has not reached a specified level during the preceding period.

Most managers take a 15 percent commission on their clients' gross income. Sometimes it happens that a manager will demand a 20 percent commission to represent a new act, on the theory that it takes 20 percent of a small income to justify the manager's expenditure of time on developing the act. This arrangement usually changes to the standard 15 percent commission deal when the act's income reaches a certain specified level. Sometimes things work in just the opposite way—the manager of a new act will take a smaller than usual percentage of the act's income until the act can earn enough to both eat on the road *and* pay the manager a 15 percent commission.

As in many music industry agreements, although the numbers are important in management agreements, they don't tell the whole story. Experienced lawyers only glance at the commission percentages specified in these agreements on their way to the paragraphs several pages later that set out exactly *what* pots of money these percentages are based on. As you might imagine, these paragraphs are usually the longest and most threatening ones in management agreements. The following paragraph illustrates the work of clever lawyers who spend hours drafting agreements that ensure that every last penny an artist earns will be captured and the manager's commission excised before the remaining money makes it to the artist's pocket. (In this agreement, the artist's lawyer has succeeded in excluding the artist's songwriting and music publishing income from the definition of commissionable income.)

Compensation: (a) In consideration of Manager's agreement hereto and as compensation for services rendered and to be rendered to Artist by Manager hereunder, Artist agrees to pay Manager as and when received a sum equal to twenty (20%) percent of any and all gross monies or other considerations received as a result of Artist's activities in any and all fields of entertainment and literature. Without in any manner limiting the foregoing, the matters upon which Manager's compensation shall be computed shall include, but shall not be limited to, any and all of Artist's activities in connection with: motion pictures, television, video, radio, literature, theatrical engagements, personal appearances, public appearances in places of amusement and entertainment, records and recordings, publications, and the use of Artist's name, likeness, and talents for purposes of merchandising, advertising, and trade. Artist likewise agrees to pay Manager a similar sum following the expiration of the term hereof upon and with respect to any and all engagements, contracts, and agreements entered into or negotiated for during the term hereof relating to any of the foregoing, and upon any and all extensions, renewals, and substitutions thereof, and upon any resumptions of such engagements, contracts, and agreements which may have been discontinued during the term hereof and resumed within a year thereafter. The term "gross monies or other considerations" shall include, without limitation: salaries, earnings, fees, recording funds and budgets, advances, royalties, commissions, gifts, bonuses, shares of profit, shares of stock, partnership interests, percentages and the total amount paid for a package of television or radio programs (live or recorded), motion picture, or other entertainment packages, earned or received directly or indirectly by Artist or Artist's heirs, executors, administrators, or assigns, or by any person, firm, or corporation on Artist's behalf. In the event that Artist receives, as all or part of Artist's compensation for activities hereunder, stock or the right to buy stock in any corporation or in any event that Artist becomes the packager or owner of all or part of an entertainment property, whether as individual proprietor, stockholder, partner, joint venturer, or otherwise, or in the event that Artist shall cause a corporation to be formed, Manager's percentage shall apply to Artist's said stock, right to buy stock, individual proprietorship, partnership, joint venture, or any other form of interest, and Manager shall be entitled to make any payment for such interest, Manager will pay its percentage share of such payment, unless Manager declines to accept its percentage share thereof.

(b) Notwithstanding anything to the contrary contained herein, Manager shall not be entitled to any fee hereunder in respect to any of Artist's compensation from the songwriting and music publishing activities of Artist.

(c) Manager shall receive Manager's twenty (20%) percent commission share whether any employment, contract, or other income-producing activity shall have been procured by Artist as a result of Manager's advice, consultation, or other efforts, and whether the term of said employment, contract, or income-producing activity shall be effective or continue before, during, or after the term of this agreement.

(d) Notwithstanding anything contained in this agreement to the contrary, Manager shall receive no commission in respect of any personal engagements procured solely by Artist prior to the commencement of this agreement.

Some managers never ask their clients to sign formal management agreements, figuring that as long as their relationships with their clients are good they don't need to put it in writing and that they don't want to try to hold on to a client who is unhappy enough to want to leave. In fact, some of the most reputable and successful managers take this approach. From the client's viewpoint, this is better than a written agreement that locks him or her into a management agreement of four to six years. However, running an important business relationship without a written document that specifies who is entitled to what for how long can also create serious problems for the client—namely, uncertainties about what income is commissionable and for how long. If you're approached by anyone who wants to act as your personal manager, even if you're not asked to sign any contract, consult an attorney before you consent to the arrangement.

Never sign any document, letter, memorandum, or cocktail napkin thinking it's not a "real" agreement—even if your manager drafts it on the spot with a swizzle stick dipped in ketchup. Any piece of writing can constitute a binding legal document, no matter how informal it looks. The "simple" agreements people draft for themselves ("There's no need to get *lawyers* involved, Bongo!") often create so many ambiguities about what the parties to the agreements meant to agree to that the only way to decide who must do or pay what under the agreement is to go to court, which is an expensive way to settle business disputes.

As a general rule, it's an extremely bad idea to agree to allow anyone on your team of professional advisors to wear more than one hat. Don't let your booking agent persuade you that he has time to be your manager, too, or your manager induce you to let her act as your music publisher or producer. Your booker should be so busy booking dates for you and other agency clients that he doesn't really have time to manage you, too. Ditto for a manager who wants to branch out into every other area of your professional life—a manager who also aspires to be your publisher or producer may be more interested in the earnings these additional roles will bring than in doing a good job for you. The more hats one person wears in your professional life, the more difficult it will be to divest yourself of that person's "help" if the relationship goes sour. And relationships do fall apart. Strangely enough, they often collapse under the stress of success, when all human beings are subject to delusions of having singlehandedly created the vast amount of income and attention that has suddenly materialized.

The possible exception to this rule is the attorney/manager. There are a lot of these around, and their clients tend to be happy. This is possibly because these hybrids know so much more about law and negotiating than most managers and so much more about building a performer's career than most attorneys that they are able to render really superior service to their clients. However, because attorney/managers wear two hats, you should carefully evaluate the potential of anyone who wants to play both roles in your life and believes he or she could really do the job of two people for you. Then, you should take the attorney/manager's agreement to another, independent lawyer for advice and negotiation.

This chapter has told you most of what you need to know about booking agents and managers. That is, you should know what they do and how to distinguish the good ones from those who are less competent, and, most of all, you should know that you shouldn't sign on the dotted line with either unless you have the blessing of a lawyer. The rest of what you need to know you *don't* really need to know, because your lawyer, the next professional who will appear on the horizon of your career, will remember it for you. Your lawyer will be critically important to your success and will play a large role in protecting you from all the things that can go wrong in your relationships with the other members of your team, as well as in creating and facilitating relationships with the music publisher, producer, and record company you hope will want a piece of your action before you get too fat to fit into a pair of spandex pants. The next chapter addresses the care and feeding of lawyers.

9

Lawyers, Guns, and Money

American lawyers may never again command the sort of respect Perry Mason got from his clients. One reason for this is that American law stopped being simple about the time Perry's show was canceled. Whole areas of law that now affect our business and personal lives were nonexistent when Perry practiced black-and-white law in our living rooms. This means our lives are much more regulated than they once were.

Most Americans resent this increased regulation, in part because they've seen a lot of TV cowboys who gave them the idea that all of us can be rugged individuals. (Marshal Matt Dillon simply shot some of the bad guys he encountered and *never* had to read the Miranda warning to the others.) In the time-honored tradition, we behead the messengers who bring us the bad news about this law or that court ruling that changes the way we must live; we get angry at lawyers. Songwriters and performers are no exception—they view lawyers as, at best, a necessary evil.

This is a misguided idea. Whatever you think about personal-injury lawyers who advertise their services in gruesome television commercials or criminal lawyers who use every trick available to keep mob bosses and drug dealers out of jail, don't make the mistake of thinking all lawyers are the same. There are as many kinds of lawyers as there are people. For anyone who aspires to a career in music, a music lawyer is indispensable. To realize your potential and maximize your earnings as a songwriter or recording artist, you need a lawyer as soon as you can get one.

The music lawyer is one of the most interesting subspecies of American lawyer. Because the music industry is made entirely out of the thin air all those hit songs fly through before they get to your radio, the only visible, tangible life of the music industry is on paper, in contracts. Contracts run the recording industry as much as music does. These contracts demand specialist lawyers to draft, negotiate, and administer them. Those lawyers are music lawyers.

Practicing music law is very different from the practice of almost any other kind of law. Music lawyers love music and believe in it as an art form or they would never have aspired to become music lawyers, because they learned almost nothing about music law in law school. They go to school for twenty years and pass a tough bar exam just to get to the stage where they can *begin* to become music lawyers. There's plenty to learn after law school.

Music lawyers have to know, do, and be a lot of things most ordinary lawyers never think of. They have to know what makes one group of four guys a band and another just a group of four musicians. They have to know what's happening with kinds of music they're too old to like and with new recording techniques they don't understand. They have to remember the names of A&R people and know when they move from one record company to another or to unemployment. They have to stay out late enough to catch their clients' acts and get up early enough for nine a.m. meetings. They have to invest time, thought, and work in clients who may never have enough money to pay their fees. And they have to be both pals and parents to their clients.

There are two basic types of music lawyers in private practice, dealmaker lawyers and shirtsleeves lawyers.

Dealmaker lawyers are the guys (mostly, they *are* guys) who shop deals for their clients. These lawyers pride themselves on who they know, and their goal is to know *everybody* who's anybody. Although most would tell you their business is based on their personal friendships, they are not given to sentiment. Their best friends are the people who have the biggest record company jobs and the most clout. They attend every music industry event in order to hobnob with industry executives, so as to get to know them well enough to send them tapes. They spend a lot of money on power lunches and parties and plane tickets and charge as much of it as possible back to their clients. When they aren't on a plane or in a tuxedo, they are on the phone in their offices, in their homes, in their cars, maybe in their pockets. Dealmaker lawyers can produce publishing contracts and record deals for talented clients, but they charge up to $300 an hour or as much as 10 percent of the deals they secure, and they are not long-distance runners; if you lose your deal or are out of the game awhile because of a little cocaine problem, all the quarters in your pocket won't get a dealmaker lawyer on the phone.

Dealmaker lawyers are like TV cameras; you're either on-screen or offscreen. To some extent, they have to be this way. Softhearted lawyers who spend their time consoling clients who have been dropped by their record companies are not going to be able to deliver for the next client who comes through the door. The music business is often hard; even musicians have to develop something like the hard shell of the dealmaker music lawyer to survive.

Dealmaker lawyers hate the shirtsleeves contract negotiation work that is necessary to finalize a publishing or record deal, so they align themselves with lawyers who don't want to be quarterbacks. These lawyers are the other primary variety of music lawyer—shirtsleeves lawyers. Most dealmaker lawyers have one or more shirtsleeves lawyers working away on the nuts and bolts of the deals they make. Shirtsleeves lawyers are more intellectual than dealmaker lawyers, and more careful and lawyerlike. They go out to hear clients play, but late nights in the clubs are not what floats their boat. They are backroom types. They read music trade publications religiously and keep up with changes in the law and can recite from memory standard paragraphs from publishing and recording contracts. They often have very good relationships with their opposite numbers in the legal departments of record companies or publishers, thanks to their years of long contract negotiations with those lawyers. Shirtsleeves lawyers won't shop your tape, but they'll protect you in every sentence of the contracts they negotiate on your behalf in ways you'll never know about.

Dealmaker lawyers and shirtsleeves lawyers are the two extreme ends of the spectrum. There are also a lot of lawyers in between who combine some of the traits of both. This is a good thing, because the clients of music lawyers are as various as the lawyers and need more choices than chocolate and vanilla.

Music lawyers perform a variety of functions for their clients, but the main service they render is contract drafting and negotiation. Most songwriter and performer clients of music lawyers don't need contracts drafted as often as they need them negotiated. This is because they're almost always asked to sign agreements drawn up by the lawyers for the music publisher or manager or record company that offers them a contract, and *whose* paper is the basis for negotiations is a point that is not open for argument. One of the things a lawyer will do is reach the basic terms of the agreement between the songwriter or performer and the publisher, manager, or record company. These basic points of agreement are called the "deal points." Then, since these agreements are always written in favor of the parties who offer them to singers and songwriters, a lawyer will negotiate the language of the standard provisions of the agreements to make them fairer to his client. In fact, "the" lawyer in these two stages of contract negotiation may be *two* lawyers; the work entailed in a major contract negotiation is often split between a lawyer who finds the deal and negotiates the deal points and one who negotiates the provisions of the rest of the long contract. (Recording agreements are often close to a hundred pages long; publishing agreements can be nearly as lengthy.)

Music lawyers sometimes also "administer" their clients' agreements. This means they monitor their clients' deals throughout the life of the contracts that establish them. They check the accuracy of royalty statements, make certain important notifications to the other contracting parties, and advise clients regarding their responsibilities at various stages of the agreements. Sometimes, usually in conjunction with contracts they have negotiated, music attorneys also collect the monies due their clients under those agreements, deposit and hold these revenues in their own trust accounts, and forward them to their clients after deducting any expenses and attorney fees that are due.

Music lawyers also often function as general career advisors to their clients, especially in the absence of experienced personal managers. Their advice can be an important resource to a client who is not yet earning enough to attract the attention and engage the services of a personal manager. Music lawyers also sometimes act as the official or unofficial general managers for their clients' business affairs. In addition to advising their clients and collecting monies for them, they coordinate the activities of the other advisors to their clients, such as their personal managers, business managers, and booking agents.

Most music lawyers don't perform all these services or play all these roles, primarily because their clients don't earn enough to pay the lawyers enough to do so. The more ordinary situation is that a music lawyer will handle *some* of the functions that aren't handled by someone else, if, of course, the client is earning enough money to make it worth the lawyer's while.

Music lawyers also perform one service that all musicians think is the primary reason music lawyers exist: "shopping" deals. Many musicians think *all* music lawyers look for deals for their clients. This is not so. While many music lawyers will take your tape around to publishers and record companies if they like your music, *most* won't, preferring to leave this time-consuming and often disappointing job to their clients or their clients' personal managers. Although you should look for a lawyer who suits your needs, remember that you need a lawyer to do the things you can't do yourself—like negotiating a complicated contract—and shouldn't look down on a music lawyer who wants to *be* a lawyer. After all, what you need from your lawyer is legal work.

Because the right lawyer is so important to anyone who expects to build a real career in music, knowing how to choose a lawyer can be critical to your success. Finding a music lawyer may not be easy for someone who doesn't yet have a big career or a fat wallet, but since you do need to look for one, you need to know what to look for. Pay no attention to the size of the firm a lawyer practices in, because the sort of work you'll have for your lawyer doesn't require much more than a phone, a photocopier, and a sharp pencil. Anyway, even large firms seldom have more than a handful of lawyers who practice music law, and some of the best music lawyers practice in very small firms or alone. Look for someone you can communicate with and believe in. Do your research when searching for an attorney, but follow your gut when you pick one.

Good music lawyers share several characteristics. If you can, hire a lawyer who demonstrates the five enumerated below.

1. *Your lawyer should understand your music and believe in you.* This does not mean your attorney has to be a musician or show up at all your performances; you want a lawyer, not just a fan. But an egghead lawyer who understands all the ramifications of the most complicated provisions of a recording agreement but doesn't know rap from rhythm and blues won't be able to give you the guidance the best music attorneys can offer their clients. The attorney and personal manager are the biggest stars in the constellation of professionals who surround an act. If one of them is weak, your career can be stalled, or worse, stopped completely, especially if you get bad advice before you have a reputation to coast on.

At the same time, avoid lawyers who are really only Elvis-wannabes in three-piece suits, because they will be more concerned with getting backstage passes than with carefully analyzing your potential, your opportunities, and your problems. There are a lot of lawyers like this lying around. The worst of them act almost like groupies. Your lawyer does not have to be as hip as you to be effective. In fact, the less you look and act and conduct business like an ordinary businessperson, the more you need someone who knows how to. Look for a lawyer who owns a pair of jeans and will come out to the clubs occasionally, but avoid an attorney who really wants to trade his or her business suit for one with spangles.

2. *Your lawyer should have a track record.* This doesn't mean you have to hire a name partner in a well-known entertainment law firm to get good service. In fact, until you're a name yourself, big-gun music lawyers will not be interested in representing you, and even if they were interested, you wouldn't be a lucrative enough client to command their full attention. You need to hook up with a young attorney (there are very few *old* music lawyers who represent struggling songwriters and performers) who has the time to represent you and who *wants* to. Look for someone who has been in practice five to ten years or is associated with an experienced attorney.

And make sure any lawyer you consider hiring has been practicing *music* law for most of the time he or she has been in practice. Just as there are a lot of people who own guitars and want to be recording artists, there are a lot of people with law degrees who want to be music lawyers. Many of them are currently practicing some sort of boring corporate law and dream of escaping. Sometimes they want to learn to be music lawyers by practicing on *you*. Don't let them.

There are two things a track record guarantees: skill as a music lawyer and knowledge of the music industry. In choosing a lawyer, you should look for one who remembers that he or she is first a lawyer. You want a lawyer who has strong enough legal skills to pilot you through the morass of contracts that you hope you'll be asked to sign. And there's simply no substitute for the sort of nose-to-nose negotiation a lawyer performs during the process of finalizing a contract for a client.

Your lawyer should also know *more* about the music industry than you do. He or she should be able to tell you which publishers and record companies to approach and should be able to advise you about the current value of your songs and/or services as a performer in the marketplace. A lawyer who doesn't know what a client is worth to a publisher or record company will destroy the possibility that a deal can be struck, burning some bridges for the client in the process. This information and the judgment it takes to use it to your benefit don't come with a law degree—they're available only through hands-on experience and good contacts.

3. *Your lawyer should listen to you.* This seems obvious, but it is so important to a good lawyer-client relationship that it bears repeating. Your lawyer works for *you*, acting on your behalf only to the extent that you authorize. The right attorney will treat you and your opinions with respect, will listen to your concerns about your career, and will, after spelling out your options in any particular situation, carefully follow your instructions. This means your lawyer should be accessible. As a time management technique, many lawyers never take phone calls but only make them. But any lawyer, no matter how skilled, who is too busy to return your phone calls within a reasonable time is not going to be much help to you. Avoid showboat attorneys who think that only they know what's best for you and lawyers who treat musicians like children. Expect your lawyer to take your career as seriously as you do.

(In fact, that's the way most lawyers *will* treat your career. If you show up for meetings stoned, don't expect your lawyer to put any extra thought or energy into your legal work. If you can't be bothered to stay straight to talk about your career, why should your lawyer do more for you than is absolutely necessary?

In fact, because music lawyers' careers prosper when their clients' do, and because clients who don't take care of business are unlikely to *have* careers for very long, it's a good career move *for your lawyer* to put you on his or her B list if you're too flaky, no matter how talented you are.)

4. *Your lawyer should have good politics.* The sort of good politics music lawyers need are good relations with music publishers and record companies. Even though it may be hard for you to land a music lawyer who lunches regularly with record company presidents, you should aim to hook up with one who is at least friendly with the A&R departments of several labels. Often a younger lawyer in a power firm can piggyback on the relationships the senior attorneys in the firm have developed. At a minimum, your lawyer should not be somebody who has a *bad* track record with publishers and record companies.

Bad blood between lawyers and music publishers or record companies can arise for many reasons. Maybe the lawyer is territorial and has a history of fighting little turf wars with publishers and record company people rather than cooperating with them to build his or her clients' careers. Maybe he or she kills deals by negotiating every contract as if it were the SALT treaty. Maybe the lawyer's songwriter and artist clients are always duds; lawyers who have never demonstrated good artistic judgment can't do much even for talented clients because publishers and A&R people won't listen to the tapes they send anymore. Whatever the reason a lawyer is in the doghouse, you don't want to borrow his or her trouble. Always ask around to find out whether having a particular lawyer represent you will hurt or help you with the people you hope will offer you fat publishing or recording contracts. And ask these questions of people who are your peers—you need to know whether some other little fish swimming in your part of the pond thinks a particular lawyer is a big fish or just a shark.

5. *Your lawyer should work with your team.* Songwriters need lawyers just as badly as performers do, but performers also need

other professionals surrounding and supporting them. Even solo acts are seldom really solo. Successful performers got there as much because of the skill of their managers, agents, and lawyers as on account of their own talents. Your lawyers should be able to work amicably with all the people around you. Vendettas between members of your team are seldom fatal for the people who are feuding, but they can kill off your career. Avoid lawyers who think that anyone who doesn't have a law degree has nothing to say, and watch out for lawyers who use their pit bull personalities on your friends as well as your adversaries.

About personalities. There is a common misconception that in order to be effective lawyers have to eat nails for breakfast and their enemies for lunch. This is not so. Having a ferocious lawyer is only an advantage when you're involved in litigation, and opinions differ about whether this is an advantage even then. Music lawyers are strategists and negotiators rather than warriors. Consequently, a lawyer who wants to fight at every juncture is a liability to his or her client. This is not to say that your lawyer shouldn't have enough moxie to ask for top dollar for you in a publishing deal and be tough enough to threaten to walk if you don't get it. You should look for an intelligent lawyer who is reasonable but street-smart and avoid attorneys with personalities that get in the way of your business.

Now that you know what to look for in a lawyer, you need to know *when* to look. The right lawyer at the wrong time (too late) may be no better than no lawyer at all. Generally, there are three circumstances that mean you need a lawyer, *now*.

1. *Somebody wants you to sign an agreement that will endure longer than a few days.* You don't need a lawyer to review most performance engagement contracts because they only deal with one or two nights of a club date. Whatever these agreements say, they will have no effect after the gig is over. This is not true of just about every other kind of agreement you may be asked to sign during your career. You need a lawyer to review and negotiate booking agreements, management agreements, tour agreements, music publishing agreements, recording agreements, producer agreements, and merchandising agreements. If your career has advanced to the stage where people approach you with fountain pens in one hand and contracts in the other, you *need* a lawyer, even if you have to hock your stereo to pay for one. Contracts drafted by the lawyers for the booker, manager, publisher, record company, producer, or merchandising company are drafted to protect *their* interests—not yours. There are very few contracts that cannot be "adjusted" slightly by a careful lawyer so that they are fairer to you. Even if the contract is a fair one, you need a lawyer to help you understand just what it is you're promising to do.

Don't be afraid that the offered contract will be withdrawn if you consult a lawyer. In the first place, a good lawyer will take pains to avoid killing your deal. Your lawyer will review the contract and offer you an opinion about it before calling or writing the other party to the contract. In fact, since you're footing the bill, you call the shots; if you don't want your lawyer to negotiate directly with the other party to the contract, you can handle your own negotiations after being advised by your lawyer what to ask for. This is never a good idea in the case of a complicated contract, like a recording agreement or exclusive publishing agreement, but may be possible in the case of a simpler agreement, such as a booking or management agreement.

2. *You enter a partnership.* If you and your band are playing for money and plan to continue to do so longer than the rest of the summer, you are a partnership and you need a partnership agreement, for all the reasons discussed in Chapter Five. If you're *really* only a pickup band, you can forgo calling a lawyer; otherwise, negotiate your partnership agreement among yourselves and get an attorney to write it down. Really.

3. *Somebody invests money in your career.* Bands often think that if they could only get their relatives and their college roommates to each contribute $1,000 to the Fund for the First Hit Album, they could (1) make a hit album, (2) sell it to a record company, and (3) get rich enough soon enough to pay everybody back before Christmas. This is seldom the way things work out. Most relatives and friends who put their money where your mouth is will never reap anything from their investments besides a carton of your cassettes. But that's not the most serious problem with seeking investors.

Unless you know exactly what you're doing, which is highly unlikely, you will fun afoul of the securities laws. These laws apply to big corporations that want to raise capital by selling stock, but they also apply to small-time operators like you. If you don't bump into *federal* securities laws, it's very probable that you will transgress state securities laws. Either way, it's a bigger headache than you want to have. Listen up. *Never* ask anyone to invest money in your career without first seeing a lawyer for advice about staying on the safe side of securities laws and a briefing on the other important concerns inherent in acquiring an investor. And if someone wants to invest a few thousand dollars in you, run to the phone and dial your lawyer's office—even if your investor says his lawyer has already drawn up the necessary paperwork.

Obviously, if you make the effort to meet a few lawyers before you absolutely, positively need the services of one, you'll be in a much better position to get satisfactory help when you really need it. The best plan is to establish some sort of relationship with a lawyer you like *before* you need one. It's not really hard to scrape acquaintance with a lawyer; after all, lawyers need clients at least as much as you need a lawyer.

Music lawyers are predictable creatures and not hard to locate. Their primary habitats are New York, Nashville, and Los Angeles, but a few of them can be found in any sizable city. Because bar association referral services usually only refer callers to the next name on their list, regardless of the areas of law in which that lawyer concentrates, these services are not a good way to find a music lawyer. You can call the offices of songwrit-

ers' organizations or industry unions or performance rights organizations or look in *The Yellow Pages of Rock!* or *The Recording
Industry Source Book* for names of music lawyers. Even if you
have a lawyer's name, you still need to get acquainted, because
what you want to establish is one of the closer and more important relationships of your business life. Sending unsolicited
tapes to music lawyers is another approach to finding one, but is
really no better, because you're still no closer to establishing a
relationship with a lawyer if no one likes your tape enough to
call you up. And although you can see music lawyers in clubs
and at concerts, they're usually there to see clients play and may
have an A&R guy in tow or similar business to attend to; in
other words, don't buttonhole a music lawyer at a club or concert, because he or she is probably trying to take care of business
and is not in a mood to hear your dreams of making music history. (If you can persuade someone to *introduce* you, that's another story.)

A better approach is to attend every music industry confab
you hear about until you meet a few music lawyers. If you don't
live in a city where events of this sort occur occasionally, find
out where they do occur and go there, even if you have to sleep
on somebody's sofa for a few days. The annual New Music Seminar in New York is one event of this sort. Music lawyers
abound at BMI, ASCAP, and SESAC events and at awards
dinners and shows of other music industry organizations. If you
meet people on the staffs of these organizations, they may be
able to introduce you to a good music lawyer.

Music lawyers also teach at colleges and law schools that offer music industry courses and speak on panels and present seminars offered by industry organizations. They show up, with time
on their hands, at regional music festivals. Every board of every
music trade organization includes at least one lawyer. Read music industry trade publications to find out when and where you
can find music lawyers; concentrate especially on the smaller
music magazines published in your area, because they'll tell you
what attorneys are prominent on your local music scene. Refer

to the list of music industry trade organizations in the Resources section of this book and call or drop by the offices of any in your area to ask about seminars, receptions, conferences, or other events they may be sponsoring.

Now, most of these conferences, seminars, and awards programs are open only to members of the organizations that sponsor them or require a registration fee, sometimes a hefty one. However, you probably don't have to register to attend a three-day conference in order to walk through a cocktail party for conference participants. But you do have to get a schedule of events, pick the one that looks easiest to crash, turn off your TV, and drive to the hotel. It's not that hard. If you have enough moxie to get up on stage and dance like James Brown, you can corner a mild-mannered music lawyer drinking a glass of Chablis at a convention cocktail party. Remember that even though you're a musician and not a music industry executive, you have to talk the talk and walk the walk at these dos. You can spike your hair and wear your favorite neon jacket, but you aren't there to drink all the free liquor in sight or to make passes at the people you meet, some of whom will be the very A&R executives or lawyers or publishers you want to impress. If you take your career seriously, take industry gatherings seriously. They're an important part of the business and can help you massage a small career into a bigger one.

Let's say you've cornered your target music lawyer at a cocktail party before an awards dinner. He's about forty and looks out of shape and a little tired, but you recognize the name on his badge and he's wearing a polka-dot bow tie with his tux, which makes you like him. (You couldn't afford a seventy-five-dollar ticket to the dinner, but you have a buddy who works in the kitchen of the hotel where it's held and she let you into the party through the service entrance.) What do you do with a music lawyer once you find him? Well, the first thing to remember is that the lawyer actually paid for the privilege of attending the dinner, so he's expecting to get something out of it, namely, some congenial networking with the music industry executives who will also attend. This does not mean you. What it does mean is that you need to respect his time at this party as much as if you were paying him his hourly rate.

Then all you have to do is act the way your folks told you when you were in the eighth grade. Stand up straight, look him in the eye, stick out your hand, and say, "Hello. I'm Bongo Jones. I'm a singer and I have a band. I'm looking for a lawyer. I know you represent The Plant Eaters. Could I call you to come in and talk for about fifteen minutes? I'd like you to hear my tape."

Lawyers are usually polite because they've spent so many years playing by the rules. Most lawyers, approached in this way, will hand you a business card and say, "Of course. Call my secretary next week, Bongo. I can see you one day after my other appointments."

Call the secretary. Get there on time. Take a tape of four songs—one you've tested beforehand to make sure it isn't blank or noisy. (Or send your tape in advance so the lawyer can listen to it before meeting with you.) Talk for fifteen minutes and then stand up to leave. Don't play your tape while you're in the lawyer's office unless he suggests it; he can listen to it later and your object in this meeting is to talk to him long enough to decide whether you could work with him. Fifteen minutes is exactly the right amount of time to ask for. It doesn't seem like a big commitment to anyone you ask to see, and turning down a request for such a small amount of time seems petty. Once you're in the door, many people will give you more than fifteen minutes—because they like you, because they're running on about their own remarkable accomplishments, because they forgot you were only supposed to take up a quarter hour of their time.

Repeat the above instructions about three times. Not every lawyer you meet will be willing to see you. Don't take it personally. Anyone who denies your request has just saved you a lot of time, because a lawyer who won't see you for a brief initial meeting is too busy or out of your league or unduly impressed

with his or her own importance. Any of these reasons is an indication that you will not be a satisfied client of that lawyer.
Move on; there are lots of lawyers. What you're asking, after all,
is to investigate the possibility that you can make a lot of
money for the lawyer you approach. It might never happen, but
it could.

You can also capture other useful industry executives in the
same way. Even if you aren't ready for a publishing deal, shake
some publishers' hands and keep their business cards. And remember that a big-time manager who wouldn't represent you
on a bet might introduce you to some new, energetic young
manager who used to work for him.

At this point you may be thinking that all you want to do is
play your guitar and sing, that your talent is sufficient to attract
the attention of a music lawyer, and that if you'd wanted to
spend your time shaking hands at cocktail parties, you would
have gone to work selling insurance with your uncle. Fine.
Have it your way. However, you may wish to note that most
successful entertainers are shameless self-promoters *in addition to*
having real talent. If you want to wait to be discovered, go sit in
a drugstore in a tight sweater with everyone else who thinks
music is magic and not really a business. It's far easier to be the
biggest *undiscovered* recording star in America than it is to become even a locally famous singer who gets an actual record
deal on a little label.

If you hire the right music lawyer, your relationship will be
profitable for you and your lawyer; you'll make money because
your lawyer will believe in you and help guide you to the money
river that flows through the recording industry, and your lawyer
will make money because you'll need a lot of legal work.

Your lawyer *will* expect to be paid. Many music lawyers, especially well-established lawyers with big reputations, won't
represent you if you can't pay them immediately. Others who
are building their reputations may agree to advise you infor-
mally until you're offered a publishing contract or recording
agreement. At that point, your lawyer will go "on the clock"

and charge you an hourly fee for the work he or she performs. Most lawyers will allow you to pay your attorney's fees out of the advance you get from your new publishing or record deal. Some attorneys, especially those who do more for a client than just contract negotiation, will ask for a percentage of the gross revenues from a deal for finding it and negotiating and administering the contract that documents it. Beggars can't be choosers, but you should be cautious in agreeing to any percentage arrangement with a lawyer. At least calculate how much money you'll be paying your lawyer under such an arrangement. Very often a lawyer will spend so much time finding, negotiating, and administering a deal that he or she loses money in a percentage fee arrangement, especially if the contract is not a very lucrative one. But just as often such fee arrangements are bonanzas for the lawyers involved. Perhaps the best arrangement is one in which your lawyer agrees to perform the work necessary to negotiate a contract for a flat fee and allows you to pay that flat fee out of your publishing or recording contract advance. But be sure you have confidence in your lawyer before entering a percentage fee agreement. A less than scrupulous lawyer could recommend that you sign *this* deal *now* in order to earn a percentage of the income from it, regardless of whether the deal is best for you.

Most lawyers will ask you to sign a fee agreement before they will undertake any significant amount of work on your behalf. (In fact, California requires an agreement of this sort.) You shouldn't be insulted by such a request because fee agreements are really an excellent idea. They let you know what you'll be paying and give you the opportunity to ask your lawyer questions about fees and billing practices. A careful lawyer will tell you that you should have another lawyer look over the fee agreement before you sign it. This is probably a good idea, but as a practical matter, most people don't go to the trouble of finding a second lawyer. At the very least, keep in mind that even a high-powered lawyer works for *you* and that you have the right to ask questions until you understand any proposed fee arrangement. Your relationship with your lawyer won't work unless it's a frank one and it won't last if your lawyer is angry with you because you can't pay your fees on time or if you are angry with your lawyer because you feel ripped off. Get it straight at the beginning of the relationship. One of the ways you keep on the good side of your lawyer is to be a good client. That may seem like an obvious statement, but any lawyer will tell you that all clients are *not* good clients; in fact, some clients give lawyers headaches.

Role Reversal

Just for a little while, imagine you're a music lawyer. You're past your youth and are getting a little gray. You worry that your clients will think you're too old and boring to understand their music and will hire the twenty-eight-year-old music lawyer who just hung up her shingle down the street. You're having problems with your marriage and you're worried that it's because you've been a lawyer too long. You woke up last night and lay awake thinking about the best way to handle an important provision of a record contract you're negotiating for your most important client, a singer whose legal fees pay most of your office overhead but who has made noises about leaving you now that he *has* an opening act rather than *is* one. It's five p.m. You have time to make one phone call before you have to show up at a BMI cocktail party and shake hands with as many grown men with ponytails as possible. You want to call one of three clients. They are:

- Raymond, called "The Incredible Hunk" by your secretary. Raymond is a talented singer and looks like Michael Bolton. His daddy arranged for a nice little trust fund for Raymond, so his accountant pays your bills on time, but you wonder whether you will ever again be able to bill Raymond for more than representing him on the occasional DUI. He *had* a record deal; now he wants another one. Unfortunately, his good looks have given him an attitude and A&R people think he is a problem child. He is typically inebriated by late afternoon, so you wonder, if you call, whether he will remember what you need to tell him—that you need five more copies of his artist tape before next week to take with you to a conference where you hope to be able to corner some A&R people who haven't heard about beautiful Raymond's bad attitude.

- Susannah, who has very little money but a lot of talent and no attitude. Your secretary calls Susannah "Susie Sunshine"—and *means* it. Susannah is a very young songwriter with a voice like a bird. She also plays her violin like Stephane Grappelli on moonshine. You are in the middle of negotiating a single song agreement for her and you think she'll be offered a publishing deal and a record deal eventually. You know you won't make much money off Susannah's fees for a while, but you like her and want to help her because she pays you $150 a month toward the $1,200 in fees she has incurred, shows up for appointments on time, and takes your tips and turns them into opportunities. You heard at lunch today that the producer for a hot country sister act is looking for songs for their new album and you want to tell Susannah to get a tape to him.

- The Red Giants, a rock band composed of two smart guys who are not very talented musicians and two not-so-smart guys who are. (Your secretary thinks the group should call itself "Two Red Giants and Two White Dwarfs.") This band keeps you awake nights. The smart guys are scared that the not-so-smart ones will leave them in the dust with only their English lit degrees to protect them. The not-so-smart guys know they can play and sing rings around their partners but are afraid to leave them because they do have a way of figuring out the next step on the road to stardom. The Red Giants need a mediator; unfortunately, they think *you* are it. You have finished negotiating a management agreement for them and you need to get them to come in for a meeting to discuss it before they sign, but you really don't look forward to hosting *Star Wars* in your office, and one of the smart guys carps about your bill at every meeting anyway.

Given these choices, the question is: *Who are you going to call?*

Obviously, the people on both sides of a relationship have to hold up their respective ends of things or the relationship will fail. This is as true for relationships between lawyers and clients as it is for any other kind of relationship. Lawyers have certain ethical obligations to their clients that they must not neglect even if they don't like their clients very well. Even though lawyers are supposed to represent their clients "zealously within the bounds of the law," as a practical matter, most lawyers reserve their zeal for clients who pay their bills and otherwise act like partners in the lawyer/client relationship rather than like spoiled children.

Music lawyers have, of necessity, a greater tolerance for clients' failings than most other sorts of lawyers, but even their patience can be exhausted. In any event, wouldn't you rather use up your lawyer's enthusiasm in negotiating the best publishing or record deal possible than wear his or her goodwill thin by your inability to cope with being an adult? There are only a few rules to remember to be a good client. Just for the heck of it, here they are:

- Show up on time for appointments with your lawyer or call to say you'll be late or can't make it if you're delayed for some *important* reason—say, if a record company executive stops you on the street and wants to talk about your career. Don't miss appointments because you can't wake up early enough. Don't miss them because you have a hangover. (Don't show up for appointments *with* a hangover, either.) Don't bring your girlfriend, boyfriend, mom, dad, or dog unless she, he, or it has something real to contribute to the meeting. Don't act the way you did in your high school civics class when you get to a meeting with your lawyer—pay attention, ask questions, and give your lawyer the information he or she needs to represent you.

- Talk to your lawyer about fees and make sure you understand what you'll be charged for. Tell your lawyer if you can't pay your bill all at once; most music lawyers are used to working out payment arrangements with their clients and will be able to suggest some creative ways to get you the legal help you need when you need it, even if that's before you can pay for it. Aside from the cost of their services, lawyers want to be reimbursed for long-distance phone calls, postage, photocopies, Federal Express charges, and other expenses incurred on your behalf, including the costs of trips they take for you. This is ordinary, but if you don't understand your lawyer's policies about reimbursement for such expenses, ask questions about this, too. However, save your complaints about your lawyer's bill for substantive problems; nothing makes a lawyer wearier than to be questioned about why so many photocopies were charged to a client on a particular statement.

- Respect your lawyer's time and privacy. No lawyer can afford to spend the time to hold your hand every time you have a creative crisis. Most lawyers will either ask you to call your mom with your personal problems or bill you for the phone calls you make to discuss them, or both. If you need a shrink, get one. Lawyers are, by and large, pretty smart, but most of them are bad therapists. In the best scenario, your lawyer will become your friend. This does not mean, however, that he or she has the time or the inclination to hear about every vicissitude of your life. Don't call your lawyer at home unless you really need advice. Even then, don't take one instance of accommodation to your busy weekday schedule for a blanket invitation to call your lawyer at home for the rest of your life. That's why they're called *business* hours. Given the hours most music lawyers work, you may find it easier to find your lawyer at the office anyway.

• Respect your lawyer's judgment. Expect your lawyer to defer to you in matters involving musical taste and creative judgment, but in matters of the law, take your lawyer's advice. Allow your lawyer to practice law. If you think you know better than your lawyer, you should either apply to law school or get another lawyer. If you lose faith in your lawyer, you should find some other lawyer you can believe in. However, make sure you really have the facts before you conclude that your lawyer is giving you bad advice. Don't make the exceedingly common mistake of confusing your hard luck in a hard industry with bad guidance from your lawyer.

Sometimes a client believes that the right lawyer can make a few phone calls and produce a publishing or recording agreement and a bag of money by this afternoon. Usually if this is true, the client is so talented that one competent music lawyer could produce these results as well as another. You'll need to evaluate your lawyer's performance just as you'll eventually need to watch the performance of your booker, personal manager, and business manager. But don't jump ship because you've leaped to the wrong conclusion about your lawyer. Make sure your expectations are reasonable and your facts are straight before you give your lawyer his or her walking papers and start the process of looking for another.

• Work at your career. Don't expect your lawyer or any of your other advisors to produce a career for you without your wholehearted participation. People have faith only in those who have faith in themselves and do something about their dreams. The best lawyer in America can't jump-start the career of an unmotivated client. Music will take everything you have to give and then some. People who have real careers in music work harder than factory laborers and are more persistent than encyclopedia salespeople. If you want to be a star, take your vitamins and tune your guitar.

Most of What You Need to Know About Written Agreements

A contract is a set of legal rights and responsibilities created by the mutual agreement of two or more people or companies; it is the body of rules, so to speak, by which a particular business relationship is to be run. A contract is the agreement itself, not the paper document that commemorates the agreement. In fact, many contracts don't even have to be in writing to be valid, although, as you'll see, written contracts are almost always a good idea.

Except in old movies, written contracts do not depend for their legal effect on complicated legal language. The goal of a good contract lawyer is to "draft," or write, a document that sets out in completely unambiguous language the agreement reached between the parties to it. This generally means that the more clearly a contract is written the more effective it is *as* a contract, but eliminating ambiguity may also require more detailed language than most people are accustomed to using and may result in a much longer written agreement than the lawyer's client thinks is really necessary. However, in a skillfully drafted agreement every provision is necessary. Even in the case of an apparently simple agreement, a good contract lawyer will write an agreement that not only provides what happens when the agreement is working but also what happens when it *stops* working.

No particular "architecture" is required to make a written document a contract. What determines whether a document is a binding agreement is the content of the language, *not* the form in which the language is arranged in the document. However, formal written agreements are customarily divided into certain standard sections.

The introductory section of a formal written agreement gives the names, and sometimes the addresses, of the parties to the agreement, indicates their legal status (an individual doing business under a trade name, a partnership, or a corporation), gives the shortened forms of the contracting parties' names by which they will be referred to in the agreement ("Reginald Jones, hereinafter referred to as the 'Writer' . . ."), and specifies the date the agreement is made or becomes effective.

The "premises" section of a formal written agreement sets out, sometimes after the word "Whereas," the set of circumstances on which the agreement is founded, or "premised." This section makes certain representations about the facts that have influenced the parties' decision to enter into the agreement and, although it may look like excess language to nonlawyers, in reality it sets out information that could be important if, in a lawsuit based on the agreement, a court had to "construe," or interpret, the written agreement in order to rule on the intent of the parties when they entered into it.

In the body of most contracts the various points of agreement between the parties are enumerated in a series of headlined paragraphs, each of which sets out one facet of the agreement and all of which probably use the word "shall" to indicate the mandatory nature of the action expected from each party. Besides all the major points of the agreement, a formal contract will contain what are sometimes entitled "miscellaneous provisions" and what lawyers often call "boilerplate." These provisions look unnecessary to most nonlawyers, since, among other things, they set out methods for handling various events that may never occur, but they can be crucially important. For example, one standard "miscellaneous" provision states that any lawsuit based on the agreement will be brought in the courts of a specified state or city and that any dispute will be decided according to the laws of that state. This sort of provision can determine whether you sue to enforce your agreement in your home city and state or, at increased expense, in a distant city.

These are the sections you'll see in agreements drafted by lawyers. You also need to know about less formal agreements, mostly so that you can recognize them and avoid them. A short "deal memo" used to set down the terms of an agreement on the spot can be a binding agreement. Music lawyers use deal memos to agree to the basic terms of complicated agreements that they have negotiated for their clients with publishing or record companies, pending the day some overworked publishing or record company lawyer can expand those basic terms to full, formal written agreements, but they know how to include a "sunset clause" in these documents, that is, a provision that if a formal agreement is not signed by a certain date, the agreement is off.

Sometimes songwriters think that if they can write a song, writing a contract can't be too hard. They sign short memorandum agreements in the mistaken belief that they are not binding. These short agreements are not only binding but are also probably ambiguous; if you sign one of these you can end up being bound by the terms of an agreement that no one can figure out without a lawsuit. Owning a typewriter and a dictionary is not qualification enough to practice law, even if you're only writing an agreement for yourself.

An exchange of letters can also constitute a contract between the people who write them if they contain the terms of the deal and show that there was agreement between the letter writers. Be careful what you write in your letters. It's wise to couch your negotiations in clearly contingent language such as "I would consider your proposal if you offered to pay me a $300-a-week draw against future royalties." Never say "I will agree to write for you exclusively if you pay me $300 a week" unless you *really* mean it and, even then, add a hedging sentence like "Of course, before I commit to any such arrangement, I would have to have my lawyer review your formal agreement." More than one innocent has been surprised that somebody thought something had been firmly promised when all that was meant was "I might."

Of course, no lawyer can include any provision in any written agreement that will compel ethical conduct from a dishonest person. The best any lawyer can do is to include provisions in a written agreement that prescribe penalties for failure to abide by the terms of the contract, and even this will not ensure that a dishonest person does not act dishonestly. Your best protection against truly dishonest people is to avoid entering agreements with them, since a true renegade has little fear of lawsuits, and in any event, having to go to court to obtain what you were due under the terms of the agreement you made is expensive, time-consuming, and frustrating.

Many creative people assume that a written contract between people who know and trust each other is unnecessary and that having a lawyer prepare a written agreement in such a case is an avoidable expense. Neither of these assumptions is true. Even if you enter an agreement with another ethical person, a written contract is a necessity, for precision and for documentation.

Even honest and knowledgeable businesspeople sometimes fail to communicate to each other *all* the terms of their agreement. Putting an agreement in writing lets both parties "see" their agreement and provides an opportunity for them to negotiate points of the agreement they have previously omitted from their discussions. Further, a written agreement serves to document the terms of the agreement throughout the life of the business arrangement. Human memory is fallible; even honest people can forget the precise terms of their agreements if they're not written down. And a written agreement can be crucial to proving the existence of the agreement if one of the parties dies.

Generally, the more complex the terms of the agreement and the longer its duration, the more it needs to be documented in writing. Further, while it may be good business practice to reduce most agreements to writing, some sorts of agreements are not valid or enforceable *unless* they're in writing. For example, almost universally in English-speaking countries, contracts that may not be performed within a year must be in writing. And the copyright statute requires transfers and exclusive licenses of copyrights to be in writing. It also provides that nothing an independent contractor creates can be a work-for-hire unless there is a written agreement to that effect signed by both the independent contractor and the person who employed him or her.

All of these are good reasons for consulting a lawyer when you enter into an agreement of any importance. A good contract lawyer who is familiar with your business can not only help you define and document your agreement, but can advise you concerning the law that governs your business relationship and suggest contract provisions that can help you reach your goals and avoid disputes.

Consulting a lawyer can be just as important, or even *more* important, when the contract was drafted by lawyers for the other party. In any business agreement you should remember that there are actually *two* sorts of possible written contracts documenting the relationship—*their* version and *your* version. This is especially true when the contracting parties are not equal in power, such as when a songwriter or recording artist is presented with an agreement drafted by lawyers for the music publisher or record company. Having your own lawyer in a situation like this can help you feel less like David confronting Goliath. Your lawyer can explain complex contract provisions to you and, by negotiating on your behalf, turn the offered agreement into one that allows you more control, gets you paid more quickly, and is generally more favorable than the unnegotiated contract you were originally offered. But your lawyer must know the music business before he or she can do the job you need. If you take your publishing contract to a lawyer who says, "By the way, how long is a copyright these days, anyway?", it's time to consult another lawyer.

Nobody ever fights over an unsuccessful project. The more successful your song or act, the more important it is to have the agreements concerning it reduced to unambiguous writing. This is true in most areas of business, but it's especially true in the music industry. Copyrights and trademarks and the personal services of performers are intangible, but they are valuable, and their ownership and the business arrangements surrounding them must be in writing, on paper, in contracts.

Appendix A:
Copyright Registration Form PA

FORM PA

For a Work of the Performing Arts
UNITED STATES COPYRIGHT OFFICE

REGISTRATION NUMBER

PA   PAU

EFFECTIVE DATE OF REGISTRATION

Month   Day   Year

DO NOT WRITE ABOVE THIS LINE. IF YOU NEED MORE SPACE, USE A SEPARATE CONTINUATION SHEET.

1 TITLE OF THIS WORK ▼

PREVIOUS OR ALTERNATIVE TITLES ▼

NATURE OF THIS WORK ▼ See instructions

2 NAME OF AUTHOR ▼

a

Was this contribution to the work a
"work made for hire"?
☐ Yes
☐ No

AUTHOR'S NATIONALITY OR DOMICILE
Name of Country
OR { Citizen of ▶
     Domiciled in ▶

DATES OF BIRTH AND DEATH
Year Born ▼   Year Died ▼

WAS THIS AUTHOR'S CONTRIBUTION TO
THE WORK   If the answer to either
                            of these questions is
Anonymous?   ☐ Yes ☐ No "Yes," see detailed
Pseudonymous? ☐ Yes ☐ No instructions.

NATURE OF AUTHORSHIP   Briefly describe nature of material created by this author in which copyright is claimed. ▼

NOTE

Under the law, the "author" of a "work made for hire" is generally the employer, not the employee (see instructions). For any part of this work that was "made for hire" check "Yes" in the space provided, give the employer (or other person for whom the work was prepared) as "Author" of that part, and leave the space for dates of birth and death blank.

See instructions before completing this space.

b

NAME OF AUTHOR ▼

Was this contribution to the work a "work made for hire"?
☐ Yes
☐ No

AUTHOR'S NATIONALITY OR DOMICILE
Name of Country
OR { Citizen of ▲
Domiciled in ▲

NATURE OF AUTHORSHIP   Briefly describe nature of material created by this author in which copyright is claimed. ▼

DATES OF BIRTH AND DEATH
Year Born ▼   Year Died ▼

WAS THIS AUTHOR'S CONTRIBUTION TO THE WORK
Anonymous?   ☐ Yes ☐ No
Pseudonymous? ☐ Yes ☐ No
If the answer to either of these questions is "Yes," see detailed instructions.

c

NAME OF AUTHOR ▼

Was this contribution to the work a "work made for hire"?
☐ Yes
☐ No

AUTHOR'S NATIONALITY OR DOMICILE
Name of Country
OR { Citizen of ▲
Domiciled in ▲

NATURE OF AUTHORSHIP   Briefly describe nature of material created by this author in which copyright is claimed. ▼

DATES OF BIRTH AND DEATH
Year Born ▼   Year Died ▼

WAS THIS AUTHOR'S CONTRIBUTION TO THE WORK
Anonymous?   ☐ Yes ☐ No
Pseudonymous? ☐ Yes ☐ No
If the answer to either of these questions is "Yes," see detailed instructions.

3
a YEAR IN WHICH CREATION OF THIS WORK WAS COMPLETED   This information must be given   Year in all cases. ▼

b DATE AND NATION OF FIRST PUBLICATION OF THIS PARTICULAR WORK
Complete this information ONLY if this work has been published.
Month ▶   Day ▶   Year ▶
◀ Nation

4 COPYRIGHT CLAIMANT(S) Name and address must be given even if the claimant is the same as the author given in space 2. ▼

TRANSFER If the claimant(s) named here in space 4 is (are) different from the author(s) named in space 2, give a brief statement of how the claimant(s) obtained ownership of the copyright. ▼

DO NOT WRITE HERE
OFFICE USE ONLY

APPLICATION RECEIVED

ONE DEPOSIT RECEIVED

TWO DEPOSITS RECEIVED

FUNDS RECEIVED

MORE ON BACK ▶   • Complete all applicable spaces (numbers 5-9) on the reverse side of this page.
• See detailed instructions.   • Sign the form at line 8.

DO NOT WRITE HERE
Page 1 of ____ pages

FORM PA

EXAMINED BY

CHECKED BY

CORRESPONDENCE
☐ Yes

FOR
COPYRIGHT
OFFICE
USE
ONLY

5

DO NOT WRITE ABOVE THIS LINE. IF YOU NEED MORE SPACE, USE A SEPARATE CONTINUATION SHEET.

PREVIOUS REGISTRATION Has registration for this work, or for an earlier version of this work, already been made in the Copyright Office?

☐ Yes ☐ No If your answer is "Yes," why is another registration being sought? (Check appropriate box) ▼

a. ☐ This is the first published edition of a work previously registered in unpublished form.

b. ☐ This is the first application submitted by this author as copyright claimant.

c. ☐ This is a changed version of the work, as shown by space 6 on this application.

If your answer is "Yes," give: **Previous Registration Number** ▼   **Year of Registration** ▼

6

DERIVATIVE WORK OR COMPILATION Complete both space 6a and 6b for a derivative work; complete only 6b for a compilation.

a. **Preexisting Material** Identify any preexisting work or works that this work is based on or incorporates. ▼

b. **Material Added to This Work** Give a brief, general statement of the material that has been added to this work and in which copyright is claimed. ▼

See instructions
before completing
this space.

7

DEPOSIT ACCOUNT If the registration fee is to be charged to a Deposit Account established in the Copyright Office, give name and number of Account.

Name ▼   **Account Number** ▼

CORRESPONDENCE Give name and address to which correspondence about this application should be sent. Name/Address/Apt/City/State/ZIP ▼

Be sure to
give your
daytime phone
▼ number

Area Code and Telephone Number ▶

8

CERTIFICATION* I, the undersigned, hereby certify that I am the

Check only one ▼

☐ author
☐ other copyright claimant
☐ owner of exclusive right(s)
☐ authorized agent of _____

Name of author or other copyright claimant, or owner of exclusive right(s) ▲

of the work identified in this application and that the statements made
by me in this application are correct to the best of my knowledge.

Typed or printed name and date ▼ If this application gives a date of publication in space 3, do not sign and submit it before that date.

_____ date ▶

☞ Handwritten signature (X) ▼

_____

MAIL CERTIFI-CATE TO

Name ▼

Number/Street/Apartment Number ▼

Certificate will be mailed in window envelope

City/State/ZIP ▼

9

YOU MUST:
• Complete all necessary spaces
• Sign your application in space 8

SEND ALL 3 ELEMENTS
IN THE SAME PACKAGE:
1. Application form
2. Nonrefundable $20 filing fee
   in check or money order
   payable to *Register of Copyrights*
3. Deposit material

MAIL TO:
Register of Copyrights
Library of Congress
Washington, D.C. 20559-6000

The Copyright Office has the authority to adjust fees at 5-year intervals, based on changes in the Consumer Price Index. The next adjustment is due in 1996. Please contact the Copyright Office after July 1995 to determine the actual fee schedule.

*17 U.S.C. § 506(e): Any person who knowingly makes a false representation of a material fact in the application for copyright registration provided for by section 409, or in any written statement filed in connection with the application, shall be fined not more than $2,500.

July 1993—300,000   ♻ PRINTED ON RECYCLED PAPER   ☆U.S. GOVERNMENT PRINTING OFFICE: 1993-342-582/80,017

Appendix B

**THE SONGWRITERS
GUILD OF AMERICA**

NOTE TO SONGWRITERS: (A) DO NOT SIGN THIS CONTRACT IF IT HAS ANY CHANGES UNLESS YOU HAVE FIRST DISCUSSED SUCH CHANGES WITH THE GUILD; (B) FOR YOUR PROTECTION PLEASE SEND A FULLY EXECUTED COPY OF THIS CONTRACT TO THE GUILD.

POPULAR SONGWRITERS CONTRACT
© Copyright 1978 AGAC

AGREEMENT made this   day of   , 19   , between
. . . .
(hereinafter called "Publisher") and
. . . .
. . . .
(Jointly and/or severally hereinafter collectively called "Writer");

WITNESSETH:

Composition
**(Insert title of
composition
here)**

1. The Writer hereby assigns, transfers and delivers to the Publisher a certain heretofore unpublished original musical composition, written and/or composed by the above-named Writer now entitled. . . . .
. . . .
(hereinafter referred to as "the composition"), including the title, words and music thereof, and the right to secure copyright therein throughout the entire world, and to have and to hold the said copyright and all

**(Insert
number of
years here)**

rights of whatsoever nature thereunder existing, for . . . .
_{not more than 40}

years from the date of this contract or 35 years from the date of the first release of a commercial sound recording of the composition, whichever term ends earlier, unless this contract is sooner terminated in accordance with the provisions hereof.

Performing
Rights
Affiliation

(Delete Two)

2. In all respects this contract shall be subject to any existing agreements between the parties hereto and the following small performing rights licensing organization with which Writer and Publisher are affiliated:

(ASCAP, BMI, SESAC). Nothing contained herein shall, or shall be deemed to, alter, vary or modify the rights of Writer and Publisher to share in, receive and retain the proceeds distributed to them by such small performing rights licensing organization pursuant to their respective agreement with it.

Warranty

3. The Writer hereby warrants that the composition is his sole, exclusive and original work, that he has full right and power to make this contract, and that there exists no adverse claim to or in the composition, except as aforesaid in Paragraph 2 hereof and except such rights as are specifically set forth in Paragraph 23 hereof.

Royalties

**(Insert
amount of
advance here)**

4. In consideration of this contract, the Publisher agrees to pay the Writer as follows:

(a) $. . . . . .as an advance against royalties, receipt of which is hereby acknowledged, which sum shall remain the property of the Writer and shall be deductible only from payments hereafter becoming due the Writer under this contract.

Piano Copies
Sliding Scale

**(Insert
percentage
here)**

(b) In respect of regular piano copies sold and paid for in the United States and Canada, the following royalties per copy:

. . . . % (in no case, however, less than 10%) of the wholesale selling price of the first 200,000 copies or less; plus

. . . . % (in no case, however, less than 12%) of the wholesale selling price of copies in excess of 200,000 and not exceeding 500,000; plus

. . . . % (in no case, however, less than 15%) of the wholesale selling price of copies in excess of 500,000.

Foreign
Royalties
**(Insert
percentage
here)**

(c) . . . . % (in no case, however, less than 50%) of all net sums received by the Publisher in respect of regular piano copies, orchestrations, band arrangements, octavos, quartets, arrangements for combinations of voices and/or instruments, and/or other copies of the composition sold in any country other than the United States and Canada, provided, however, that if the Publisher should sell such copies through, or cause them to be sold by, a subsidiary or affiliate which is actually doing business in a foreign country, then in respect of such sales, the Publisher shall pay to the Writer not less than 5% of the marked retail selling price in respect of each such copy sold and paid for.

Orchestrations
and Other
Arrangements,
etc.

**(Insert
percentage
here)**

(d) In respect of each copy sold and paid for in the United States and Canada, or for export from the United States, of orchestrations, band arrangements, octavos, quartets, arrangements for combinations of voices and/or instruments, and/or other copies of the composition (other than regular piano copies) the following royalties on the wholesale selling price (after trade discounts, if any):

. . . . % (in no case, however, less than 10%) on the first 200,000 copies or less; plus

. . . . % (in no case, however, less than 12%) on all copies in excess of 200,000 and not exceeding 500,000; plus
. . . . % (in no case, however, less than 15%) on all copies in excess of 500,000.

Publisher's Song Book Folio, etc.

(e) (i) If the composition, or any part thereof, is included in any song book, folio or similar publication issued by the Publisher containing at least four, but not more than twenty-five musical compositions, the royalty to be paid by the Publisher to the Writer shall be an amount determined by dividing 10% of the wholesale selling price (after trade discounts, if any) of the copies sold, among the total number of the Publisher's copyrighted musical compositions included in such publication. If such publication contains more than twenty-five musical compositions, the said 10% shall be increased by an additional $^{1}/_{2}$% for each additional musical composition.

Licensee's Song Book, Folio, etc.

(ii) If, pursuant to a license granted by the Publisher to a licensee not controlled by or affiliated with it, the composition, or any part thereof, is included in any song book, folio or similar publication, containing at least four musical compositions, the royalty to be paid by the Publisher to the Writer shall be that proportion of 50% of the gross amount received by it from the licensee, as the number of uses of the composition under the license and during the license period, bears to the total number of uses of the Publisher's copyrighted musical compositions under the license and during the license period.

(iii) In computing the number of the Publisher's copyrighted musical compositions under subdivisions (i) and (ii) hereof, there shall be excluded musical compositions in the public domain and arrangements thereof and those with respect to which the Publisher does not currently publish and offer for sale regular piano copies.

(iv) Royalties on publications containing less than four musical compositions shall be payable at regular piano copy rates.

Professional Material and Free Copies

(f) As to "professional material" not sold or resold, no royalty shall be payable. Free copies of the lyrics of the composition shall not be distributed except under the following conditions: (i) with the Writer's written consent; or (ii) when printed without music in limited numbers for charitable, religious or governmental purposes, or for similar public purposes, if no profit is derived, directly or indirectly; or (iii) when authorized for printing in a book, magazine or periodical, where such use is incidental to a novel or story (as distinguished from use in a book of lyrics or a lyric magazine or folio), provided that any such use shall bear the Writer's name and the proper copyright notice; or (iv) when distributed solely for the purpose of exploiting the composition, provided, that such exploitation is restricted to the distribution of limited numbers of such copies for the purpose of influencing the sale of the composition, that the distribution is independent of the sale of any other musical compositions, services, goods, wares or merchandise, and that no profit is made, directly or indirectly, in connection therewith.

Mechanicals. Electrical Transcription, Synchronization, All Other Rights

(g) . . . . % (in no case, however, less than 50%) of:

All gross receipts of the Publisher in respect of any licenses (including statutory royalties) authorizing the manufacture of parts of instruments serving to mechanically reproduce the composition, or to use the composition in synchronization with sound motion pictures, or to reproduce it upon electrical

(Insert
percentage
here)

transcription for broadcasting purposes; and of any and all gross receipts of the Publisher from any other source or right now known or which may here after come into existence, except as provided in paragraph 2.

Licensing (h)
Agent's
Charges

If the Publisher administers licenses authorizing the manufacture of parts of instruments serving to mechanically reproduce said composition, or the use of said composition in synchronization or in timed relation with sound motion pictures or its reproduction upon electrical transcriptions, or any of them, through an agent, trustee or other administrator acting for a substantial part of the industry and not under the exclusive control of the Publisher (hereinafter sometimes referred to as licensing agent), the Publisher, in determining his receipts, shall be entitled to deduct from gross license fees paid by the Licensees, a sum equal to the charges paid by the Publisher to said licensing agent, provided, however, that in respect to synchronization or timed relation with sound motion pictures, said deduction shall in no event exceed $150.00 or 10% of said gross license fee, whichever is less; in connection with the manufacture of parts of instruments serving to mechanically reproduce said composition, said deductions shall not exceed 5% of said gross license fee; and in connection with electrical transcriptions, said deduction shall not exceed 10% of said gross license fee.

Block Licenses (i)

The Publisher agrees that the use of the composition will not be included in any bulk or block license heretofore or hereafter granted, and that it will not grant any bulk or block license to include the same, without the written consent of the Writer in each instance, except (i) that the Publisher may grant such licenses with respect to electrical transcription for broadcasting purposes, but in such event, the Publisher shall pay to the Writer that proportion of 50% of the gross amount received by it under each such license as the number of uses of the composition under each such license during each such license period bears to the total number of uses of the Publisher's copyrighted musical compositions under each such license during each such license period; in computing the number of the Publisher's copyrighted musical compositions for this purpose, there shall be excluded musical compositions in the public domain and arrangements thereof and those with respect to which the Publisher does not currently publish and offer for sale regular piano copies; (ii) that the Publisher may appoint agents or representatives in countries outside of the United States and Canada to use and to grant licenses for the use of the composition on the customary royalty fee basis under which the Publisher shall receive not less than 10% of the marked retail selling price in respect of regular piano copies, and 50% of all other revenue; if, in connection with any such bulk or block license, the Publisher shall have received any advance, the Writer shall not be entitled to share therein, but no part of said advance shall be deducted in computing the composition's earnings under said bulk or block license. A bulk or block license shall be deemed to mean any license or agreement, domestic or foreign, whereby rights are granted in respect of two or more musical compositions.

Television and (j) New Uses	Except to the extent that the Publisher and Writer have heretofore or may hereafter assign to or vest in the small performing rights licensing organization with which Writer and Publisher are affiliated, the said rights or the right to grant licenses therefor, it is agreed that no licenses shall be granted without the written consent, in each instance, of the Writer for the use of the composition by means of television, or by any means, or for any purposes not commercially established, or for which licenses were not granted by the Publisher on musical compositions prior to June 1, 1937.
Writer's (k) Consent to Licenses	The Publisher shall not, without the written consent of the Writer in each case, give or grant any right or license (i) to use the title of the composition, or (ii) for the exclusive use of the composition in any form or for any purpose, or for any period of time, or for any territory, other than its customary arrangements with foreign publishers, or (iii) to give a dramatic representation of the composition or to dramatize the plot or story thereof, or (iv) for a vocal rendition of the composition in synchronization with sound motion pictures, or (v) for any synchronization use thereof, or (vi) for the use of the composition or a quotation or excerpt therefrom in any article, book, periodical, advertisement or other similar publication. If, however, the Publisher shall give to the Writer written notice by certified mail, return receipt requested, or telegram, specifying the right or license to be given or granted, the name of the licensee and the terms and conditions thereof, including the price or other compensation to be received therefor, then, unless the Writer (or any one or more of them) shall, within five business days after the delivery of such notice to the address of the Writer hereinafter designated, object thereto, the Publisher may grant such right or license in accordance with the said notice without first obtaining the consent of the Writer. Such notice shall be deemed sufficient if sent to the Writer at the address or addresses hereinafter designated or at the address or addresses last furnished to the Publisher in writing by the Writer.
Trust for (l) Writer	Any portion of the receipts which may become due to the Writer from license fees (in excess of offsets), whether received directly from the licensee or from any licensing agent of the Publisher, shall, if not paid immediately on the receipt thereof by the Publisher, belong to the Writer and shall be held in trust for the Writer until payment is made; the ownership of said trust fund by the Writer shall not be questioned whether the monies are physically segregated or not.
Writer (m) Participation	The Publisher agrees that it will not issue any license as a result of which it will receive any financial benefit in which the Writer does not participate.
Writer Credit (n)	On all regular piano copies, orchestrations, band or other arrangements, octavos, quartets, commercial sound recordings and other reproductions of the composition or parts thereof, in whatever form and however produced, Publisher shall include or cause to be included, in addition to the copyright notice, the name of the Writer, and Publisher shall include a similar requirement in every license or authorization issued by it with respect to the composition.

Writers'
Respective
Shares

5. Whenever the term "Writer" is used herein, it shall be deemed to mean all of the persons herein defined as "Writer" and any and all royalties herein provided to be paid to the Writer shall be paid equally to such persons if there be more than one, unless otherwise provided in Paragraph 23.

Release of
Commercial
Sound
Recording
(Insert period
not exceeding
12 months)

6. (a) (i) The Publisher shall, within. . . . . months from the date of this contract (the "initial period"), cause a commercial sound recording of the composition to be made and released in the customary form and through the customary commercial channels. If at the end of such initial period a sound recording has not been made and released, as above provided, then, subject to the provisions of the next succeeding subdivision, this contract shall terminate.

(Insert amount
to be not less
than $250)

(Insert period
not exceeding
six months)

(ii) If, prior to the expiration of the initial period, Publisher pays the Writer the sum of $ . . . . (which shall not be charged against or recoupable out of any advances, royalties or other monies theretofor paid, then due, or which thereafter may become due the Writer from the Publisher pursuant to this contract or otherwise), Publisher shall have an additional . . . . months (the "additional period") commencing with the end of the initial period, within which to cause such commercial sound recording to be made and released as provided in subdivision (i) above. If at the end of the additional period a commercial sound recording has not been made and released, as above provided, then this contract shall terminate.

(iii) Upon termination pursuant to this Paragraph 6(a), all rights of any and every nature in and to the composition and in and to any and all copyrights secured thereon in the United States and throughout the world shall automatically re-vest in and become the property of the Writer and shall be reassigned to him by the Publisher. The Writer shall not be obligated to return or pay to the Publisher any advance or indebtedness as a condition of such re-assignment; the said re-assignment shall be in accordance with and subject to the provisions of Paragraph 8 hereof, and, in addition, the Publisher shall pay to the Writer all gross sums which it has theretofore or may thereafter receive in respect of the composition.

Writer's
Copies

(b) The Publisher shall furnish, or cause to be furnished, to the Writer six copies of the commercial sound recording referred to in Paragraph 6(a).

Piano Copies,
Piano
Arrangement
Arrangement
or Lead Sheet
(Select (i)
or (ii))

(c) The Publisher shall

☐ (i) within 30 days after the initial release of a commercial sound recording of the composition, make, publish and offer for sale regular piano copies of the composition in the form and through the channels customarily employed by it for that purpose;

☐ (ii) within 30 days after execution of this contract make a piano arrangement or lead sheet of the composition and furnish six copies thereof to the Writer.

In the event neither subdivision (i) nor (ii) of this subparagraph (c) is selected, the provisions of subdivision (ii) shall be automatically deemed to have been selected by the parties.

Foreign
Copyright

7. (a) Each copyright on the composition in countries other than the United States shall be secured only in the name of the Publisher, and the Publisher shall not at any time divest itself of said foreign copyright directly or indirectly.

Foreign
Publication   (b) No rights shall be granted by the Publisher in the composition to any foreign publisher or licensee inconsistent with the terms hereof, nor shall any foreign publication rights in the composition be given to a foreign publisher or licensee unless and until the Publisher shall have complied with the provisions of Paragraph 6 hereof.

Foreign
Advance   (c) If foreign rights in the composition are separately conveyed, otherwise than as a part of the Publisher's current and/or future catalog, not less than 50% of any advance received in respect thereof shall be credited to the account of and paid to the Writer.

Foreign
Percentage   (d) The percentage of the Writer on monies received from foreign sources shall be computed on the Publisher's net receipts, provided, however, that no deductions shall be made for offsets of monies due from the Publisher to said foreign sources; or for advances made by such foreign sources to the Publisher, unless the Writer shall have received at least 50% of said advances.

No Foreign
Allocations   (e) In computing the receipts of the Publisher from licenses granted in respect of synchronization with sound motion pictures, or in respect of any world-wide licenses, or in respect of licenses granted by the Publisher for use of the composition in countries other than the United States, no amount shall be deducted for payments or allocations to publishers or licensees in such countries.

Termination
or Expiration
of Contract   8. Upon the termination or expiration of this contract, all rights of any and every nature in and to the composition and in and to any and all copyrights secured thereon in the United States and throughout the world, shall re-vest in and become the property of the Writer, and shall be re-assigned to the Writer by the Publisher free of any and all encumbrances of any nature whatsoever, provided that:

(a) If the Publisher, prior to such termination or expiration, shall have granted a domestic license for the use of the composition, not inconsistent with the terms and provisions of this contract, the re-assignment may be subject to the terms of such license.

(b) Publisher shall assign to the Writer all rights which it may have under any such agreement or license referred to in subdivision (a) in respect of the composition, including, but not limited to, the right to receive all royalties or other monies earned by the composition thereunder after the date of termination or expiration of this contract. Should the Publisher thereafter receive or be credited with any royalties or other monies so earned, it shall pay the same to the Writer.

(c) The Writer shall not be obligated to return or pay to the Publisher any advance or indebtedness as a condition of the re-assignment provided for in this Paragraph 8, and shall be entitled to receive the plates and copies of the composition in the possession of the Publisher.

(d) Publisher shall pay any and all royalties which may have accrued to the Writer prior to such termination or expiration.

(e) The Publisher shall execute any and all documents and do any and all acts or things necessary to effect any and all re-assignments to the Writer herein provided for.

Negotiations
for New or
Unspecified
Uses   9. If the Publisher desires to exercise a right in and to the composition now known or which may hereafter become known, but for which no specific provision has been made herein, the Publisher shall give written notice to the Writer thereof. Negotiations respecting all the terms

and conditions of any such disposition shall thereupon be entered into between the Publisher and the Writer and no such right shall be exercised until specific agreement has been made.

Royalty
Statements
and Payments

10. The Publisher shall render to the Writer, hereafter, royalty statements accompanied by remittance of the amount due at the times such statements and remittances are customarily rendered by the Publisher, provided, however, that such statements and remittances shall be rendered either semi-annually or quarterly and not more than forty-five days after the end of each such semi-annual or quarterly period, as the case may be. The Writer may at any time, or from time to time, make written request for a detailed royalty statement, and the Publisher shall, within sixty days, comply therewith. Such royalty statements shall set forth in detail the various items, foreign and domestic, for which royalties are payable thereunder and the amounts thereof, including, but not limited to, the number of copies sold and the number of uses made in each royalty category. If a use is made in a publication of the character provided in Paragraph 4, subdivision (e) hereof, there shall be included in said royalty statement the title of said publication, the publisher or issuer thereof, the date of and number of uses, the gross license fee received in connection with each publication, the share thereto of all the writers under contract with the Publisher, and the Writer's share thereof. There shall likewise be included in said statement a description of every other use of the composition, and if by a licensee or licensees their name or names, and if said use is upon a part of an instrument serving to reproduce the composition mechanically, the type of mechanical reproduction, the title of the label thereon, the name or names of the artists performing the same, together with the gross license fees received, and the Writer's share thereof.

Examination
of Books

11. (a) The Publisher shall from time to time, upon written demand of the Writer or his representative, permit the Writer or his representative to inspect at the place of business of the Publisher, all books, records and documents relating to the composition and all licenses granted, uses had and payments made therefor, such right of inspection to include, but not by way of limitation, the right to examine all original accountings and records relating to uses and payments by manufacturers of commercial sound recordings and music rolls; and the Writer or his representative may appoint an accountant who shall at any time during usual business hours have access to all records of the Publisher relating to the composition for the purpose of verifying royalty statements rendered or which are delinquent under the terms hereof.

(b) The Publisher shall, upon written demand of the Writer or his representative, cause any licensing agent in the United States and Canada to furnish to the Writer or his representative, statements showing in detail all licenses granted, uses had and payments made in connection with the composition, which licenses or permits were granted, or payments were received, by or through said licensing agent, and to permit the Writer or his representative to inspect at the place of business of such licensing agent, all books, records and documents of such licensing agent, relating thereto. Any and all agreements made by the Publisher with any such licensing agent shall provide that any such licensing agent will comply with the terms and provisions hereof. In the event that the Publisher shall instruct such licensing agent to furnish to the Writer or his representative statements as provided for herein, and to permit the inspection of the books, records and documents as herein provided, then if such licensing agent should refuse to comply with the said instructions, or any of them, the Publisher agrees to institute and prosecute diligently and in good faith such action or proceedings as may be necessary to compel compliance with the said instructions.

(c) With respect to foreign licensing agents, the Publisher shall make available the books or records of said licensing agents in countries outside of the United States and Canada to the extent such books or records are available to the Publisher, except that the Publisher may in lieu thereof make available any accountants' reports and audits which the Publisher is able to obtain.

(d) If as a result of any examination of books, records or documents pursuant to Paragraphs 11(a), 11(b) or 11(c) hereof, it is determined that, with respect to any royalty statement rendered by or on behalf of the Publisher to the Writer, the Writer is owed a sum equal to or greater than five percent of the sum shown on that royalty statement as being due to the Writer, then the Publisher shall pay to the Writer the entire cost of such examination, not to exceed 50% of the amount shown to be due the Writer.

(e)   (i) In the event the Publisher administers its own licenses for the manufacture of parts of instruments serving to mechanically reproduce the composition rather than employing a licensing agent for that purpose, the Publisher shall include in each license agreement a provision permitting the Publisher, the Writer or their respective representatives to inspect, at the place of business of such licensee, all books, records and documents of such licensee relating to such license. Within 30 days after written demand by the Writer, the Publisher shall commence to inspect such licensee's books, records and documents and shall furnish a written report of such inspection to the Writer within 90 days following such demand. If the Publisher fails, after written demand by the Writer, to so inspect the licensee's books, records and documents, or fails to furnish such report, the Writer or his representative may inspect such licensee's books, records and documents at his own expense.

(ii) In the further event that the Publisher and the licensee referred to in subdivision (i) above are subsidiaries or affiliates of the same entity or one is a subsidiary or affiliate of the other, then, unless the Publisher employs a licensing agent to administer the licenses referred to in subdivision (i) above, the Writer shall have the right to make the inspection referred to in subdivision (i) above without the necessity of making written demand on the Publisher as provided in subdivision (i) above.

(iii) If as a result of any inspection by the Writer pursuant to subdivisions (i) and (ii) of this subparagraph (e) the Writer recovers additional monies from the licensee, the Publisher and the Writer shall share equally in the cost of such inspection.

Default in Payment or Prevention of Examination

12. If the Publisher shall fail or refuse, within sixty days after written demand, to furnish or cause to be furnished, such statements, books, records or documents, or to permit inspection thereof, as provided for in Paragraphs 10 and 11 hereof, or within thirty days after written demand, to make the payment of any royalties due under this contract, then the Writer shall be entitled, upon ten days' written notice, to terminate this contract. However if the Publisher shall:

(a) Within the said ten-day period serve upon the Writer a written notice demanding arbitration; and

(b) Submit to arbitration its claim that it has complied with its obligation to furnish statements, books, records or documents, or permitted inspection thereof or to pay royalties, as the case may be, or both, and thereafter comply with any award of the arbitrator within ten days after such award or within such time as the arbitrator may specify;

then this contract shall continue in full force and effect as if the Writer had not sent such notice of termination. If the Publisher shall fail to comply with the foregoing provisions, then this contract shall be deemed to have been terminated as of the date of the Writer's written notice of termination.

Derivative Works
13. No derivative work prepared under authority of Publisher during the term of this contract may be utilized by Publisher or any other party after termination or expiration of this contract.

Notices
14. All written demands and notices provided for herein shall be sent by certified mail, return receipt requested.

Suits for Infringement
15. Any legal action brought by the Publisher against any alleged infringer of the composition shall be initiated and prosecuted at its sole cost and expense, but if the Publisher should fail, within thirty days after written demand, to institute such action, the Writer shall be entitled to institute such suit at his cost and expense. All sums recovered as a result of any such action shall, after the deduction of the reasonable expense thereof, be divided equally between the Publisher and the Writer. No settlement of any such action may be made by either party without first notifying the other; in the event that either party should object to such settlement, then such settlement shall not be made if the party objecting assumes the prosecution of the action and all expenses thereof, except that any sums thereafter recovered shall be divided equally between the Publisher and the Writer after the deduction of the reasonable expenses thereof.

Infringement Claims
16.(a) If a claim is presented against the Publisher alleging that the composition is an infringement upon some other work or a violation of any other right of another, and because therof the Publisher is jeopardized, it shall forthwith serve a written notice upon the Writer setting forth the full details of such claim. The pendency of said claim shall not relieve the Publisher of the obligation to make payment of the royalties to the Writer hereunder, unless the Publisher shall deposit said royalties as and when they would otherwise be payable, in an account in the joint names of the Publisher and the Writer in a bank or trust company in New York, New York, if the Writer on the date of execution of this contract resides East of the Mississippi River, or in Los Angeles, California, if the Writer on the date of execution of this contract resides West of the Mississippi River. If no suit be filed within nine months after said written notice from the Publisher to the Writer, all monies deposited in said joint account shall be paid over to the Writer plus any interest which may have been earned thereon.

(b) Should an action be instituted against the Publisher claiming that the composition is an infringement upon some other work or a violation of any other right of another, the Publisher shall forthwith serve written notice upon the Writer containing the full details of such claim. Notwithstanding the commencement of such action, the Publisher shall continue to pay the royalties hereunder to the Writer unless it shall, from and after the date of the service of the summons, deposit said royalties as and when they would otherwise be payable, in an account in the joint names of the Publisher and the Writer in a bank or trust company in New York, New York, if the Writer on the date of execution of this contract resides East of the Mississippi River, or in Los Angeles, California, if the Writer on the date of execution of this contract resides West of the Mississippi River. If the said suit shall be finally adjudicated in favor of the Publisher or shall be settled, there shall be released and paid to the Writer all of such sums held in escrow less any amount paid out of the Writer's share with the Writer's written consent in settlement of said action. Should the said suit finally result adversely to the Publisher, the said amount on deposit shall be released to the Publisher to the extent of any expense or damage it incurs and the balance shall be paid over to the Writer.

(c) In any of the foregoing events, however, the Writer shall be entitled to payment of said royalties or the money so deposited at and after such time as he files with the Publisher a surety company bond, or a bond in other form acceptable to the Publisher, in the sum of such payments to secure the return thereof to the extent that the Publisher may be entitled to such return. The foregoing payments or deposits or the filing of a bond shall be without prejudice to the rights of the Publisher or Writer in the premises.

Arbitration   17. Any and all differences, disputes or controversies arising out of or in connection with this contract shall be submitted to arbitration before a sole arbitrator under the then prevailing rules of the American Arbitration Association. The location of the arbitration shall be New York, New York, if the Writer on the date of execution of this contract resides East of the Mississippi River, or Los Angeles, California, if the Writer on the date of execution of this contract resides West of the Mississippi River. The parties hereby individually and jointly agree to abide by and perform any award rendered in such arbitration. Judgment upon any such award rendered may be entered in any court having jurisdiction thereof.

Assignment   18. Except to the extent herein otherwise expressly provided, the Publisher shall not sell, transfer, assign, convey, encumber or otherwise dispose of the composition or the copyright or copyrights secured thereon without the prior written consent of the Writer. The Writer has been induced to enter into this contract in reliance upon the value to him of the personal service and ability of the Publisher in the exploitation of the composition, and by reason thereof it is the intention of the parties and the essence of the relationship between them that the rights herein granted to the Publisher shall remain with the Publisher and that the same shall not pass to any other person, including, without limitations, successors to or receivers or trustees of the property of the Publisher, either by act or deed of the Publisher or by operation of law, and in the event of the voluntary or involuntary bankruptcy of the Publisher, this contract shall terminate, provided, however, that the composition may be included by the Publisher in a bona fide voluntary sale of its music business or its entire catalog of musical compositions, or in a merger or consolidation of the Publisher with another corporation, in which event the Publisher shall immediately give written notice thereof to the Writer; and provided further that the composition and the copyright therein may be assigned by the Publisher to a subsidiary or affiliated company generally engaged in the music publishing business. If the Publisher is an individual, the composition may pass to a legatee or distributee as part of the inheritance of the Publisher's music business and entire catalog of musical compositions. Any such transfer or assignment shall, however, be conditioned upon the execution and delivery by the transferee or assignee to the Writer of an agreement to be bound by and to perform all of the terms and conditions of this contract to be performed on the part of the Publisher.

Subsidiary Defined 19. A subsidiary, affiliate, or any person, firm or corporation controlled by the Publisher or by such subsidiary or affiliate, as used in this contract, shall be deemed to include any person, firm or corporation, under common control with, or the majority of whose stock or capital contribution is owned or controlled by the Publisher or by any of its officers, directors, partners or associates, or whose policies and actions are subject to domination or control by the Publisher or any of its officers, directors, partners or associates.

Amounts 20. The amounts and percentages specified in this contract shall be deemed to be the amounts and percentages agreed upon by the parties hereto, unless other amounts or percentages are inserted in the blank spaces provided therefor.

Modifications 21. This contract is binding upon and shall enure to the benefit of the parties hereto and their respective successors in interest (as hereinbefore limited). If the Writer (or one or more of them) shall not be living, any notices may be given to, or consents given by, his or their successors in interest. No change or modification of this contract shall be effective unless reduced to writing and signed by the parties hereto.

The words in this contract shall be so construed that the singular shall include the plural and the plural shall include the singular where the context so requires and the masculine shall include the feminine and the feminine shall include the masculine where the context so requires.

Paragraph Headings 22. The paragraph headings are inserted only as a matter of convenience and for reference, and in no way define, limit or describe the scope or intent of this contract nor in any way affect this contract.

Special Provisions 23.

Witness:	Publisher ....
....	By ....
Witness:	Address ....
....	Writer ....(L.S.)
Witness:	Address ....
....	Soc. Sec. # ....
Witness:	Writer ....(L.S.)
....	Address ....
	Soc. Sec. # ....
	Writer ....(L.S.)
	Address ....
	Soc. Sec. # ....

FOR YOUR PROTECTION,
SEND A COPY OF THE FULLY
SIGNED CONTRACT TO THE GUILD.
★★★★

Special Exceptions to apply only if filled in and initialed by the parties.

☐   The composition is part of an original score (not an interpolation) of

☐   Living Stage Production   ☐   Motion Picture   ☐   Night Club Revue
☐   Televised Musical Production

which is the subject of an agreement between the parties dated   , a copy
of which is hereto annexed. Unless said agreement requires compliance with Paragraph
6 in respect of a greater number of musical compositions, the Publisher shall be deemed
to have complied with said Paragraph 6 with respect to the composition if it fully performs the terms of said Paragraph 6 in respect of any one musical composition included
in said score.

Appendix C

NOTICE
TO MY HEIRS AND EXECUTORS

If the procedures specified in Sections 203 and 304(c) of the U.S. Copyright Act of 1976 are followed and certain requirements are met, the ownership of the copyright in the song described below may be regained, by me or by my spouse, children, or grandchildren, even though I previously assigned all or some part of my copyright to a music publisher, as described below.

If the date of transfer listed below is before January 1, 1978, it is possible that the transfer may be terminated 56 years after copyright protection was secured.

If the date of transfer listed below is after January 1, 1978, it is possible that the transfer may be terminated between 35 and 40 years after it was made.

The copyright described below may be very valuable. If the termination of the transfer of this copyright is not carried out correctly, the right to regain ownership of the copyright may be lost. This notice and any attachments should be taken to a copyright lawyer not more than ten years and not less than three years (a) before the 56th anniversary of a transfer made prior to January 1, 1978 or (b) before the 35th anniversary of a transfer made after January 1, 1978.

Title of Song:

_____

_____

Songwriter(s) (indicate percentage share of authorship for each writer):

_____

_____

_____

_____

_____

Date Transfer of Copyright by Me: _____

Percentage of Entire Copyright Transferred by Me: _____

Copyright Transferred To (indicate name of publisher, most current address and phone number available, and performing rights society affiliation, i.e., BMI, ASCAP, or SESAC):

_____

_____

_____

_____

_____

_____

_____

_____

_____

_____

_____

_____

_____

_____

_____

Appendix D:
Trademark Cease and Desist Letter

ROMANO AND TORTELLINI, ATTORNEYS
205 Waterman Street
Belmont, California 62245

November 17, 1994

Via Certified Mail, Return Receipt Requested

Mr. Edouardo Sanchez
Senior Vice President, Business Affairs
Mega Records, Inc.
1000 Wilshire Boulevard
Los Angeles, CA 52242

Mr. Sanchez:

I am writing on behalf of my clients, the band DANCEARAMA of Vancouver, British Columbia, Canada, and in regard to your new act, a Los Angeles group of the same name.

The Canadian band DANCEARAMA has been performing under that name in Canada since December of 1991 (and is the owner of a

Letter to Mr. Sanchez
November 17, 1994
Page Two

Canadian trademark registration for the name) and in the United States since at least as early as August of 1992. In addition, their trademark DANCEARAMA has become well-known in the U.S. through sales of their recordings and promotional clothing made in conjunction with their tours here in 1992 and early 1994, fan magazine advertising, various fan promotions and giveaways, touring directory listings, and articles in numerous publications such as *Kerrang!*, *Rock Hits*, and *Metal Edge*. They recently signed a recording agreement with a small Vancouver label. My clients plan to continue to market their services, records, and merchandise in the United States; their new record will be placed in U.S. record stores through a U.S. distributor and promoted widely to U.S. radio stations.

The facts that both bands consist of four members, perform roughly the same sort of music, and appeal to the same segment of the record-buying public, when coupled with the circumstance that the names of the two bands are verbally identical, guarantee that consumer confusion will result. Indeed, such confusion has *already* occurred. I enclose a photocopy of a short piece from the last issue of the London-based magazine *Kerrang!* in which a picture of my clients is erroneously used to illustrate a short article concerning the signing of the Los Angeles band to a recording agreement with your company. Further, letters received from fans indicate that fans are confusing the two bands because of their identical names. Industry professionals are also confused; one Italian distributor wrote my clients to congratulate them on "their" Mega Records signing.

According to statements made by members of the Los Angeles band in various published interviews, that band was formed only eight months ago. As you know, in the United States trademark rights accrue by use. This means, of course, that the Los Angeles band's use of the DANCERAMA name in the United States is an infringement of my clients' rights under U.S. law. Performance by the Los Angeles band under that name in Canada or any Canadian release of any record by that band using the DANCERAMA name

Letter to Mr. Sanchez
November 17, 1994
Page Three

would constitute an infringement of my clients' *Canadian* trademark rights.

My clients' management has had several discussions with various people associated with the Los Angeles band, including an attorney representing that band and someone from your A&R department. It is my clients' perception that these people are refusing to acknowledge that a conflict exists and are simply hoping that the problem will disappear. I assure you that this is not likely.

My clients intend to do whatever is necessary to protect their rights in their name, including bringing trademark infringement lawsuits in both the United States *and* Canada, if necessary. I hope you will see the necessity for the Los Angeles band's abandonment of the DANCEARAMA name and any claims to the right to use it and will advise your band accordingly. If the Los Angeles group will agree to adopt another name immediately and to desist from any further use of the DANCEARAMA name, I am authorized to state that my clients will forego requiring payment of any settlement amount in compensation for the damage your band's use of the name has caused them. Of course, any such settlement would have to be documented in an appropriate agreement, the other terms of which, such as the disposition of your band's tee shirts, cassette tapes, etc. which bear the DANCEARAMA name, would have to be negotiated.

Every day that the present situation persists further damages my clients' rights. Because your company has not yet released an album for the Los Angeles band, it would seem that the best time for that group to adopt another name is *now*, before albums are released under the DANCEARAMA name, complicating the existing situation and increasing the risk of harm to your company and your band. Please respond to me within ten business days of your receipt of this letter to let me know whether your band will agree to cease use of the DANCEARAMA name and enter a settlement agreement with my clients. Pending your response, I will not make any recommen-

228 MAKING IT IN THE MUSIC BUSINESS

Letter to Mr. Sanchez
November 17, 1994
Page Four

dations to my clients regarding the course they should take in this matter.

This letter is written for purposes of settlement only; all rights and remedies of my clients are specifically reserved.

Sincerely,

ROMANO AND TORTELLINI, ATTORNEYS

Sigrid Romano

SIGRID ROMANO

SR/dcr

Enclosures

Appendix E:
Trademark Search Opinion Letter

ROMANO AND TORTELLINI, ATTORNEYS
205 Waterman Street
Belmont, California 62245

May 22, 1992

Aaron Bowers, Robert Wilson, Will St. Charles
P.O. Box 72890
Indianapolis, IN 46260

Gentlemen:

I am writing to report the results of the trademark search you recently had me commission for your proposed mark THE LAW OF NATURE and to give you my evaluation of that search and my opinion regarding the advisability of your adopting and using that proposed mark. Based on the results of the trademark search, I believe that THE LAW OF NATURE is available for use as the name of your band.

Trademark infringement usually occurs because someone adopts a trademark for a product or services which is very similar or identical

Letter to Mr. Bowers, Mr. Wilson, and Mr. St. Charles
Page Two
May 22, 1992

to an established mark used for the same or similar products or services. Similarity between marks is judged by the "sight, sound, and meaning" test; that is, is the new mark so similar to the established mark in the way it looks, the way it sounds when spoken, and in its meaning that consumers are likely to be confused if they encounter the new mark in connection with products or services that are very similar or identical to those the established mark names? This evaluation must be made for every mark that appears in the search report that is reasonably similar to your proposed mark.

There are several sections of the enclosed search report; each reports a particular sort of trademark record. The first section of the search report lists trademarks that are registered federally, that is, registered in the U.S. Patent and Trademark Office. The second section of the search report lists trademarks that are registered in the states. The third section of the search report is called the "common law" section and lists trademarks that are in use but unregistered. Since trademark rights accrue by *use* of a trademark rather than by either federal or state registration of the mark, the "common law" section of the search report, which compiles information taken from trade directories and publications, phone directories, etc., can be important.

Federal (U.S. Patent and Trademark Office) Records

Federal trademark registrants are usually the most vigilant group of trademark owners in terms of acting against infringers. This means that the section of the search report that reports federally-registered marks is especially important to our evaluation whether your proposed mark is available for use. The services that your proposed mark would name would be properly classified in International Class 41 (Education and Entertainment Services), which is also the class in which your proposed mark would be registered. (The corresponding U.S. classification number is 107.) This means that similar marks registered in that class and similar marks registered in other classes that name *related* goods or services are of special interest to us. Of the

Letter to Mr. Bowers, Mr. Wilson, and Mr. St. Charles
Page Three
May 22, 1992

marks listed in the federal registrations section of the search report,
the following marks are pertinent to our evaluation of the availability
of your proposed mark:

Mark	Class	Services or Goods	Registration/ Application Status
NATURALIS (the English translation of the word "Naturalis" is "The Law of Nature")	Int. Cl. 42	retail, wholesale and mail-order sales, services of products, jewelry, and apparel made from recycled materials	pending
THE LAW	Int. Cl. 41	entertainment services in the nature of a musical performing and recording group	pending
MARSHAL LAW	Int. Cl. 41	entertainment services in the nature of a musical group	published
ABOUT THE LAW	Int. Cl. 41	entertainment services in the nature of a television program series in the field of legal affairs	pending
L.A. LAW	Int. Cl. 41	entertainment services rendered through the medium of television— namely, a television dramatic series	registered
NATURA MUSIC	Int. Cl. 42	music composition for others	registered
THE LAW LOTTERY	Int. Cl. 41	entertainment services, namely gambling and casino services	abandoned
THE LAW AND YOU	Int. Cl. 41	entertainment services; namely, an educational television series dealing with legal matters	pending
MARTIAL LAW	Int. Cl. 41	band name	pending
M.C. LAW	Int. Cl. 41	a rap album for educational and entertainment purposes	pending

Letter to Mr. Bowers, Mr. Wilson, and Mr. St. Charles
Page Four
May 22, 1992

LOOKING AT THE LAW	Int. Cl. 41	entertainment services in the nature of a radio program	registered
2ND NATURE	Int. Cl. 41	entertainment group title (musical)	abandoned
SECOND NATURE	Int. Cl. 41	musical entertainment services rendered by a vocal and instrumental group	registered
BROTHER NATURE	Int. Cl. 41	entertainment services and other services; namely, live performances rendered by a musical group in all media	pending
THE ART OF NATURE	Int. Cl. 41	entertainment services in the nature of multi-media concerts	pending
NAUGHTY BY NATURE	Int. Cl. 41	entertainment services by a musical band; namely, live and recorded performances	pending
NAUGHTY BY NATURE	Int. Cl. 41	musical performing group	pending
NATURE	Int. Cl. 41	entertainment services in the nature of a weekly natural history television series	registered
THE MOST COUNTRY MUSIC ALLOWED BY LAW	Int. Cl. 38	radio broadcasting services	registered

State Trademark Records

The state registrations section of the search report lists these marks which are pertinent to our evaluation of your proposed mark:

Mark	Class	Services or Goods	Registration/ Application Status
LAW RECORDING	Int. Cl. 16 U.S. Cl. 38	record label	registered (NJ)

Letter to Mr. Bowers, Mr. Wilson, and Mr. St. Charles
Page Five
May 22, 1992

LAW	U. S. Cl. 107	band	registered (WI)
LAW LINE	U. S. Cl. 107	education and entertainment	renewed (OH)
COUNTRY MUSIC'S FIRST OUT-LAW	U. S. Cl. 107	education and entertainment	registered (TN)
THE LAW	Int. Cl. 41 U. S. Cl. 41	a dance band	registered (NM)
THE LAW AND YOU	U. S. Cl. 107	education and entertainment	registered (OK)
NATURE'S CHILDREN	U. S. Cl. 107	band	registered (WI)

Common Law Trademark Records

The "common law" section of the search report includes the following information on marks which are similar to your proposed mark:

Mark	Class	Services or Goods	Registration/ Application Status
LAW & ORDER	not stated	pop group	not stated
THE LAW	not stated	pop group	not stated
NATURAL BEAUTY	not stated	pop group	not stated
NATURE'S WAY	not stated	pop song	not stated

Letter to Mr. Bowers, Mr. Wilson, and Mr. St. Charles
Page Six
May 22, 1992

Evaluation

In my opinion, none of the marks reported is so similar to your proposed mark as to constitute a valid basis for challenging the use or registration of that mark for musical entertainment services rendered by a band. All the other reported marks that name bands or similar services are so dissimilar to THE LAW OF NATURE as to all but eliminate any possibility that their owners could raise any legitimate objection to your use of that mark. Further, all the reported marks that include the word LAW or the word NATURE or variations of those words name very different services, or are different enough verbally from your proposed mark to eliminate any likelihood of confusion between the marks, or both.

The enclosed trademark search report was prepared by a nationally-known trademark search service; I consider the information it contains to be reliable. However, it is a search only of United States records and does not contain information concerning marks valid in other countries. The information contained in a U.S.-only search report is inadequate to predict conflicts that may exist between your proposed mark and trademarks used and/or registered in other countries where you may, or may in future, offer products or services. The only way to eliminate such possible problems is to search the availability of a mark in all the countries where it is expected to be used. I would be happy to investigate and quote the costs of any such additional searches.

Further, there may be some mark in use somewhere in the United States which is not reported in this search that is similar enough to your proposed mark that the owners of that mark could object to your use of THE LAW OF NATURE. There is always at least some possibility that there is a conflicting mark in prior use that is not reported in a search report and it is difficult to eliminate this small chance of a conflict.

Letter to Mr. Bowers, Mr. Wilson, and Mr. St. Charles
Page Seven
May 22, 1992

Since the information in trademark search reports quickly becomes "stale," I recommend that, if you do decide to adopt and use your proposed mark, you do so reasonably quickly and that you commence the process of obtaining federal registration for that mark as soon as you decide to adopt it. If you have not yet begun to use your proposed mark outside your home state but want to notify the world that you intend to do so you should file an "intent-to-use" application; this sort of federal trademark registration application confers the benefit that the date of filing of the application eventually becomes the constructive date of first use of the mark, that is, the date your rights in the mark begin. If you have used your new name outside your home state you may file a "use" application.

My statement is enclosed. I'll call you next week to determine whether you wish to apply for federal trademark registration for THE LAW OF NATURE.

Sincerely,

ROMANO AND TORTELLINI, ATTORNEYS

Hubert Tortellini

HUBERT TORTELLINI

HT/dcr

Enclosures

Appendix F

Designer's Agreement and Assignment of Copyright

This Designer's Agreement and Assignment of Copyright (hereinafter called the "Agreement") is made as of the *FIRST, SIXTH, ETC.* day of *MONTH*, 199_ by and between *NAME OF DESIGNER* (hereinafter called "the Designer") and *NAMES OF BAND MEMBER(S)* doing business as *NAME OF BAND*, (hereinafter called "*NAME OF BAND*").

This Agreement is made with reference to the following facts:

A. That the Designer has prepared, at the instruction, from a concept, and under the direction of *NAME OF BAND*, a certain Design (hereinafter referred to as "the Design").

B. That the Design, a photocopy of which is attached hereto and is incorporated herein by this reference, may be described and identified as follows:

*DESCRIPTION OF DESIGN OR LOGO
CREATED BY THE DESIGNER*

C. That *NAME OF BAND* desire to obtain ownership of all rights of every nature in and to the Design and of all physical objects which embody it and to employ the Design in the manufacture of various materials and merchandise, including tee shirts, which *NAME OF BAND* will sell or allow others to sell.

In consideration of the above premises and of the mutual promises contained herein, *NAME OF BAND* and the Designer mutually agree as follows:

1. That the Designer hereby assigns, transfers and conveys to *NAME OF BAND* all right, title, and interest in and to the Design described above together with the copyright(s) therein and the right to secure copyright registration therefor, in accordance with Sections 101, 204 and 205 of Title 17 of the United States Code, the Copyright Law of the United States. The above assignment, transfer, and conveyance includes, without limitation, any and all features, sections, and components of the Design and any and all works derived therefrom, the United States and worldwide copyrights therein and any renewals or extensions thereof and any and all other rights which the Designer now has or to which the Designer may become entitled under existing or subsequently-enacted federal, state, or foreign laws, including, but not limited to, the following rights: to reproduce, publish, and display the Design publicly, to prepare derivative works of and from the Design, to incorporate the Design into merchandise and other materials and to otherwise exploit and control the use of the Design. The above assignment further includes any and all causes of action for infringement of the Design, past, present, and future, and any and all proceeds from such causes accrued and unpaid and hereafter accruing.

2. That *NAME OF BAND* shall have the right to crop, edit, alter or otherwise modify the Design to the extent deemed necessary, in the sole discretion of *NAME OF BAND*, to conform the Design to the style, design, or physical dimensions of the merchandise or materials into which it is incorporated or to suit it to such other use(s) as *NAME OF BAND* may choose to make of it.

3. That the Designer warrants that the Designer is the owner of copyright in the Design and possesses full right and authority to grant the rights herein granted. That the Designer further warrants that the Design does not infringe the copyright(s) in any other work(s) whatsoever, and does not invade any privacy, publicity, trademark, or other rights of any other person. The Designer agrees to indemnify and hold *NAME OF BAND* harmless in any litigation or other dispute in which a third party challenges any of the warranties made by the Designer in this paragraph.

4. That the Designer shall use copyright notice in the following form on any merchandise or materials which incorporates the Design and which is or are manufactured by the Designer at the request of *NAME OF BAND*:

© 199__ *NAME OF BAND*

Further, that the Designer shall refrain from applying the Designer's name or copyright notice to any merchandise or materials which incorporate the Design.

5. That the Designer further hereby transfers to *NAME OF BAND* title to each and every piece of artwork of any nature in existence which embodies the Design, in whole or in part. Notwithstanding the foregoing, the Designer may retain possession of any such artwork until *NAME OF BAND* request that possession of any such artwork be surrendered to *NAME OF BAND* and may display any such artwork at Designer's place of business or in trade shows or art competitions. However, in no event shall the Designer alter or destroy any such artwork or transfer possession of any such artwork to any third party without specific authorization from *NAME OF BAND*.

6. That in compensation for the services of the Designer in preparing the Design, and for the promises and undertakings of the Designer, the assignment of copyright by the Designer, and the transfer of ownership of all physical objects which embody the Design contained herein, *NAME OF BAND* shall pay to the Designer on or before a date thirty (30) days from the date first written above the sum of *AMOUNT* Dollars ($ 000.00), which sum shall constitute the Designer's entire fee and only payment.

7. That this Agreement shall be binding upon the heirs, assigns, and successors of the parties hereto.

"NAME OF BAND*"

By: *NAMES OF BAND MEMBER(S)* doing business as
     NAME OF BAND
     ADDRESS OF BAND
     CITY, STATE, AND ZIP OF BAND
     SIGNATURE FOR BAND   *DATE OF SIGNATURE*
     (Partner)   (Date of signature)

PRINTED NAME OF PERSON SIGNING
(Print Name)

and

"DESIGNER"

By: *NAME OF DESIGNER*
      ADDRESS OF DESIGNER
      CITY, STATE, AND ZIP OF DESIGNER

SIGNATURE OF DESIGNER   *DATE OF SIGNATURE*
(Authorized signature)   (Date of signature)

*PRINTED NAME OF
PERSON SIGNING*   *TITLE OF PERSON SIGNING*
(Print Name)   (Title)

Acknowledgment

State of _____
County of _____
Personally appeared before me, _____, a notary public
in and for the said state and county, the within-named *NAME OF
DESIGNER*, with whom I am personally acquainted and who exe-
cuted the foregoing instrument, for the purposes therein contained.
Witness my hand and official seal at _____, this _____ day of
_____, 19___.

_____   My commission expires: _____
Signature of Notary

Glossary

access— the first element of the three-part test for copyright infringement. That is, in a case for infringement of a musical composition, did the defendant have access to the plaintiff's song so that copying was possible? Usually access must be proved before the two other parts of the copyright infringement test are considered.

actual damages— the profits a copyright infringer made from the infringing song and the money the plaintiff lost because of the infringement. A court deciding a copyright infringement case may award either actual damages or statutory damages.

assignment of copyright— the customary method of transferring the ownership of song copyrights from songwriters to publishers. An assignment of copyright is like a sale of the copyright. In the case of a song copyright, a transfer of ownership of the copyright from the songwriter to the publisher is made in return for the promises the publisher makes in the music publishing agreement regarding what share of the royalties produced by the song will be paid to the songwriter, and how often. Ownership of the copyrights in the master recordings that embody the performances of a recording artist is assigned by the artist to his or her record company in the recording agreement between them. The copyright statute requires that the transfer of ownership of any sort of copyright be made in a written document signed by the person assigning the ownership of the copyright to someone else; no verbal transfer of copyright ownership is possible. Anyone who acquires any right of copyright by assignment can, in turn, sell that right to someone else unless the written assignment document provides otherwise. (Assignment of copyright is one of *three* ways that ownership of rights in copyright is transferred to someone besides the author of the copyrighted work; the other two are license and work-for-hire.)

author— in the language of the U.S. copyright statute, the creator of any copyrightable work, whether that work is a book, photograph, painting, poem, play, or musical composition.

booking agent— a person who secures employment for performers in return for a fee of 10 percent of the proceeds of the contracts secured. Booking agents are also called talent agents.

business manager— someone who charges a fee, usually 5 percent of the income of the client, to manage that income.

case law— law that originates in the decisions of courts, as opposed to written laws passed by state legislatures or Congress, which are called "statutes."

cease and desist letter— a letter written by the lawyer for the plaintiff telling the defendant to immediately cease certain specified actions that infringe the plaintiff's copyright or trademark and thereafter desist from any further such actions. These letters are usually the first indication a defendant has that his or her actions have violated the plaintiff's rights. Depending on the merits of the plaintiff's claims of infringement, a defendant will decide to comply with the plaintiff's demands and try to settle the infringement dispute out of court or to fight the plaintiff's assertions of infringement in court. An example of a trademark cease and desist letter is reproduced in the Appendixes of this book.

compulsory (mechanical) license— a limitation on the exclusive right of song copyright owners to control the preparation of copies of the song. The U.S. copyright statute provides that if a song has been recorded with the permission of the copyright owner and the recording was distributed within the United

States in the form of phonorecords, anyone can issue another recording of the song, subject only to the obligations imposed by the statute to notify the owner of the song copyright in advance of releasing the new phonorecord, to pay to the copyright owner royalties at the rate prescribed in the statute, and to furnish the copyright owner with monthly royalty statements. Because a copyright owner cannot deny permission to record a song under these circumstances, the right to do so—the "license" to prepare a recording—is called a "compulsory" license.

constructive notice— the presumption that because a copyright registration is reflected in the records of the Copyright Office, which are public, everyone knows of the claim of copyright ownership the registration embodies, regardless of whether any examination of those records is actually made.

contingency fee— a lawyer's fee taken from an award of damages to the plaintiff. Copyright infringement suits are often filed by lawyers who agree to work for a contingency fee, that is, such a lawyer agrees that the fee for his or her work is to be taken from and is contingent upon an award by the court in favor of the plaintiff. If the plaintiff loses, the lawyer is not paid a fee. Usually a plaintiff is still responsible for bearing the costs of the suit, such as his or her lawyer's travel expenses, the costs of court reporters for depositions, and the fees of expert witnesses. Lawyers never agree to work on a contingency fee basis for defendants, who have no expectation of any awards.

controlled composition— a song copyright written or owned by an artist who records it. By means of "controlled composition clauses" in recording contracts, record companies commonly negotiate the right to pay even less than the statutory mechanical royalty rate set by the Copyright Royalty Tribunal for the use of songs in phonorecords.

copublishing agreement— an exclusive publishing agreement in which a music publisher agrees to own less than the entire copyright in the songs produced by the songwriter who is the other party to the agreement, to take less than the half share of the royalties produced by those songs that are customarily due the publisher, and to treat the songwriter like a publisher, at least to the extent of paying him or her part of the royalties otherwise due the publisher.

copying— the second part of the three-part test for copyright infringement. That is, in a case for infringement of a musical composition, was part of the protected expression of the plaintiff's song copied by the defendant? Usually a defendant must be found to have copied significant portions of the melody or the lyrics (or both) of a plantiff's song before this part of the copyright infringement test is satisfied. The mere fact that two songs share certain similarities, even if those similarities are significant, is not sufficient to prove infringement *unless* the defendant *copied* from the plaintiff's song. Coincidental creation of a similar song, without copying, is not actionable under the U.S. copyright statute, even if the songs in question are so similar as to be nearly identical.

copyright— the set of exclusive rights that are granted, initially to the creators of copyrightable works, by the various copyright statutes that exist in most countries.

copyright infringement— the unauthorized exercise of any of the exclusive rights reserved by law to copyright owners. The most usual sort of copyright infringement lawsuit involving musical compositions claims that the defendant is guilty of unauthorized copying from the plaintiff's song. In this situation, copyright infringement is judged by a three-part circumstantial evidence test: (1) Did the accused infringer have *access* to the song that is said to have been infringed, in order to make copying possible? (2) Is the defendant actually guilty of *copying* from the plaintiff's song part of the plaintiff's protectable expression? and (3) Is the accused song *substantially similar* to the work the plaintiff says was copied? Coincidental creation of a song similar to an existing copyrighted composition is not infringement; the gist of most copyright infringements is unauthorized *copying*.

copyright notice— the three elements that legally serve to give notice to the world that a copyright owner is claiming ownership of a particular work. Copyright notice consists of three parts: the word "copyright" or the "©" symbol (or, for sound recordings, the ℗ symbol), the year of first publication of the work, and the name of the copyright owner. No formalities are required in order to use copyright notice, and although it is no longer required to secure copyright protection, use of copyright notice does confer certain valuable procedural benefits (in the case of a copyright infringement lawsuit) on the copyright owner.

copyright protection— the protection the law gives copyright owners from unauthorized use of their works during the term of copyright.

copyright registration— the registration of a claim to ownership of a copyright, made in Washington, D.C., in the U.S. Copyright Office, a division of the Library of Congress. Copyright registration enhances the rights an author gains automatically by the act of creating a copyrightable work but does not, of itself, create those rights. The PA Form is used to register the copyrights in songs; the SR Form is used to register the copyrights in sound recordings.

copyright statute— in the United States, the written copyright law passed by Congress, as opposed to copyright law that originates in the decisions of courts, which is called "case law." The current United States copyright statute became effective January 1, 1978, and changed significantly many aspects of copyright law operative under the previous statute. Because the copyright statute is a federal statute and federal law outranks state law, there is no such thing as a state copyright statute. Most other countries also have copyright statutes, the provisions of which often vary from those of the U.S. statute.

corporation— a form for doing business, created under state law as an entity separate from those who form it and called an "artificial person" because it has most of the legal rights and powers the law grants to human beings. Corporations are a popular business form for bands or performers who want to insulate themselves from some of the liability created by their activities. If someone sues an individual performer or a partnership, all the assets of that performer or of the partners are at risk; that is, those assets can be claimed by a plaintiff to satisfy a court judgment against the performer or the partnership. Owners of a corporation, who are called stockholders, risk only their investments in the corporation because only the assets *of the corporation* are at risk in litigation. Sometimes corporations are owned in whole or in part by an investor, or "backer," and the performer or band is simply employed by the corporation. These investor corporations are not uncommon, but they are often viewed as less desirable than partnerships or performer-owned corporations because they usually offer much less control to the artist or musician over his or her life as a professional performer.

deal points— basic points of an agreement that must be agreed upon before the remaining, auxiliary, points of a contract are negotiated.

derivative rights— the right to prepare alternate versions of a work or create a derivative work from it.

derivative work— an alternate version of a copyrighted work, i.e., a work "derived" from the original work. The right to prepare derivative works from a copyrighted work is one of the exclusive rights of copyright reserved to copyright owners in the U.S. copyright statute.

direct license— a permission to record a song obtained directly from the owner of the song copyright. Because the copyright statute sets out strict and specific accounting regulations by which record companies must abide when they record songs under the compulsory mechanical license provision of the statute, record companies prefer to obtain permission to record songs by "direct license," rather than by exercising their right to record the songs under compulsory licenses.

exclusive publishing agreement— a written contract that gives a music publisher the right to publish all the songs written by a named songwriter during a specified period and to collect royalties from any exploitation of those songs. These rights are given to the music publisher by the songwriter in return for the publisher's promise to pay to the songwriter, at stated intervals, certain specified percentages of the revenues produced by commercial exploitations of the songwriter's songs. The songwriter also usually receives a weekly or monthly "draw" against the royalties that are anticipated to become due him or her under the agreement; this draw is what is known as an "advance," that is, an advance payment of royalties, and is always recoverable ("recoupable") from royalties produced by the songwriter's songs before any further payments are made to the songwriter by the publisher.

exclusive rights of copyright— those rights pertaining to copyright that may be exercised only, or *exclusively*, by the owner of that copyright. The exclusive rights of copyright applicable to musical compositions are the right to reproduce the copyrighted song in phonorecords or otherwise make copies of it, the right to distribute copies or phonorecords of the song to the public, the right to create derivative works (alternate versions) of the song, and the right to perform the song publicly. Owners of sound recording copyrights have similar rights, with the exception that they do not have the right to control performances of their recordings, or the right to prohibit copying of the performances embodied in those recordings by anyone who wishes to create "soundalike" recordings.

exploitation— the use of a work to produce income. Song copyrights are usually exploited by music publishers who enter into contracts with the authors of the songs to pay those authors certain specified percentages of the revenues produced by commercial exploitations of the songs. The copyrights in master recordings belong to record companies under the provisions of the recording agreements the recording artists enter with those companies, which similarly promise to pay certain percentages of revenues from record sales to those artists.

fair use— a use of another's copyrighted work that does not, because of the circumstances surrounding it, constitute an infringement of the copyrighted work. "Fair" uses of copyrighted works usually are very limited uses of those works, made in noncommercial settings, that do not impair the market for the copyrighted works. Because songs are short, there are few fair uses of musical compositions.

First Amendment— the first amendment to the Constitution of the United States. This amendment, which most U.S. citizens do not realize gives them rights not enjoyed by citizens of many other countries, guarantees, among related rights, the right of free speech. Censorship encroaches upon the right of free speech by limiting what ideas may be expressed, or how. Copyright law is also somewhat at odds with free speech because it allows copyright owners to control the public display or performance of their works and prohibits the use, in a new work, of any significant portion of a copyrighted work by anyone besides the author without the author's permission. However, the copyright law and the First Amendment are, in our free-enterprise system, the foundations of the entire music industry, and without the privileges they guarantee everyone in the United States, the industry would not exist, or, at least, would exist only in a vastly different form.

fixation— the U.S. copyright statute provides that the moment a work is "fixed" in any tangible form that allows the work to be perceived by the senses (with or without the aid of a mechanical device, such as a CD player), that work is automatically protected by copyright; fixing the work in a tangible form is called "fixation."

foreign royalties— payments that result from the use of copyrights outside the United States. In the case of song copyrights, these royalties, which are created primarily by foreign mechanical and performance uses, are usually collected by foreign subpublishers under the terms of agreements with U.S. music publishers.

grand performing rights— for songs, the grand performing rights are primarily the right to perform the song in a musical play or as a part of a television show or movie in a way that advances the plot.

grant-of-rights clause— the clause in every music publishing agreement that contains the language that formally transfers ownership of the U.S. and foreign copyrights in the song or songs to which the agreement applies to the music publisher from the songwriter.

hook— the repeated lyrical phrase in a popular song that is the "punch line" for the song. Because a song's hook line is in many cases the most memorable section of its lyrics, hooks are consequently usually granted more protection by courts considering copyright infringement cases than other lyrical phrases of equivalent length.

indemnity provision— a provision found in every music publishing agreement that, when read in conjunction with the warranty clause of the agreement, makes the songwriter responsible, legally and financially, for claims of copyright infringement made against the song transferred to the publisher in the agreement.

injunction— a court order that directs the enjoined party to do something or, more typically, to cease doing something and to refrain from doing it in future. Plaintiffs in copyright and trademark infringement suits typically seek injunctions to stop defendants from continuing to infringe the plaintiffs' copyrights or trademarks. The most common sort of injunction in music-related litigation is the injunction that orders that shipments of records that include an infringing song or that are sold under an infringing trademark be halted, or even that those records be pulled from store shelves. The scope of an injunction and whether a litigant's motion for one is granted is at the discretion of the judge who hears the suit. A temporary restraining order is usually granted at the same time a suit is filed and endures only ten days. A preliminary injunction is granted by a judge after hearing arguments for and against the injunction from both the plaintiff and the defendant and usually lasts until the end of the lawsuit, when it may ripen into a permanent injunction by means of a paragraph to that effect in the judge's order rendering his or her decision.

leaving-member clause— a clause in many band partnership agreements that typically provides, among other things, that a group member who wants to resign as a partner must give the other partners advance notice of his or her intention to resign, that the existing partnership will continue after the exit of the resigning partner, and that the partnership will pay an amount equal to the value of the resigning partner's share of the partnership assets to him or her (often in installment payments over a specified period) and the appropriate share of royalties (from previously recorded records and other related revenue sources) when the partnership receives them.

license of copyright—   if an assignment of copyright is like a sale of the copyright, a license of copyright is like a lease. In the context of the music industry, many uses are customarily made of songs through license. These are numerous, and include the right to record a song and release it as a phonorecord (a "mechanical license"), the right to synchronize a song with visual images (a "synch license"), and the right to prepare and sell sheet music for a song or include it in written form in a songbook (a "print license"). These licenses are typically granted by the owner of the copyright in the song that is licensed—usually the music publisher. Record companies license master recordings for various uses, such as use of the recording in a K-Tel–type collection of rereleased hits or a use in the soundtrack for a movie (this license for the use of a *recording* of a song is different from the synch license granted by the publisher of the song for the use of the song itself). License of copyright is one of *three* ways that ownership of rights in copyright are transferred to someone besides the author of the copyrighted work; the other two are assignment of copyright and work-for-hire.

mechanical rights—   the right to reproduce a song in the form of records, tapes, CDs, and other phonorecords.

mechanical royalties—   the royalties (also referred to as "mechanicals") paid by record companies for the use of songs in the form of phonorecords.

music publisher—   a company set up to exploit song copyrights, which it acquires by assignment of copyright from the songwriters who write the songs. The transfer of ownership of a copyright from a songwriter to a publisher is made in return for the promises the publisher makes in the music publishing agreement regarding what share of the royalties produced by the song will be paid to the songwriter, and how often.

ordinary observer test— the test courts use in determining whether substantial similarity exists in copyright infringement cases. In the case of musical copyrights, courts try to decide whether an ordinary observer, hearing two similar songs for the first time, would believe that the defendant's song and the plaintiff's song are the same. If so, substantial similarity, the third part of the three-part test for copyright infringement, exists.

parody— a work that satirizes another work. Musical copyrights are difficult to parody without infringing the parodied song because many parody songs depend for their effect on the use of the melodies of the songs that are parodied, a practice that is usually viewed as copyright infringement by music publishers and their lawyers. Such a parody also constitutes creation of an alternate version of the parodied song, which is a separate violation of another exclusive right of the owner of copyright in the parodied song, that of creating derivative works from the song. However, *securing permission* from the owner of the copyright in a parodied song to use the melody of that song in the creation of a parody is not copyright infringement. This is the method most successful song parodists use to avoid infringement suits.

partnership— "an association of two or more persons [who] carry on as co-owners a business for profit," as defined in the Uniform Partnership Act, a model law on which many state partnership statutes are based. This definition applies regardless of the intent of the partners and even without a written partnership agreement; many bands are partnerships, even if the band members don't realize it, and in the absence of a written partnership agreement that varies the rules stated in the applicable state partnership statute, their business affairs are governed by those rules regardless of whether the partners believe otherwise.

performance rights— the right to perform a copyrighted work publicly, which is one of the exclusive rights of copyright reserved to copyright owners in the U.S. copyright statute. Performance rights are divided into "small performing rights" and "grand performing rights."

performing rights organizations— in the United States,

the three organizations, BMI, ASCAP, and SESAC, that collect the small performing rights royalties created by the public performances of songs.

personal manager— someone who directs and supervises the progress of the career of a performer in return for a percentage, usually 15 percent, of the performer's income from entertainment-related employment.

phonorecords— the term "phonorecords" is used in the U.S. copyright statute to mean vinyl records, cassette tapes, CDs, and all other material objects, *except* audiovisual recordings, that embody recordings of copyrighted works.

pipeline money— royalties that are on the way ("in the pipeline") for some exploitation of a song but have not yet been paid to a music publisher and therefore are not yet due to be paid to the songwriter.

print rights— the right to reproduce a song in the form of sheet music, songbooks, and other printed reproductions of its words and music.

protectable expression— those elements of a work which are protected by copyright. The most basic premise of copyright law is that copyright does not protect ideas, only *expressions* of ideas. Therefore, the idea on which a copyrighted work is based is not granted protection under copyright law. Other unprotectable elements of songs are themes, titles, short slogans or lyrical phrases, short musical phrases, the structure of a song, and, in many cases, the arrangement of a song.

publication— generally, selling or otherwise distributing copies of a work to the public constitutes, for copyright purposes, publication of the work. In the case of a song, selling or distributing copies of the song in the form of sheet music or phonorecords would constitute publication, but a public performance of the song onstage or on the radio does not *of itself* constitute publication. Because publication, in the context of copyright, can determine the expiration of the term of copyright for a song written as a work-for-hire or under a pseudonym, it can be very important to determine whether and when such a song has been published within the meaning of the copyright statute.

public domain— works for which copyright protection has expired. The U.S. copyright statute is based on the assumption that creative people will be encouraged to create if they are given exclusive control for a period over the use of their works. After that control ends, the public will benefit from the right to make unlimited use of the previously protected creations. When a song falls into the public domain the song has become available for use in any way by anyone.

reversion clause— a type of clause sometimes included in music publishing agreements that provides that ownership of the song copyright(s) transferred under the agreement will revert to the songwriter after a certain period. Reversion is sometimes dependent on the nonoccurrence of a certain event, such as a commercial recording of the song secured through the efforts of the publisher. The reversion is said to be "automatic" if no effort is required from the songwriter to trigger reversion.

secondary meaning— the trademark significance that a slogan or song, movie, or book title, etc., can gain when it achieves widespread fame. Although slogans and titles are not protected by copyright law, they can become so famous and so associated with one particular entertainment project that they gain something like the protection accorded trademarks and become unavailable for use by anyone else as the name of another entertainment project, under the principles of unfair competition law, which, among other things, prohibits the sale of any product or service by use of any name, image, etc., that indicates a false source for the product or service.

single song agreement— a written contract that gives a music publisher the right to publish a song and collect royalties from any exploitation of it. This right is given to the music publisher by the songwriter in return for the publisher's promise to pay to the songwriter, at stated intervals, certain specified percentages of the revenues produced by commercial exploitations of the songwriter's song.

six-bar rule— a mostly mythological "rule" related to musical copyright infringement that supposedly says that anyone who steals fewer than six bars from a song is not guilty of copyright infringement. This so-called rule apparently has its origins in a 1923 copyright decision that held that six bars copied from a plaintiff's composition, when used in the defendant's new composition of 450 bars, did not constitute copyright infringement. In actuality, since the test for copyright infringement is both quantitative *and* qualitative, it is never safe to consciously lift *any* number of bars from any song still protected by copyright.

small performing rights— for a song, the small performing rights are primarily the right to perform it on radio and television, in clubs, concert halls, and parks, and in restaurants and other businesses on public address systems.

Songwriters Guild contract— also sometimes called an "AGAC contract" (after the former name of the Guild), this is a model single song agreement drafted by Guild lawyers with the interests of songwriters at heart. Most music publishers will not sign the Songwriters Guild contract, which is available as a blank form for use by Guild members, because they believe it is too favorable to songwriters. However, the contract can be useful to any songwriter as an example of a contract favorable to the songwriter, which is sometimes hard to find elsewhere. The Songwriters Guild contract is reprinted in the Appendixes of this book.

soundalike recording— a kind of copying that is never infringement, no matter how closely the soundalike recording mimics the original, imitated, recording. Because the U.S. copyright statute does not protect *performances* of songs, anyone can create a soundalike recording of any recording artist's performance without committing copyright infringement under U.S. law. However, no matter how much a recording sounds like the original performance, the marketers of the soundalike must make clear to consumers that they are not selling copies of the original recording or they run the risk of a suit for unfair competition (by falsely indicating the origin of the soundalike recording) and infringement of the "right of publicity" of the original performer (by trading on the fame of that performer to sell the soundalike recording), which are two sorts of law that, if violated, can result in a lawsuit as quickly as copyright infringement, even though they have nothing to do with copyright law.

statute— a written law passed by a state legislature or Congress, as opposed to law that originates in the decisions of courts, which is called "case law."

statute of limitations— the period within which a suit must be filed under a given statute. The U.S. copyright statute provides that a suit for copyright infringement must be filed within three years of discovery of the infringement or it will be barred by the court.

statutory damages— a range of money damages the copyright statute allows courts to award a plaintiff in a copyright infringement suit instead of the money lost by the plaintiff as a result of an infringer's actions plus the actual amount by which the infringer profited from the use of the plaintiff's song. Because actual damages can be very difficult, time-consuming, expensive, or impossible to prove during infringement lawsuits, and because infringers often do not profit from their infringements, awards of statutory damages are often desirable.

stock devices— common literary or dramatic conventions, such as star-crossed lovers or the pauper who is actually the lost heir to a fortune. Such devices are a variety of idea and are therefore, in themselves, not protected by copyright, although particular *expressions* of these conventions are protectable.

substantial similarity— the third part of the three-part test for copyright infringement. That is, in a case for infringement of a musical composition, is the defendant's song substantially similar to the plaintiff's song? Substantial similarity is more than isolated, insignificant similarities, but the "infringed" song and the accused song need not be identical for substantial similarity to be found.

synch (or synchronization) rights— the right to use a song for a television or movie soundtrack, that is, to "synchronize" it with the images embodied in videotape or motion picture film.

term of copyright— the period during which copyright protection endures for a copyrightable work. For any song written after December 31, 1977, copyright protection begins the moment the song is first fixed in a tangible form. How long it lasts depends to a large extent on who wrote it and under what circumstances. Under the ordinary circumstance, copyright protection lasts for the remainder of the life of the songwriter, plus fifty years; if two or more songwriters compose a song, copyright protection will endure until fifty years after the last of the songwriters dies. If a song is written as a work-for-hire, anonymously, or under a fictitious name, the term of copyright will be either one-hundred years from the date the song was created or seventy-five years from the date it is published, whichever period expires first.

termination of transfers— a right given authors (and certain of their heirs) in the current U.S. copyright statute by which they may recover ownership of copyrights previously assigned or licensed to someone else. The termination-of-transfers provision of the statute specifies precise procedures for exercising this right of recovery, and these procedures require that good records be kept of copyrights that are transferred to others. The rules for copyrights created before 1978 and those created after December 31, 1977, are significantly different. The Appendixes of this book include a form for this recordkeeping called "Notice to My Heirs and Executors." In most cases, consulting a copyright lawyer is an important step in ensuring that the required termination-of-transfers procedures are followed and the termination is effected.

trademark— a word, phrase, sound, or symbol that represents in the marketplace the commercial reputation of a product or service. The names of bands and individual performers are trademarks, since they represent the services of particular performers and performing groups to consumers, who buy records and concert tickets by the names of the artists. In this country, trademark ownership accrues by virtue of use of a trademark rather than by regis-tration, although trademark registration significantly enhances the rights of trademark owners. Roughly speaking, trademark owners acquire ownership of trademarks commensurate with the duration and scope of their use of their marks. Unlike copyright law, which is solely federal law, U.S. trademark law is founded both in a fed-eral statute and in state trademark statutes. Most other countries also have trademark laws, but their provisions often differ signifi-cantly from those of the U.S. trademark statute.

trademark infringement— the use of a trademark without permission of the trademark owner or of a trademark that is confusingly similar to a trademark owned by someone else. A common sort of music trademark infringement lawsuit claims that a newcomer defendant band is guilty of using a name that is so similar to the established name of the plaintiff's band that consumers are likely to confuse one group with the other. Trademark infringement is judged by the "sight, sound, and meaning test." That is, the new name is compared to the estab-lished trademark for similarities of appearance, sound, and meaning. If the two marks are so similar that the average buyer is likely to confuse the products or services the marks name, or to believe that they are somehow related, the new name in-fringes the older mark. Unlike the situation that exists with similar copyrights, where only copying is actionable and coinci-dental creation of a work similar to an earlier copyrighted work is *not* infringement, *intent is immaterial* in evaluating most trade-mark infringement cases. In other words, use of a trademark that is confusingly similar to an established trademark will cre-ate problems whether or not it was an intentional effort to trade on the good commercial reputation of the established mark.

trademark registration— the registration of a claim to ownership of a trademark, made in Washington, D.C., in the U.S. Patent and Trademark Office, a division of the Department of Commerce. Trademark registration enhances the rights an owner gains by virtue of the use of a trademark but does not of it-self create those rights. While it is possible to register a trademark with the secretaries of state in the states where it is used and in the (federal) U.S. Patent and Trademark Office if it is used in interstate or international commerce, federal registration is usually sought by trademark owners who can qualify for it because it confers much greater benefits than state trademark registration. Unlike copyright registration, which is usually readily granted after a registration process that is simple enough that copyright owners can generally accomplish it themselves, federal trademark registration is so difficult to get that applying for registration usually requires the services of a lawyer experienced in trademark law.

trademark search— a survey of data on existing trademarks performed by a trademark search service in order to clear a proposed trademark for use or, alternately, eliminate it from consideration because it is determined to infringe an established mark. The results of trademark searches are reported in trademark search reports and are interpreted in trademark search opinion letters, an example of which is reproduced in the Appendixes of this book.

transcription license— the right to use a song as the "soundtrack" for a radio ad.

transfer of copyright— another term for assignment of copyright ownership.

unregistrable trademarks— names (or logos) for products or services that, because of certain inherent characteristics, are deemed by the U.S. trademark statute to be unworthy of registration. The nine statutory grounds for denial by the U.S. Patent and Trademark Office of an application to register a name (or logo) as a trademark are: the name (or logo) does not function as a trademark; the name (or logo) is immoral, deceptive, or scandalous; the name (or logo) disparages or falsely suggests a connection with persons, institutions, beliefs, or national symbols or brings them into contempt or disrepute; the name (or logo) consists of or simulates the flag, coat of arms, or other insignia of the United States or of a state, municipality, or foreign nation; the name (or logo) is the name, portrait, or signature of a particular living individual who has not given consent to use the name, portrait, or signature or of a deceased president of the United States during the life of his widow, unless she has given her consent to the use; the name (or logo) is confusingly similar to a trademark that is already registered for a similar product or service; the name (or logo) is merely descriptive or is deceptively misdescriptive of the product or service to which it is applied; the name (or logo) is primarily geographically descriptive or geographically deceptively misdescriptive of the product or services to which it is applied; or the name is primarily a surname.

work-for-hire—   a copyright that is created by an independent contractor (a freelancer) *if* the work falls into one of nine categories of specially commissioned works named in the U.S. copyright statute *and* both the independent contractor and the person who commissions the creation of the work agree in writing that it is to be considered a work-for-hire or a copyright that is created by an employee as a part of his or her full-time job. Works-for-hire belong to the employers of the people who create them, and those employers are considered the authors of those works *for copyright purposes* from the inception of the works. Except in a very few special situations, work-for-hire has little application in the lives of songwriters, who customarily transfer the copyrights in the songs they write to music publishers by means of assignments of copyright. (Work-for-hire is one of *three* ways that ownership of rights in copyright are transferred to someone besides the author of the copyrighted work; the other two are assignment of copyright and license.)

work—   in the language of the U.S. copyright statute, any copyrightable product of the imagination, whether it is a book, photograph, painting, poem, play, musical composition, or other sort of work.

Resources

Recommended Books

The ability to read books may be just as important to your success in the music business as the ability to read music. There are lots of books on the market for those who earn their living making music and those who aspire to. Some of them are more worth the time it takes to read them than others. The books listed below are especially worthwhile. If you read them, you'll be better equipped to achieve your potential and better protected from your own mistakes and the inadequacies or treachery of others than someone who sets out to build a music career armed only with a bass guitar.

If you want to buy one of the titles recommended but can't find it at your local bookstore, ask the sales staff to order it for you. Specially ordered books don't cost any more, and bookstores are usually happy to make sales they otherwise would not have rung up.

Books About Songwriting and Copyright

How To Protect Your Creative Work: All You Need to Know About Copyright. David A Weinstein. John Wiley and Sons, 1987. $16.95 (paperback).

Protecting Your Songs and Yourself. Kent J. Klavens. Writer's Digest Books, 1989. $15.95 (paperback).

Books About the Music Industry Generally

All You Need to Know About the Music Business. Donald S. Passman. Prentice Hall, 1991. $24.95.

Hit Men. Frederick Dannen. New York Times Books, 1991. $12.00 (paperback).

Music, Money, and Success. Jeffrey Brabec, Todd Brabec. Schirmer Books, 1994. $30.00.

The Musician's Business and Legal Guide. Mark Halloran, ed. Prentice Hall, 1991. $29.95 (paperback).

Music Business Directories

Billboard International Talent and Touring Directory. Published annually by Billboard Publications, One Astor Plaza, 1515 Broadway, New York, NY 10036 (212-764-7300). $75.00.

This directory lists hundreds of recording artists and tells you who their agents, managers, and record companies are and where to contact the agents and managers.

The Recording Industry Source Book. Published annually by Anscona Group, Inc., 8800 Venice Boulevard, Los Angeles, CA 90034 (310-841-2700). $34.95.

This directory contains the names and addresses of big and little record companies, music publishers, agents, lawyers, managers, etc., and lots of other useful information.

Yellow Pages of Rock! Published annually by Album Network, 120 N. Victory Boulevard, Burbank, CA 91502 (818-955-4000). $90.00.

This directory lists everybody who is anybody or might be in rock music—just like the yellow pages in your hometown phone book, but hipper and much more informative for rock singers and songwriters. This book is expensive enough that you may want to try to find a copy in a library to consult once in a while rather than buying it.

Books by Mail

Perhaps the best source for good books about all facets of working as a musician, performer, or songwriter is Mix Bookshelf, a bookstore-by-mail service connected with *Mix* magazine. The people at Mix Bookshelf read most books published on any topic related to popular music and stock the best ones for their customers. Their book catalog is almost an education in itself. Write for it at Mix Bookshelf, 6400 Hollis Street, #12, Emeryville, CA 94608, or call 800-233-9604 to get a current copy.

You can also buy any of the titles listed above with a credit card by phone. There are two good services for this; both will deliver books to your door within a few days. These services are:

Book Call
59 Elm Street
New Canaan, CT 06840
800-ALL-BOOK [255-2665]

Book Call accepts orders between 9:00 a.m. and 6:00 p.m. EST, Monday through Friday.

The Book Resource
41 E. 11th Street, Third Floor
New York, NY 10003
212-254-6031

The Book Resource advertises that it offers "100 percent of all books in print, 100 percent of the time." It offers discounts to frequent buyers. Call between 9:30 a.m. and 5:30 p.m. EST, Monday through Friday.

Libraries

If you're a starving musician, ask the nice folks at your local public library whether the library has these titles or other books about the music business. Librarians are employed to help readers—it's what they wake up for every day—and they can help you find *any* kind of information, not just the principal products of Argentina for your sixth-grade social studies paper. If you don't have a library card, apply for one—it's free, and it's your ticket to learning what you need to know.

If your hometown library is too small to have any books that are useful to songwriters or performers, you can go to any public library and many college and university libraries and read their books on the spot even if you can't check the books out. Ask a librarian to help you find the books you want.

Another route is to ask your local library to borrow books for you from other libraries through the interlibrary loan system. History professors and English teachers and their ilk do this all the time to see books they can't find in their own school libraries. There's no reason why you can't do the same to find books about *your* profession—music. Interlibrary loan is free or nearly free—you may be asked to pay the cost of mailing the book to your local library, where you will go to check it out when it arrives from Chicago or Duluth or Houston.

Copyright

The best information and publications on copyright are available from the Copyright Office free of charge.

To speak to a Copyright Information Specialist, call 202-707-3000 between 8:30 a.m. and 5 p.m., Monday through Friday (except holidays); recorded information is available twenty-four hours a day and seven days a week. (Copyright Information

Specialists are knowledgeable and helpful, but the Copyright Office does not give legal advice and will not advise you regarding copyright infringement or bringing an infringement suit, disputes over copyright ownership, music publishing agreements, or collecting royalties due you. You need a music lawyer for this sort of advice.)

To write the Copyright Office Information Section, send your letter to: Information Section, LM-401, Copyright Office, Library of Congress, Washington, DC 20559.

To order blank copyright registration forms and copies of the free Copyright Office publications listed below, call the Copyright Office forms hotline at 202-707-9100.

Songwriters, musicians, and performers are likely to want either Form PA or Form SR. Form PA is used to register the copyrights in works of the performing arts, including published and unpublished musical compositions, whether or not those compositions include lyrics. Form SR is used to register the copyrights in sound recordings, such as recordings of performances of musical compositions, whether or not those compositions include lyrics. Form SR may also be used to register both the sound recording and the musical work fixed in the phonorecord (the tape, disk, cassette, record, etc., that embodies the sound recording) *if* the same person or organization owns the copyrights in the sound recording *and* the underlying musical composition.

The following Copyright Office publications are of interest to songwriters, musicians, and performers. These publications are short and well written, and they're free. Use the numbers beside the titles to order the ones you want.

Copyright Basics. (Circular 1)
Copyright Notice. (Circular 3)
Mandatory Deposit of Copies or Phonorecords for the Library of Congress. (Circular 7d)
Works-Made-for-Hire Under the 1976 Copyright Act. (Circular 9)

Duration of Copyright. (Circular 15a)

How to Investigate the Copyright Status of a Work. (Circular 22)

Copyright Registration for Musical Compositions. (Circular 50)

Copyright for Sound Recordings. (Circular 56)

Copyright Registration of Musical Compositions and Sound Recordings. (Circular 56a)

Copyright Law of the United States of America. (Circular 92) (This is a pamphlet copy of the copyright statute.)

The Copyright Office has compiled information kits on a variety of topics. The kits that are of most interest to songwriters and musicians are listed below.

Fair Use. (Kit 102)

Music. (Kit 105)

Copyright Searches. (Kit 116)

Sound Recordings. (Kit 121)

Trademarks

Almost the only useful, reliable information on trademark registration that is available to anyone but lawyers is the pamphlet "Basic Facts About Trademarks," from the U.S. Patent and Trademark Office. This booklet contains all the information necessary to federally register a trademark, along with the necessary forms and instructions. The bad news is that anyone but a trademark lawyer may have a hard time preparing a trademark registration application using this booklet, not because it's badly written or incomplete, but because the regulations that apply to everyone who wants to register a trademark are complex and particular and can frustrate even lawyers. Call the Trademark Office's Public Information Line at 703-308-HELP [4357] to request a copy of "Basic Facts About Trademarks." Read it for the information it contains and to convince yourself that you need to know more to register your trademark than you can find out from any booklet. Then call a trademark lawyer, who won't be learning how to file a registration application by practicing on yours.

Music Industry Unions and Organizations

Academy of Country Music (ACM)
P.O. Box 508
Hollywood, CA 90078
213-462-2351

American Federation of Musicians (AFM)
(The AFM maintains about 450 local union offices around the country. Call the Los Angeles, Nashville, or New York office to find the AFM office nearest you.)

Los Angeles office:
817 Vine Street
Hollywood, CA 90038
213-462-2161

Nashville office:
11 Music Circle N.
Nashville, TN 37212
615-244-9514

New York office:
1501 Broadway
Paramount Building, Suite 600
New York, NY 10036
212-869-1330

American Federation of Television and Radio Artists (AFTRA)
(AFTRA operates numerous offices around the country. Call the Los Angeles, Nashville, or New York office to find the AF-TRA office nearest you.)

Los Angeles office:
6922 Hollywood Boulevard
8th Floor
Hollywood, CA 90028

Nashville office:
1108 Seventeenth Avenue S.
Nashville, TN 37212
615-327-2944

New York Office:
260 Madison Avenue
New York, NY 10016
212-532-0800

Country Music Association (CMA)
7 Music Circle N.
Nashville, TN 37203
615-244-2840

Gospel Music Association (GMA)
7 Music Circle N.
Nashville, TN 37203
615-242-0303

Nashville Songwriters Association International (NSAI)
15 Music Square W.
Nashville, TN 37203
615-256-3354; 800-321-6008

National Academy of Recording Arts and Sciences (NARAS)
National office:
3402 Pico Boulevard
Suite 902
Santa Monica, CA 90405

Atlanta chapter:
1227 Spring Street, N.W.
Atlanta, GA 30309
404-875-1440

Chicago chapter:
1946 North Hudson
Chicago, IL 60614
312/440-1350

Nashville chapter:
1017 Sixteenth Avenue S.
Nashville, TN 37212
615/327-8030

New York chapter:
157 West 57th Street
Suite 902
New York, NY 10019
212/245-5440

San Francisco chapter:
245 Hyde Street
San Francisco, CA 94102
415-441-0662

National Academy of Songwriters (NAS)
6381 Hollywood Boulevard
Suite 780
Hollywood, CA 90028
213-463-7178

Recording Industry Association of America, Inc. (RIAA)
1020 19th Street, N.W.
Suite 200
Washington, DC 20036
202-775-0101

The Songwriters Guild of America (SGA)
  Los Angeles chapter:
  Suite 1002
  6430 Sunset Boulevard
  Hollywood, CA 90028
  213-462-1108

Nashville chapter:
1222 Sixteenth Avenue S.
Suite 25
Nashville, TN 37212
615-329-1782

New York chapter:
276 Fifth Avenue
New York, NY 10001
212-686-6820

Performing Rights Organizations

There are three performing rights organizations that collect royalties due songwriters and music publishers for public performances of their songs. They are the American Society of Composers, Authors and Publishers (ASCAP), Broadcast Music, Inc. (BMI), and SESAC. Each organization operates offices in the U.S. cities that are centers for the music industry.

ASCAP
  Chicago office:
  350 West Hubbard
  Chicago, IL 60610
  312-527-9775

  Los Angeles office:
  7920 Sunset Boulevard
  Suite 300
  Los Angeles, CA 90046
  213-883-1000

  Nashville office:
  2 Music Square W.
  Nashville, TN 37203
  615-742-5000

New York office:
One Lincoln Plaza
New York, NY 10023
212-621-6000

BMI
  Los Angeles office:
  8730 Sunset Boulevard
  Third Floor
  Los Angeles, CA 90069
  310-659-9109

  Nashville office:
  10 Music Square E.
  Nashville, TN 37203
  615-291-6700

  New York office:
  320 West 57th Street
  New York, NY 10019
  212-586-2000

SESAC
  New York office:
  421 West 54th Street
  New York, NY 10019
  212-586-3450

  Nashville office:
  55 Music Square E.
  Nashville, TN 37203
  615-320-0055

VOLUNTEER LAWYERS FOR THE ARTS

Volunteer Lawyers for the Arts (VLA) was founded in 1969 as the first legal aid organization for artists and arts organizations. If a musician meets certain financial eligibility criteria, VLA will review and negotiate contracts on his or her behalf. These and other matters may be handled in-house by VLA's staff attorneys or referred to one of more than eight hundred attorneys in the New York area who volunteer their time through VLA at no cost to VLA clients. In addition, VLA operates an Art Law Line (212-319-2910) which musicians may call for answers to their music law questions. The Art Law Line also refers callers who live outside New York to the nearest of the other more than forty volunteer lawyers for the arts organizations that exist around the country.

Index